Challenging Hierarchies

Society and Politics in Africa

Yakubu Saaka
General Editor

Vol. 5

PETER LANG
New York • Washington, D.C./Baltimore • Boston
Bern • Frankfurt am Main • Berlin • Vienna • Paris

Challenging Hierarchies

Issues and Themes in Colonial and Postcolonial African Literature

Edited by

Leonard A. Podis & Yakubu Saaka

PETER LANG
New York • Washington, D.C./Baltimore • Boston
Bern • Frankfurt am Main • Berlin • Vienna • Paris

Library of Congress Cataloging-in-Publication Data

Challenging hierarchies: issues and themes in colonial and postcolonial African
literature/ [edited by] Leonard A. Podis and Yakubu Saaka.
p. cm. — (Society and politics in Africa; vol. 5)
Includes bibliographical references.
Partial contents: The African woman writer
as "killjoy"—A critical debate on Achebe's depiction of women—Eurocentric
challenges to colonialism—Afrocentric challenges to colonial and
postcolonial hegemony—Envisioning successful challenges.
1. African literature—History and criticism. 2. African literature
(English)—History and criticism. 3. Achebe, Chinua—Criticism and interpretation.
I. Podis, Leonard A. II. Saaka, Yakubu.
PL8010.C466   809'.8896—dc21   97-14652
ISBN 0-8204-3710-7
ISSN 1083-3323

Die Deutsche Bibliothek-CIP-Einheitsaufnahme

Challenging hierarchies: issues and themes in colonial
and postcolonial African literature/ Leonard A. Podis and Yakubu Saaka, eds.
–New York; Washington, D.C./Baltimore; Boston; Bern;
Frankfurt am Main; Berlin; Vienna; Paris: Lang.
(Society and politics in Africa; Vol. 5)
ISBN 0-8204-3710-7

The paper in this book meets the guidelines for permanence and durability
of the Committee on Production Guidelines for Book Longevity
of the Council of Library Resources.

∞

© 1998 Peter Lang Publishing, Inc., New York

To Abrafi and JoAnne

Contents

Preface

Looking over the titles of the selections in this anthology, we are reassured that the title we have chosen for the book, *Challenging Hierarchies*, remains an apt one. For example, the title of Micere Mugo's second selection, "The South End of a North-South Writers' Dialogue," speaks eloquently to the notion of hierarchies and the attempts of African writers to call them into question. Not only does much contemporary African literature offer resistance to the hierarchical relationship usually evoked by the "North-South" pairing, it also raises similar doubts about typical understandings of "Western vs. Third-World," and "colonizer vs. colonized," among others. A special focus of this collection is the challenging of hierarchies that have relegated African women and African women writers to a subordinate position.

When we were preparing to co-teach our first course in African literature a decade ago, we knew that we wanted to include a number of works by women, and we were pleased to find that there existed a wider range of high quality material than even we suspected: works not only by Aidoo, Emecheta, and Nwapa, but also Bâ, Dangarembga, Mugo, and others. At the same time, we were chagrined to learn that there was relatively little critical commentary to be found on African women writers. Indeed, at the time, there were no book-length critical studies devoted to any of the women writers as there were to the works of Achebe, Ngugi, or Soyinka. (Even as of this writing, a decade later, Odamtten's recent study of Aidoo is the only such study extant.) Aside from the anthology, *Ngambika*, and one or two other survey works, there was nothing to be found. Even chapters within scholarly books on African literature were rare. We recall, for instance, eagerly opening Gerald Moore's *Twelve African Writers*, certain that we would find at least one of the twelve to be a woman, only to wonder in disappointment and disbelief at the total omission of women writers.

The focus on women writers, particularly in the first two sections of our book, is appropriate in that African women's writing challenges traditional and contemporary hierarchies not only through what it has to say, but also through its very existence as a presence that undermines the hegemony of male writing. In devoting prominent attention to it in our book, we mean to challenge the critical hierarchy that has tended to relegate it to a lesser sphere of importance through misjudging, dismissing, or ignoring it.

Acknowledgments

Our special focus on African women's writing and women's issues would have been difficult to accomplish without the assistance of Ama Ata Aidoo, whom we got to know during her stay as a Visiting Distinguished Professor of English at Oberlin College. She helped us a great deal, not only by allowing us to include her work in the anthology, but by guest lecturing to our class, discussing important issues with us, and offering us her friendship. We are deeply indebted to her.

Of course we owe immense thanks to all of the authors who contributed selections for this book, and we hereby thank them heartily once again.

We also wish to thank our colleagues and students at Oberlin College who have assisted us along the way. Indeed, this book has its origins in our collaboration as co-directors of the Danenberg Oberlin College in London Program approximately a decade ago. A hallmark of that program has been interdisciplinary team-teaching, with instructors from varying fields designing new courses that would make use of the resources of London. Since one of us is a specialist in literary criticism and the other a scholar of African politics and cosmology, we developed a course with colonial and postcolonial (mainly African) literature at its core, but in which the literature would be read primarily as a reflection of sociocultural, historical, and political realities. The course evolved over time as we imported it back to our college to be taught as part of the Mellon Colloquium program. Many of the issues and themes that we have used to organize this collection are a result of discussions, analyses, and debates that took shape in our classes.

For their help and encouragement at various points in the development of our course and the shaping of the book, we also wish to thank Abu Abarry of Temple University, Lawrence I. Buell of Harvard University, and Biodun Jeyifo of Cornell University.

Special thanks also go to Terri Mitchell of Oberlin College for her word-processing assistance and to Kabuki Moore for helping with computer conversions.

Finally, we thank Owen Lancer, our editor at Peter Lang, who has been supportive and accommodating throughout all phases of the project, and Scott Gillam, whose meticulous copyediting set a standard for us to emulate.

Introduction

With the emergence of a vast and vital body of postcolonial African literature, many issues have surfaced: questions of the role of tradition, the nature of the new literary discourses, and the relationship of the postcolonial era to colonialism and neocolonialism, among others. In this collection the authors whose work we have assembled are also concerned with a variety of pressing issues. However, as we see it, the one overarching consideration that connects so much of the discourse and debate now occurring is that of the continued and persistent challenge to preexisting hierarchies. The most obvious and prominent of these hierarchies is, of course, that of imperial hegemony, the legacy of colonialism that permeates postcolonial societies and pervades their literatures. But there are also other hierarchies. For example, much of the significant contemporary literature is concerned with women's issues and with challenging not only colonially inspired domination of women but also traditional patriarchy, with its lingering effects in postcolonial societies. Yet another hierarchy to be challenged is that represented by repressive and illegitimate neocolonial governments, rife with corruption and bent on maintaining power.

Since nearly all of the pieces included in this collection are concerned with postcolonial literature, they generally share in the particular challenge that such literature has directed toward the hierarchy of the western literary canon. Indeed, among writers and critics alike there is consensus that, in the postcolonial era, those who constitute the western literary establishment are still engaged in a form of colonization: they continue to imperialize postcolonial literature by treating it as second-class, inferior, or otherwise subsidiary to "serious" western literature. Thus the writers who contribute to this book (save Adekoya) are all engaged in challenging the hierarchy of western literary domination.

Implicit (if not explicit) in these discussions is the view that postcolonial literatures (here represented almost exclusively by African works) are at least as artistically worthy as are contemporary western works. What needs to be understood, as has been pointed out by Chinweizu, Jemie, and Madubuike (*Toward the Decolonization of African Literature*), is that the standards of the western hierarchy must not be used to judge postcolonial works as inferior. Rather, we must recognize the appropriate standards that apply to the emerging postcolonial literatures. For example, anyone approaching contemporary African fiction should be aware that the literature conforms to particular aesthetic and contextual criteria that may differ from those that apply to western narratives. A list of such criteria would include the following:

1. Skillful use of proverbs or aphoristic language
2. Depiction of social behavior and customs
3. Incorporation of cultural myths
4. Evocation of traditional African spirituality
5. Concern with issues of political significance to the society
6. Conciseness and succinctness of style

To recognize and use appropriate standards such as these is indeed to challenge the edifice of the Eurocentric hierarchy in letters. For instance, using these criteria allows us to place high value on a book such as *Our Sister Killjoy*. Using a western value system that deplores the political in serious literature as "unaesthetic," some western critics might question the obvious "political" nature of the work as well as its concise narrative style, thus enabling them to judge it as inferior to the "great western masterpieces." The use of criteria 5 and 6, however, reveals that such characteristics are positive, not negative. Indeed, the brevity of Aidoo's book is considered an achievement, not a demerit, for the same reason that the use of proverbs (criterion 1) is valued: proverbs allow the communication of the maximum meaning through the minimum number of words, evoking a great deal without necessitating what African writers might see as the verbosity of many western narratives, which employ many words but might in fact say very little of true importance.

Although the stereotypical hierarchy of "superior western literature/inferior postcolonial literature" still dominates most literary study, it is clear that the establishment of Afrocentric criteria poses an important challenge to the traditional patterns. Not all of the hierarchies are so clearly drawn, nor are they so firmly entrenched as one might believe. While we have become used to discussing sociocultural and literary hierarchies in absolute, "black and white" terms (or, in the jargon of poststructuralism, as "binary oppositions"), the nature of these hierarchies is complex and overlapping. Conceived of strictly as oppositions, such hierarchies do appear to be fixed and immutable, incorporating paired phenomena such as colonizer/colonized, power/resistance, tradition/modernization, patriarchal/feminist, and so forth, with all of the conventional assumptions about which position sits atop the hierarchy. However, in actuality, the conventional hierarchies implied by such binary oppositions are often dubious, questionable, or variable, particularly from the point of view of those who are intent on challenging them. For example, with regard to tradition/modernization, within the world of a work such as Soyinka's *Death and the King's Horseman*, modernization is clearly at the top of the hierarchy created by the imperialization of Yoruba culture by the British. From the viewpoint of the playwright and the major characters in the play, however, tradition occupies the top rung of the hierarchy, to the extent that even Olunde the medical student, the embodiment of modernizing Nigeria, commits suicide to preserve it. In light of this variability in the hierarchies, it is indeed a complex matter to discern the exact nature of the challenges being made to them.

Similarly, while it is broadly true that contemporary African writers have been concerned with challenging the hierarchy of "oppressor/oppressed," it is not often clear who occupies the specific rungs of this hierarchy. As we will see in the debate conducted in Section II about Achebe's depiction of women, the African male may be seen to occupy simultaneously the role of oppressed (in relation to the colonial masters) and oppressor (in relation to the African woman). In other words, Achebe's work embodies a hierarchy within a hierarchy, and one question that the articles collected here examine is the extent to which those hierarchies are challenged or simply acknowledged and accepted. Adding to this debate is Micere Mugo's observation (in Section I) that the position of the woman writer is generally held to be inferior to that of the male writer. Deploring the "cult of giants and celebrities," she notes that the preoccupation with the work of supposedly eminent figures (i.e., men of letters) works against the efforts of women writers to have their voices heard. In this regard, she suggests another "hierarchy within a hierarchy," one that parallels that which is present in Achebe's fictional world. This hierarchy of "men of letters/minor women writers" is also, ironically, a replication of the hierarchy of "western canon/inferior postcolonial literature" that we discussed above. Moreover, as we will see in the introduction to Section I, Aidoo's "The Genesis of 'Male-ing Names in the Sun'" posits a discourse community or contemporary cultural situation in which the conventional shape of this hierarchy ("men of letters/minor women writers") is challenged and finally inverted. From the position afforded them by their literary accomplishments, postcolonial women writers have succeeded in envisioning for themselves a space of power and even privilege, a space from which the conventionally understood location of men of letters and imperial writers at the top of the hierarchy may be viewed as spurious.

On a related matter we might observe that, given the overlapping and intertwined nature of hierarchical structures in contemporary African literature, there exists the real possibility that such attempts to challenge one sort of hierarchy might simultaneously work to support other hierarchies, or, put another way, to undermine a writer's attempts to challenge other hierarchies. For example, in Section I, which is centered on the works of Ama Ata Aidoo and Micere Mugo, an important question that emerges is whether feminist challenges to traditional African patriarchy serve to undermine more generally Afrocentric challenges to Eurocentric hegemony. That is, does the critique of patriarchal sexism weaken the critique of colonialist racism by undermining the credibility of the struggle waged by African men against imperial oppression? When African women writers call attention to the chauvinistic behavior of African men, does their critique of those men weaken the efforts of Africans in general to gain moral support for their struggle against the legacies of colonialism? Both Aidoo and Mugo offer unique perspectives on this issue as they manage to fuse the two types of challenges into one. Their work resists presenting the so-called patriarchal behavior of African male characters as something traditionally African, thereby enabling them to *merge* their challenge to sexism with their challenge to western domination. In the view of Aidoo and Mugo, in other words, to challenge patriarchy is to reinforce the challenge to Eurocentrism.

Yet not all contemporary writers or critics are concerned with challenging the hierarchies we have been discussing. In Section III, for example, Adekoya's "Criticizing the Critic" takes Achebe to task for challenging (in "An Image of Africa") the conventional western view that Conrad's *Heart of Darkness* is anti-imperialist. Adekoya maintains that to challenge Conrad's depictions of Africa and Africans as racist is wrongheaded, since *Heart of Darkness* on one level challenges the imperialist enterprise of the late nineteenth century. Exemplifying the "universalism" decried by theorists such as Wallerstein and Spivak, Adekoya sees no problem with the Eurocentric vision that suffuses Conrad's book and himself accepts the elements of anti-imperialism as exonerating it of any charges against Conrad.

By contrast, in the other article in Section III, "Narrative Distancing and the (De)Construction of Imperialist Consciousness in 'The Man Who Would Be King' and *Heart of Darkness*," Podis does attempt to challenge colonial hierarchy in discussing two classic works of late-nineteenth-century British short fiction. While he concedes, with Adekoya, that *Heart of Darkness* is, in its overt message, at least partially anti-imperialist, Podis insists, with Achebe, that the novella is both racist and imperialist at its Eurocentric core. Yet, he further argues, this racist mentality finally proves to be its own undoing, a fact which is perhaps evident to some extent to Conrad even as he exercises the deeply Eurocentric vision that characterizes the novel. Comparing *Heart of Darkness* with another central narrative of the era of high imperialism, Kipling's "The Man Who Would Be King," Podis demonstrates that both works do in fact undermine or "deconstruct" their own invidious assumptions about the colonized world. In this sense, he argues, they can profitably be read as colonial precursors to the more direct attacks on Eurocentric hegemony that are made by postcolonial African writers. In other words, a careful reading of these Eurocentric works from our contemporary perspective suggests that, while the racism Achebe decries is abundantly present, the works themselves are rife with evidence that such racist and imperialist assumptions are artifically constructed and tenuously sustained—that, in effect, they ultimately collapse in on themselves and belie the supposed superiority of the Eurocentric vision that permeates them.

While the bulk of the pieces collected here fall under the heading of literary criticism, we have also included some autobiographical writing and even a short sample of fiction. Indeed, one of the hierarchies that must inevitably be challenged in such a collection is that of traditional scholarly discourse, which has tended to elevate the formal, analytic essay to the highest stature. Certainly the feminist autobiographical challenge to "male-centered," logocentric discourse and the multicultural challenge to the predominance of Eurocentric discourse and the traditional canon must be reflected in any collection of contemporary work on postcolonial literature. As Kofi Anyidoho's article in Section IV illustrates, the impulse toward autobiographical scholarship is definitely not limited to women writers, even though feminism has taken a leading role in legitimizing such an approach. By incorporating verse and "creative" writing in his piece, Anyidoho further underscores the fact that contemporary African writers, like many of their western counterparts, are bent on challenging the hierarchy of genre that has existed within the scholarly world.

Although our discussion of the challenges to western hegemony is focused mainly on the modern and contemporary periods, it is important to note that, as Chris Kwame Awuyah points out in "Nationalism and Pan-Africanism in Ghanaian Writing" (Section IV), there is a tradition of using literature to challenge hierarchies dating back at least to the eighteenth century. In examining the works of Ottobah Cugoano, Joseph E. Casely-Hayford, and Ayi Kwei Armah, Awuyah establishes that, in the case of Ghana, the contemporary concern with questioning colonial hegemony has antecedents in both the era of high imperialism and the period of slavery. In doing so, Awuyah seeks to militate against the tendency of the western critical tradition first to dismiss such works as unworthy of canonization altogether and second to appropriate them as examples of "universal" art. While such appropriation is, at one level, a form of endorsement or acceptance, it ultimately, in the words of Vincent O. Odamtten, is a form of "critical (mal)practice[:] . . . the insensitive distortion and . . . destruction of the text-work as a historically constituted aesthetic and ideological product, unique in its portrayal of a specific condition." (*Aidoo*, 3) Such an approach, Odamtten asserts, says more about "the general ideological character of the [western critic's] society" than about the African literary texts under consideration. (Odamtten, 15–16)

Valuable and vital as these Afrocentric challenges are, it is important to recognize that they are not mounted effortlessly and that they are often characterized by troubling undercurrents of self-doubt and insecurity. Saaka and Podis's article on the depiction of sons and daughters in modern African literature underscores the fact that the project of challenging hierarchies tends to be accompanied by significant social stresses which play themselves out in the struggles of those sons and daughters to choose between traditional and modern (often westernized) paths. Perhaps the clearest example of this social stress is seen in the case of highly controversial traditions (e.g., Olunde's insistence on killing himself in his father's place) being used as, in effect, weapons of resistance or assault upon western hegemony. In such cases, we see African youth making choices, as Sissie in *Our Sister Killjoy* enjoins, based not upon "which factors out of both the past and present represent for us the most dynamic forces for the future" (Aidoo, 116) but upon a fierce determination to use tradition, at whatever cost, as an instrument to resist domination.

In this body of literature, another impediment to the realization of a dynamic future is political corruption, especially in neocolonial regimes. Podis and Saaka's essay on *Anthills of the Savannah* and *Petals of Blood* (Section V) focuses on the efforts of Achebe and Ngugi to envision a positive new order, one which can arise only out of a conscious rejection of the present order, a major aspect of which is corrupt and repressive neocolonial rule. In this case, the new postindependence governments (of Kangan—Nigeria—and of Kenya) would appear to have eliminated the kind of pernicious hierarchies that characterized the colonial regimes that predated them. However, as both writers make clear, that is not the case: Oppression and corruption live on in the form of the new African rulers. Only the color of the occupants in the imperial palace has changed. For both Ngugi and Achebe, the problem can only be solved by a thorough reconceptualization of (in fact, for Ngugi, actually a revolutionary transformation of) the present system. Only governments that are based on a platform of abiding African values can have legitimacy. Current models that simply project the spirit of colonialism must be abolished in favor of systems rooted in African heritage. Both novels challenge neocolonial hierarchy, as Podis and Saaka observe, by envisioning non-hierarchical, Afrocentric alternatives to the current sociopolitical order.

The other article in Section V, Obioma Nnaemeka's "Marginality as the Third Term: A Reading of Kane's *Ambiguous Adventure*," is concerned with the challenge to imperial hierarchy in an even more encompassing sense. Through an analysis of *Ambiguous Adventure*, Nnaemeka demonstrates a new understanding of the notion of African "otherness." Rather than seeing such "otherness" as an expression of the African's place on the outside or at the bottom of the hierarchy, she sees Kane's novel as illustrating the idea of a "hybrid" third term, one that does not position itself as inferior to the West, but which mediates and conflates, resulting in a sense of agency. Thus the struggle involved in working through colonialism/neocolonialism centers on the self-determination that results from being neither the first nor second term, but rather the third term. The novel celebrates the agency to recreate oneself, in other words, in a way that abolishes the traditional sense of hierarchy.

By this point we hope to have made clear our rationale for categorizing the pieces as we do. In addition, we will preface each of the five sections to follow with a brief introductory statement that further elucidates the issues and themes being considered within that section. We intend to keep such editorial comments to a minimum in the belief that the selections should be allowed, by and large, to speak for themselves.

Works Cited

Aidoo, Ama Ata. *Our Sister Killjoy*. London: Longman, 1977.

Chinweizu, Onwuchekwa Jemie, and Ihechukwa Madubuike. *Toward the Decolonization of African Literature*. Washington: Howard University Press, 1983.

Odamtten, Vincent O. *The Art of Ama Ata Aidoo: Polylectics and Reading Against Neocolonialism*. Gainesville, FL: University Press of Florida, 1994.

I

THE AFRICAN WOMAN WRITER AS "KILLJOY"
UNDERSTANDING HER CHALLENGE

Just as it is appropriate to title this section with an allusion to the work of Ama Ata Aidoo, so it is appropriate to begin the section with an essay by her, "Literature, Feminism, and the African Woman Today." In this article, Aidoo, in seeking "to get the world to look at the African woman properly," openly challenges western notions of the African woman as a powerless beast of burden as well as the attitudes of patriarchal African male critics and the arrogant, self-righteous views of white feminists. In all, the spirit of the African feminist challenge to a range of oppressive hierarchies is evident in each of the six selections presented in this section.

Micere Mugo's survey, "The Woman Artist in Africa Today: A Critical Commentary" (previously published in *Africa Development*, 19 [1994]: 49–69), continues with the thread established by Aidoo, as she inquires:

> Why is it that criticism has paid such scanty attention to our women's artistic productivity? Why the imposed invisibility, in the face of so much harvest all around us?

Mugo's opening anecdote, in which a visiting man ignores the presence of several children and females ("I say! Are people not here today?") suggests that the pattern of denigrating the contributions of women derives from a wider societal attitude, and her extension of the debate into the abuses of "orature culture" reveals that the efforts of women storytellers are often not merely ignored, but shamelessly exploited by those at the top of the political hierarchy.

The complexity of the challenges represented in efforts of African women writers to "get the world to look . . . properly" is perhaps best seen in "The Genesis of 'Male-ing Names in the Sun.'" Here Aidoo provides us with a prime example of the blurring or reversal of hierarchies that characterizes much of the discourse on colonial and postcolonial African literature. As she observes, the women writers present in Sydney, Australia, to choose the winners of the Commonwealth Writer's Prize are clearly representatives of the central postcolonial challenge to the colonial/neocolonial hierarchy. Their presence in Sydney, despite its "wholesome" nature, is viewed as "a rather potent symbol of our humiliation as a people." Here the conventional understanding of the oppressor/oppressed hierarchy is foregrounded. However, as the piece progresses, we are made aware of—indeed drawn into—an oppositional and counterbalancing point of view: namely that of the postcolonial women writers as ironically *in control*. It is those women writers who have gathered in Australia to be judges who have the last laugh on their putative oppressors. Aidoo puts it this way:

> As the current propagators of English and therefore upholders of "The Empire" were we not an odd bunch? . . . We could not resist to conclude that if they could see us now, the original Empire builders would surely turn in their far-flung graves. . . .

With considerable exuberance, Aidoo observes an essential point about the tendency of colonial hierarchy to be challenged in two ways simultaneously: (1) directly and precipitously, through resistance to, and criticism of, oppression; and (2) indirectly, or more subtly and gradually, through the recognition that, over the long term, the oppressors have essentially failed in their attempts to dominate. In other words, she puts her finger on a truth about the relationship of colonization and decolonization—that the former carries within it the seeds of the latter.

Ama Ata Aidoo's "Male-ing Names in the Sun" (which previously appeared in *Unbecoming Daughters of the Empire*, Shirley Chew and Anna Rutherford, eds., Dangaroo Press, 1993) takes a satiric look at the "colonial mentality" adopted by some Africans during the colonial era. This tongue-in-cheek collection of *tolis* (stories) mocks those people who upheld the imperial hierarchy by attempting to replicate the ways of the colonizers, rejecting their "primitive" customs in order to adopt the "modern" practices of the Europeans. Aidoo vigorously challenges the hierarchy in two ways: first, with her biting irony toward the supposedly enlightened behavior of the people of Oguaa, who "set about the business of Europeanizing themselves with panache," especially the Methodist "Osofo" and the Shillingsons; and second, through the spirited refusal of Achinba, the fiancée of Dr. Kwesi Shillingson, to adopt his "silly" surname.

In the final selection in Section I, "Beside Every Good Woman Was a Good Man," Vincent O. Odamtten examines the ways in which Aidoo's *No Sweetness Here* challenges the notion that sexism results strictly from either traditional patriarchy or the imposition of colonial or neocolonial influences. While demonstrating the obstacles that both women and men face in forging mutually supportive relationships, Aidoo, according to Odamtten, is consistently concerned to undercut the simplistic assumption that the African man is a one-dimensional oppressor of the African woman. Rather, Odamtten believes that Aidoo's stories effectively challenge such a hierarchy by positing the existence of "good men" who stand beside good women.

Chapter 1

Literature, Feminism, and the African Woman Today

Ama Ata Aidoo

There was always a temptation or an encouragement for those of us who lived in the Euro-American world, or at least visited it frequently, to approach the vital discourses in the African world as opportunities to respond to stimuli received from the West. This kind of response was inevitable and necessary because the stimuli were nearly always, and regrettably, negative. The danger lay in considering that commitment as our only responsibility. It was not.

The most harrowing experiences some of us had in North America were on college and university campuses: teaching literature. Our colleagues in the English departments left us in no doubt that they did not think that what we had come all the way from another continent to offer was literature. Never mind that they had never bothered to read a single African novel, volume of short stories, or collection of poetry. As far as they were concerned, our courses were only needed so that those students who wanted to take them to fulfill the requirement to study something on "diversity" or "multiculturalism"—read "blacks" and "women"—could do so. Yet we should be careful about running too fast to knock even that requirement. Fighting for these areas of study had sometimes cost people tenure and other positions in institutions that they had come to virtually consider as home. Meanwhile, our colleagues in the women's studies departments behaved, consciously or unconsciously, as though we should have felt and appeared grateful that African women's literature was considered worthy of being offered alongside the works of major Western women writers. In practical terms, some even reacted to us as though we should have been aware that the opportunity to teach on the same

An earlier, abridged version of this essay appeared in *Reconstructing Womanhood, Reconstructing Feminism*, ed. Delia Jarrett-Macauley (London: Routledge, 1996).

*campuses as them was a major lease on life for us, for which we had
to pay–either with a slavish agreement with them on relevant current discourses, including issues relating to Africa, Africans, and
African women, or with our silence.*

*On these campuses, people were still convinced that any African
knowledge, in any field, still belonged to anthropology. Meanwhile,
all of these opinions and attitudes had been and were being communicated on a regular basis to the students. As a result, we found
ourselves quite often teaching literature to young people who managed to convey to us that we should feel flattered that they had conde-
scended to take our courses. On one occasion, a student reported me
to the head of the English Department and then dropped my course,
after I had refused to let her bully me to agree with her that the
women in Flora Nwapa's* Efuru *sounded "mythical" because they
were much more independent than she knew "real African women
can possibly be." She could not possibly have been alone in holding
that opinion, either. From early age, young people in the West are
bombarded with images of Africa and Africans that can only be described as wicked and defamatory. A couple of examples from the last
few years should help to illustrate what is meant here.*

First there was Bob Geldorf's Band Aid, which was staged
to raise both the international community's awareness of the
plight of and funds for Ethiopia's drought victims.[1] Then there
was the more enduring picture of U.S. marines landing am-
phibiously, to feed Somalia's starving populations. No doubt,
both these events were extremely well-intentioned. However,
there is also no doubt that they helped to confirm and petrify
a specific image of the African woman in the minds of the
world. She was breeding too many children she could not take
care of and whom she should not expect other people to pick
up the tab for. She was hungry, and so were her children. In
fact, it had become an idiom of the photo-journalism for the
U.S. and other Western visual media that the African woman
looked old beyond her years; she was half-naked; her drooped
and withered breasts were well exposed; there were flies buzz-
ing around the faces of her children, and she had a permanent
begging bowl in her hand.[2] Then just as people thought they
had had enough of staring at Africa's shame, in 1994 they were
given Rwanda.

The notion that some women in contemporary African literature are stronger, more articulate, and more independent than "real African women" is a widely held view, which invariably got expressed in one way or another about the eponymous Anowa and Efuru, and Iyaloja of Soyinka's *Death and the King's Horseman,* and which we found ourselves compelled to resist literally with every class to which we taught African literature in foreign lands. Unfortunately, an equally articulate young woman like Sissie in *Our Sister Killjoy* complicates the debate when she expresses unease with her own liberal impulses:

> Someone should have taught me how to grow up to be a woman. I hear in other lands a woman is nothing. And they let her know this from the day of her birth. But here . . . they let a girl grow up as she pleases until she is married. And then she is like any woman anywhere: in order for her man to be a man, she must not think, she must not talk. . . . (Aidoo 1988, 112)

Some critics have pointed out, especially Odamtten, that although Anowa was supposed to have lived in the latter part of the nineteenth century, she seemed to have expressed so well some of the dilemmas and concerns of the African woman today; that, for example, she "identifies with the plight of mothers, though childless herself, a significant step toward a mature understanding of the complex nature of oppression." (Odamtten, 72) In fact, at another point, Odamtten assesses her in even more universalist terms and concludes that "by stressing her opposition to the acquisition of slaves, Anowa is upholding the right of persons, female or male to work and enjoy the fruits of their labor. . . ." (Odamtten, 76)

As remarked elsewhere, to a certain extent, African women are some sort of a riddle. This is because, whether formally educated or not, traditional or modern, they do not fit the accepted (Western) notion of themselves as mute beasts of burden, and they are definitely not as free and as equal as African men (especially some formally educated) would have us believe. In fact, they fall somewhere between those two notions.

What is clear, however, is that like others everywhere, African women struggle to be independent (and articulate) at all mother of Esi in *Changes* epitomizes this capacity the African woman has always had to formulate clear and critical opinions in order that she would understand her position and be able to deal with it. When Esi goes to consult her on whether she should go ahead and become Ali's *second* wife, the old lady takes her time and presents her analysis of what she sensed Esi was up to:

> "You are asking me whether you should marry this Ali of yours—who already has got his wife—and become one of his wives? Leave one man, marry another. What is the difference? Besides, you had a husband of your own . . . whom you have just left because you say he demanded too much of you and your time. But Esi tell me, doesn't a woman's time belong to man?"[3]

Esi would never know whether Nana had actually wanted her to answer any of these questions or she had meant them rhetorically, because without pausing, Nana proceeds to answer them herself:

> "Remember, my lady, the best husband you can ever have is he who demands all of you and all of your time. Who is a good man if not the one who eats his wife completely, and pushes her down with a good gulp of alcohol?" (Aidoo 1991, 109)

She goes on to warn Esi:

> "My Lady Silk,. . . a woman has always been diminished in her association with a man. A good woman was she who quickened the pace of her own destruction. To refuse, as a woman to be destroyed, was a crime that society spotted very quickly and punished swiftly and severely." (Aidoo 1991, 109–110)

It was important to quote her substantially to enable the rationality and logic of her thoughts to unfold. Again, incredible as it may sound, we are aware that some readers in the Western world have complained, both in our absence and to our faces that as far they know a character like Esi's grandmother "doesn't sound like an old African woman . . . she sounds like some contemporary educated European or American feminist." The only reasonable response to such criticisms is that they can only come from people who do not know old African women. Rather, what a Ghanaian, for instance, might legitimately argue is that of course it is easy for Nana to talk, for with age comes wisdom. What this means is that the society has no tolerance for a "foolish old person." In fact, that would be considered a major oxymoron, all puns intended!

However, as the Old Man in *Anowa* was quick to point out:

> "It is not too much to think that the heavens might show something to children of a latter day which is hidden from them of old." (Aidoo 1987, 101)

Intelligence and clarity of perception do not have to come with grey hairs and wrinkles only. Sissie in *Our Sister Killjoy* was in her early twenties when she left her secure West African environment to go to Europe. Yet she could see, feel, and *say* a whole lot in her letter to her lover:

> Maybe I regret that I could not shut up and meekly look up to you even when I knew I disagreed with you. But you see, no one had taught me such meekness. And I wish they had.
>
> . . . No, My Darling: it seems as if so much of the softness and meekness you and all the brothers expect of me and all the sisters is that which is really western. Some kind of hashed-up Victorian notions, hm? Allah, me and my big mouth!! (Aidoo 1988, 117)

The women in Lauretta Ngcobo's *And They Didn't Die* are no less assertive. MaBiyela (the mother-in-law of Jezile, the protagonist) "had so much power. . . . Conscious of her power, not only within the family, but in the community as well, she had to set an example. . . . She had exerted as much authority over Siyalo [her son]. . . ." On the other hand, she and other older women in the community prove to be all too human even in their strength. "They were capable, they were strong. They had to be. They were lonely and afraid." (Ngcobo, 17)

As a people who had to cope *daily* at the vicious end of apartheid, not to mention regular harassments and other provocations from the regime, they could not avoid a certain cumulative bitterness that somehow corroded their good will towards one another. So they were "prone to gossip about each other's failures and misfortunes." (Ngcobo, 99)

The younger generation of women have had to learn to improve on the manner in which they relate to one another. They have had to teach themselves that survival lies only in collective strength. When pressed, they rise to the occasion with awesome courage, strength, and clarity. Arrested and jailed for organizing a protest march against pass laws and other indignities, they cheer one another up with speeches linking their struggles to other African struggles, and prop up the weak among them:

> The women around Nosizwe drew closer, so close that from a distance the watchful guard could not count her flagging strokes. In quick, deft movements Jezile dragged a mound of broken (stone) pieces in front of Nosizwe, a pile larger than any in front of the others. That evening, the women went back to prison happy that they had shielded her from the guard. (Ngcobo, 99)

Perhaps critics are quick to tag some of us as "feminist" writers because we make it possible for our women characters to be themselves, without any of the assumed dumbness and pretended weaknesses which all societies expect from women and women in fiction. Perhaps that is not only to be expected but even granted. However, we also have to be careful with the use of the term. Simply writing about women does not make us "feminist writers." Just making women the protagonists of drama or fiction is not feminist. Men writers are not necessarily male chauvinist pigs because they write about men. A writer is not an African nationalist simply because he or she writes about Africa and Africans. Nor is any writer a revolutionary for just writing about poor oppressed humanity. Women writers write about women because when we wake up in the morning and look in the mirror, we see women. It is the most natural thing to do. It does not require any extra commitment and of course, that should explain why men write about men. *Any writer's feminism comes out in her writing only when she deals with women's issues with concern and commitment in ways that go beyond what would be of general interest to the author herself, as well as her potential readership.* The same should be applicable to any writer and her or his ideological leanings.

One of the most rabid expressions of prejudice and lack of clarity in the academy on this and other aspects of the field of women and literature came out in Oladele Taiwo's *Female Novelists of Modern Africa.* The book's publishers blurbed it as "an important study," and the author himself claimed in the preface that it is a "celebration of the literary activities of female novelists of modern Africa." For any writing woman, reading that "important study" should be a sobering experience. Taiwo manages to see the books he discusses only in one-dimensional categories. He does not attempt to do any comparative analysis. What is even more bewildering is that he treats the female authors of those novels (and short stories when the spirit moves him) as though they were his co-wives, to whom he dishes out his whimsical favors. He constantly remarks on their intelligence or storytelling capabilities in the best "dancing dog" tradition or as if the writers were a bunch of precocious six year olds who had demonstrated some special abilities to the head teacher.[4] *Inter alia*, he declares rather censoriously of *Our Sister Killjoy*:

> It may be the intention of the author to prove that women can do without men in their private relationships. . . . Ms. Aidoo is quite entitled to put women at the helm of affairs in her novel. But it is an error to think that they can live a full life without men. . . . (Taiwo, 11)

The most cursory reading of *Our Sister Killjoy* would confirm that it is not about women proposing to "live a full life without men." So it is difficult to fathom how anybody could have read the book well enough to attempt to do a professional commentary on it and still manage to come away with such an impression. Put bluntly, we cannot help wondering whether Taiwo really reads the books he comments on. Often, his very strong remarks seem to have less to do with the books the authors wrote, than a determination on his part to put the women in their place. Indeed, he as much as asks them how they came to dare write at all. More germane to the concerns of this paper, though, is the fact that he ends that particular paragraph with a solid warning to the effect that "if such a situation is tenable in Europe, it has no chance of succeeding here [in Africa]." (Taiwo, 11)

The rest of his critique is comprised entirely of an attempt to scold the writers for what he suspects were all sorts of dangerous, new-fangled notions they had filled their heads with, *without his permission*! Since it is possible for an intermediary to be unfair, we should listen to Taiwo himself. To begin with, because the writers are women (and as far as he is concerned, all women's writing *is* "kitchen literature") he suggests in regard to the authors that

> their economic and literary contributions and their important functions in home and family life [should be] compared with their preoccupations as novelists *to see what transfer of knowledge and skill has taken place.* (Taiwo, 34)

The literary critic then proceeds with a homily on how to raise children:

> A happy and stable family life is essential for the child's success. His future happiness depends to a large extent on the kind of environment provided for him as a child by his parents. . . . Every occasion should be exploited [including] family dinners. (Taiwo, 36)

He has more to say on the relationship between a woman as a novelist and what society (or Taiwo!) expects of her as a mother and the welcome outcome when such expectations are well fulfilled:

> If the correct attitude is fostered at home, in school and the community, the child has no difficulty in interacting with people and serving his nation loyally as an adult. It is only then that the mother can claim she has successfully carried out the more important obligation of parenthood [read "womanhood"], which is the proper upbringing of children. (Taiwo, 26)

Can anything of the sort of the foregoing be imagined in a study of the works of male novelists like Achebe, Armah, Ngugi, Mphahlele, and Soyinka? Yet Taiwo does not only conceive of its possibility in this context but seems to have considered it an essential part of his study, because he is discussing books written by women writers: Bâ, Emecheta, Head, Nwapa, Aidoo, and others. In the main body of his discussion, he regularly calls up for scolding those he considers sassy, and none is spared his patronizing tone.

Taiwo says grandly of *Efuru*:

> In this work the novelist pursues her interest in home and family life. She portrays different kinds of marital connections in order to highlight what factors make for success or failure in married life. (Taiwo, 26)

He leaves one speculating as to whether Flora Nwapa could not have gone to less trouble and done much better by writing a book with a title like *How to Avoid Disastrous Marriages*! Of *Daughter of Mumbi* by Charity Waciuma, he remarks with avuncular approval that "the author quite rightly [sic!] concentrates on the sufferings of the individual Kikuyu." One cannot help wondering what is so right about concentrating on the suffering of an individual in any community? Is this because the agonies of whole communities are not real tragedies? Taiwo comes down heavily on Buchi Emecheta for *The Joys of Motherhood*, too:

> The novelist's treatment of polygamy is uninspiring. By making Nnaife so completely ineffective as the head of the extended family she may be suggesting that polygamy is one of the traditional practices which need to be changed. (Taiwo, 184)

(An inspiring treatment of polygamy from the pen of a woman? Dear Dr. Oladele, please be realistic! For the creation of such a work, perhaps the reading world must look to a male writer.)

Taiwo's self-righteousness is as pervasive as it is laced with a baffling insensitivity. This comes out clearly in his comments on the works of Bessie Head. At one point, he asks with marked rhetorical exasperation:

> Why does a man like Makhaya not stay on and fight the system from within, instead of fleeing to another country. . . . ? One does not change . . . "false beliefs" by running away from the situation which they have helped to generate. (Taiwo, 44–45)

Does this critic really know what he is talking about? How can any African in the early 1980s manage to arrive at the conclusion that the black people of South Africa helped to "generate" apartheid? One thing is clear: Taiwo would not have dared assume such posturings vis-à-vis *When Rain Clouds Gather* if it had been written by a man. In his zeal to play the stern schoolmaster, he forgets, as so many other critics do, what must be a fundamental hypothesis in the science that should be literary criticism: *that any writer can be judged only on what she (or he) wrote, and against the background of what is perceived to be her (or his) intentions.* There should be, and indeed there are, other considerations, but they can only be secondary to that.

Taiwo regularly falls into his own and everybody else's traps, one of them being an incredible but widely accepted assumption in traditional literary discourses: that Literature (of course with the big *L*) is better served only through the portrayal of heroic (or even antiheroic) male protagonists, as they grapple with the problems and challenges of existence. Taiwo, for instance, wails that in Aidoo's *Our Sister Killjoy* and Bâ's *So Long a Letter,* the scene is almost completely "monopolised by women." In fact, he consistently and rather ridiculously accuses every single one of the women writers of writing a novel that "is packed full of women"!

*All this works out to a fairly simple formula. Male writers should write about men and women writers should write about men. This article of faith is itself a product of the question of what—not to mention who!—defines literature. Because it is clear here that **if women writers want their works to be considered as "literature," then their characters, or at least the main ones, should be men.***

Perhaps one should hasten to add at this stage that as writers, women are not looking for approbation. What we have a right to expect, though, is that commentators try harder to give our works, too, some of their best in time and attention, as well as the full weight of their intelligence and scholarship, just as they do for the works of our male counterparts. In this regard, Vincent Odamtten has made a very impressive and ground-breaking contribution with *The Art of Ama Ata Aidoo: Polylectics and Reading Against Neocolonialism.* What is also rather interesting about this study—to date the only one?—of the works of one African woman writer is that Odamtten not only gives the texts a close reading, but he also treats their contents seriously. As a result, he comes out with some extremely profound insights into the material he works on, as well as into contemporary African literature, and indeed, literature generally.

But unfortunately in the eyes of most literary critics, men are the only fit subjects for literature; women are unfit. This is a smoothly insidious notion that does violence to women. Yet it is firmly fixed in literary aesthetics. It is also at the root of the question which interviewers for the print and electronic media and all manner of researchers invariably ask *any* woman writer:

"Why do you write about women?"[5]

The only honest response to which should of course be the counter question:

"Whom else should women writers write about?"

Since deep down in everyone's soul (including the souls of female freelance journalists and researchers), there is a conviction that even women writers must write about men, the logical conclusion is that when a woman writer writes about women, it is abnormal; it is perverse; it is because she is a "feminist." From all of which we conclude that any writing that focuses attention on women is feminist literature. Of course, this is unfair, wrong and false. But it is also the central reality in popular notions about "feminist writing."

Currently, there is a hot and widespread debate in African and other black academic circles on the issue of feminism and African women and other women of African descent. It has become common to dismiss feminism as a foreign ideology, zealously imported into Africa to ruin good African women and stultify intellectual debate. It is also easy, and a trap we all fall into every now and then, to feign disinterest in the discourse. A third attitude is to airily maintain that "we don't need feminism" because "African women were feminists long before feminism." Needless to say, none of these positions is completely convincing. Besides, even if any of them were, the implied conclusion that therefore we do not need to bother with contemporary and global forms of feminist struggles is flawed.

Feminism is an essential tool in women's struggles everywhere. And that includes African women. In fact, whenever some of us are asked rather bluntly whether we are feminists, we not only also bluntly answer, "yes," but even go on to assert that every woman, as well as every man, should be a feminist—especially if we believe that we Africans should take charge of our land and its wealth and our own lives and the burden of our reconstruction from colonialism and slavery. For, with that belief comes another awareness: that at least half of the entire population of Africa are women; and therefore if Africa is to develop, then first, African women too must get the best that the environment can offer for their well-being and development. Meanwhile, what we refer to as the "well-being and development" of women should cover areas like primary health care, shelter, adequate nourishment, accessibility to the best and highest possible education, availability of suitable and adequate career opportunities, freedom from sexual harassment in the workplace, freedom over our wombs, and the end to all other forms of marginalization and tokenism. For some of us, our demand that society acknowledge and provide these fundamentals constitutes the most important element in *our* feminist thought.

Certainly for Micere Mugo of Kenya the issue is equally clear. She sees feminism as the means by which, as a woman, she can break out of the prison of confining roles. In "The Woman's Poem" the recurrent image she uses to define women's aspirations and feminism, which she considers synonymous, is breaking out, being free:

> *Ta imagini* that
> we exploded
> > > chilling silences
> defrosted
> > > refrigerated womanhood
> pestled and mortared
> > > the chains
> > > that grate
> > > and grind us! (Mugo, 45)

She is even more direct in the poem that—yes—she titled "To Be a Feminist Is." She introduces the poem as being part of the

> *effort to liberate the concept of feminism from abduction by Western bourgeois appropriators and in the spirit of naming the essence, rather than simply peeling off the label.* (Mugo, 36)

Among so many other illuminating ways in which she defines what it is to be a feminist, she says she also declares with glorious determination that for her

> to be a feminist is
> > to burst all the non-space
> > between the bedroom
> > and the kitchen
> > of my life

it is
to grow wings
and fly
to unlimited heights
it is
to ride the sun
of my visions. (Mugo, 38)

Nevertheless, we are aware that "feminism" as a contemporary ideology carries other meanings and concepts of life and living, including, and especially, lesbianism. However, equating feminism with lesbianism is ridiculous. The latter is a sexual preference. Feminism, on the other hand, is an ideology, a world view, a specific notion of how life must be organized and lived by half of the entire humanity here on this earth. What is being emphasized here is that women everywhere can, and in fact often do, have feminist concerns. On the other hand, it would be a violent untruth to assert that in the last decade of the twentieth century, the major preoccupation of the majority of African women was the debate on society's perception of female (or male) homosexuality.

Like all other ideologies, feminism carries its own imperatives and particular commitments. On the other hand, being lesbian is no more feminist or ideological than being heterosexual is fascistic. Lack of clarity on these matters confuses the issues for everybody, especially young women, whether they are feminist but not lesbian, lesbian and feminist, or lesbian but not necessarily feminist—although it has to be granted that the latter seems to be the rarest category of all.

However, as we try to sort these issues out, we should also be aware that the entire field is mined. One area of special concern is that to a number of men, and women too, the thought of women independently providing a construct to challenge the patriarchal underpinnings of *all* human society has enormous subversive implications. For such people, it is easy to equate feminism with lesbianism, raise lesbianism itself to a moral issue, and then of course, wail against the advent of Sodom and Gomorrah!

Perhaps a desire to clarify matters somewhat was what inspired Alice Walker to open one of the most interesting fronts in the discourse when she proposed that we substitute the term "womanist" to describe the global African woman's particular concerns. Titled *In Search of Our Mothers' Gardens*, Walker's book of seminal essays on "black" women, especially African Americans, is subtitled *Womanist Prose*. The volume came out in 1983. Since then, the terminology has generated some truly enormous international controversies. In her contribution to the debate, Chikwenye Okonjo Ogunyemi states that

> more often than not, where a white woman may be a feminist, a black woman writer is likely to be a "womanist." That is, she would recognize that along with her consciousness of sexual issues, she must incorporate racial, cultural, national and political considerations into her philosophy. (Ogunyemi, 64)

Unfortunately for some of us, the real problem is not the racially sensitive "black/white" polarization that white feminists seem to be so worried about. What bothers us about the seemingly harmless etymological polarization implicit in the "feminist/womanist" formulation is, rather, its effects on us, black women. For, if women of African descent are "womanist" while other women are "feminist," then by implication, are we more women than other human females while managing not to be feminine, while other women may have feminist concerns and still manage not to be women enough, and so on? It gets quite unclear. The fear, in the long run, is that by essentializing our own experiences, we women of African descent are also inadvertently limiting our capacity to understand ourselves—which, in turn, could weaken our capacity to deal effectively with the predicament we find ourselves in.

On the other hand, black women did not create the black women/white women polarization. It is a historical fact based on the realities of Africa's conquest by Europe and the consequent enslavement of her peoples in the Americas, the Caribbean, and on the continent of Africa—the latter normally and euphemistically described as "colonization"—and the consequent racism and marginalization of black people everywhere, in the twentieth century. This fact created a major schism in the fortunes of African and European women that must inevitably—and most, most unfortunately—haunt the relationship between the two groups for a very long time to come.

The situation is not improved by the arrogance with which some white feminists handle current feminist discourses, especially in relation to African and other black women. In October 1988, a persistent nightmare got played out all over again in an incredible scenario in a European city (Hamburg) where a group of African writers had been invited to a workshop on African literature. One of the panels had been dedicated to issues about African women and African women writers. However, it soon became apparent, after the panelists had made their statements and the discussions had been opened to the floor, that on the question of the status of African women in their own societies, the audience was split into clear factions.

On one side were European feminists who were almost bullying us, the African women and African women writers on the panel, to declare for their brand of feminism. As far as they were concerned, they knew much more about the oppression of African women than the African women writers who had been flown all the way from wherever they had been, ostensibly to go and tell them about themselves and their environment. In fact, one of the women had declared that we supposedly bourgeois African women were in no position to speak for the ordinary African woman in the village. Naturally, it had not struck her that by the same token, it was even more ridiculous that she, a European bourgeois woman, was herself trying to speak for that ordinary African woman. Talk about colonial legacies!

Another part of the audience was made up of African male students, workers and professionals who, it turned out, had also come to the meeting with a clear-cut mission: to order the African women writers to say that we did *not* want feminism at all in Africa. Along the way, they tried to also get us to convey to the European women that our men, too, knew better when it came to what the African woman in Africa needed—and that whatever that was, it definitely did not include feminism! In the end, and out of sheer exasperation, we had to tell both the European feminists and the African men resident in Europe that strange as it might seem, African women, including African women writers, are quite capable of making up their own minds and speaking for themselves: on feminism and a few other issues, too.

For some of us, the tragedy of the non-communication between some African women and European feminists seemed to have finally bloomed around Mineke Schipper's book: *Source of All Evil: African Proverbs and Sayings on Women*. From its cover, its subtitle, the dedication, and not to mention the editing of the proverbs, it seemed there was not a single aspect of the book that did not hurt some African sensibility or other.

In response to a message I had sent her objecting to her decision to dedicate the book to me and two other African writers, Schipper sent me a letter in which she said, among other lines of defense, that she considered a dedication to be a gift to somebody she felt close to. She had dedicated other books to her parents, husband, children, and old friends. She also went on to say how much she admired my so-called strength and other aspects of my personality and to mention the names of other Africans she had previously dedicated books to. Needless to say, this was a rather non-response to my concerns.

In the end, I felt that the issues that had been raised were so important, I should put my views down. The decision crystalized in what finally became an open letter to her of which the following comprises the main text.[6] I first confirmed "my feeling of unease about" her book or rather, its title and subtitle. The letter continues:

> However . . . [we are] getting more and more convinced that . . . the European (or Western) woman believes that her position in society is the highest of all women's positions in the world. That conversely, the position of the African woman in society is the lowest. This is in line with the normal European way of looking at Africa and Africans. It is also a dichotomy of conquest. You are the conquerors. We are the vanquished. It stands to reason then that you would think you should represent the superior, and we the inferior, in all things. *The only problem arises when, as now, elements from the defeated community refuse to share such a belief and resist pressures (or refuse to be used) to endorse positions that do violence to themselves.*
>
> For years, some of us have been struggling to get the world to look at the African woman properly. Hoping that with some honesty, it would be seen that vis-à-vis the rest of the world, the position of the African woman was not only *not* that bad, but in actual fact, in some of the societies, as in West Africa, she had been far better off than women of so many other societies. That when the African woman's position fell into the pits it was as a result of colonial intervention. . . . I may be wrong. But I suspect that any *traditional* African woman would be aghast contemplating the evidence of other people's dehumanization of women: from the complete depersonalization of the woman through name change after marriage which was invented only in modern Europe (can you imagine?!) and now slavishly copied around the world, to foot-binding in China and widow-burning in India. At the

very least, I hoped we could agree that the African woman never went through worse.

So what hurts about your book or its title and subtitle is that they reaffirm the prejudices we are struggling so hard to change. And from someone like you, that is really quite unforgivable. Surely, a scholar of your standing cannot be unaware that almost any data from any research can be manipulated to tell any tale we would want told, depending on our aims and objectives? Or that perhaps, even more than any other material, proverbs are highly susceptible to such manipulation? Had you considered the very different impression you would have created if you had titled and subtitled your book differently, using some other proverb from even your highly selective compilation? *MOTHER IS GOLD: African Proverbs and Sayings about Women*[7] for instance? . . . But of course, your aim was not to supply your readers with *positive* ideas about women from Africa. Plainly put, Mineke, I am just tired of the way *Africa always surfaces first whenever there is something negative on someone's agenda.* I am happy for you that UNESCO has adopted the project. But you see, the African opening was necessary. Or wasn't it? With those kinds of a title and subtitle, I genuinely think that it would have been more valid if you had begun the project from your own society. You could have laid your foundation with Dutch and European *negative* sayings on women, and then moved out to the rest of the world in search of parallels among other peoples: including Africans. (Aidoo 1992)

I then proceeded to discuss what could or could not be done with the offending dedication, thanked her for the copy of the book, and remarked on the fact that "it makes very interesting, if quite often controversial reading." The letter ended with the normal year's end and New Year greetings.

What seems to emerge from my letter to the author of *Source of All Evil: African Proverbs and Sayings on Women* is unmistakable. Even after one hundred years, and more, some sections of contemporary African society are not weary of the need to express our frustration and exasperation with the cavalier use of African artistic and creative material by sundry Western happy hunters who prey on Africa in order to valorize themselves and their cultures.

On the other hand, and in the long run, the more serious obstacle in the path of African women, African women writers and African women in literature—and elsewhere—is the almost total absence of support or recognition from our menfolk. Even when, as in Oladele Taiwo's full-length study of the prose works of some contemporary African women writers, we are given some recognition, it comes pathetically compromised. Yet, we have to express some gratitude to people like Taiwo. Like all artists, writers know that there is almost nothing like bad publicity, and so, to paraphrase oneself from some other time, we also know that when a critic refuses to discuss your work he is willing you to die.

Epilogue: There We Go Again, Poor African Women Writers, Getting Dissed Out of History!

On a bitterly cold day in Massachusetts, an American (white) teacher showed me a clipping from *West Africa* (9–16 January 1995) of a piece in which Ivor Agyeman-Duah interviews Kwame Anthony Appiah.[8] As she was showing me, the woman was telling me all the while how "mad" she was about the piece and that she suspected that I would be "mad" about it, too. My curiosity aroused, I began to read the piece and soon understood the source of her concern. The interview was partly on the state of African literature today. Yet neither in the interviewer's framing of the lead question nor in Appiah's response to it had either of them found it necessary to mention a single woman writer or her work. As I was reading the piece, the woman was watching me intently. When I failed to be "mad," she wondered why. I just told her quite calmly that I and other African women writers are used to being ignored. Isn't that sad?

Notes

Parts of this paper are comprised of sections from the following sources: "Women and Books," a paper given to the Writers' Workshop, Harare International Bookfair 1983; "Changing Relations Between the Sexes in the African Experience—A Quick Look at the Status Quo," a keynote address to a conference organized by the forum of African Students in Toronto (FAST), York City, October 1989; "The African Woman Today," *Dissent* magazine (New York, 1992); and a letter to Mineke Schipper in response to *Source of All Evil: African Proverbs and Sayings on Women*. In all cases, the pieces were revised and updated.

1   Also referred to as LIVE AID, Geldorf organized it in 1985. It galvanized the world. Among the honors Geldorf received were a knighthood bestowed by the Queen of England and the 1986/87 Third World Prize. The Western media consequently fell over itself paying him a well-deserved homage, calling him "Santa Bob," "Sir Bob," and "St. Bob."

2   This picture is the first part of a trifocal image the media gives the world of Africa. Travel agents, holiday tour operators, and airlines insist on two others: both of them to do with nature. So the second Africa we get is the land of exotic flora, and vanishing fauna, as in for example, the threatened elephant and the vanishing black rhino. Then finally we get the Africa of "golden" beaches, great lakes against crimson sunsets, calm rivers, breathtaking waterfalls, and always, white folks having fun! The press in Africa is no better. Check *The Insider* (Harare, Zimbabwe) No. 13, February, 1992, p. 1.

3   Ama Ata Aidoo, *Changes* (London: The Women's Press, 1991), p. 109. I must confess that I firmly believe that it is not only academics who can ratiocinate or analyze. Formal education and training only sharpen our basic intellect and allow us a certain breadth of field for comparisons.

4   "Dancing dog" is a reference to a general attitude that views a woman performing in any capacity as a "dog's walking on his hind legs. It is not done well, but you are surprised to find that it is done at all"!!— Dr. Johnson, quoted by Virginia Woolf in *A Room of One's Own*. Making these observations does not mean that we do not appreciate the fact that to date, Taiwo's book seems to be the only full-length study of the works of any group of contemporary African women writers.

5   Frankly, the regularity with which journalists and researchers ask this
     question is impressive. From Harare to London and New York, they
     never disappoint. Plus the interrogator always comes with such ease
     of manner, such confidence. As though of course it is absolutely all
     right to ask it! I have been asked this almost each time, everywhere
     and by everyone I have been interviewed by. In fact, in response to
     the incessant questioning, I felt compelled to do a paper titled "Why
     Women Writers Write About Women," which I first presented at the
     University of Richmond (Virginia) in 1989. In April/May 1991, I had
     to relive the nightmare over and over again, when I was in London for
     the production of *Anowa* at the Gate Theatre, and to promote *Changes*,
     which had just come out.

6   Letter to Mineke Schipper, January 30, 1992. Actually, I am ashamed
     now to confess that I let myself be discouraged from distributing the
     letter. I had made the mistake of showing a copy to an African male
     colleague whose intellect and intellectual integrity I had always re-
     spected. His response after reading it? "Ama, you better be careful.
     She is powerful."

7   The whole Yoruba proverb is "mother is gold, father is mirror."

8   *West Africa* is a weekly magazine published in London on West Afri-
     can affairs and on the affairs of the educated elite of West Africa on
     their regular visits to Britain and especially London. Established nearly
     one hundred years ago, it now comments generally on much of Africa
     south of the Sahara. Ivor Agyeman-Duah is a Ghanaian journalist.
     Kwame Anthony Appiah is a British/Ghanaian Professor of Afro-
     American Studies and Philosophy at Harvard University and the au-
     thor of *In My Father's House* (New York: Oxford University Press, 1992).

Works Cited

Aidoo, Ama Ata. *Changes*. London: The Women's Press, 1991.

———. *The Dilemma of a Ghost and Anowa*. London: Longman, 1987.

———. Letter to Mineke Schipper, 30 January 1992.

———. *Our Sister Killjoy: or, Reflections from a Black-Eyed Squint*. London: Longman, 1988.

Mugo, Micere Githae. *My Mother's Poem and Other Songs*. Nairobi: East African Educational Publishers, 1994.

Ngcobo, Lauretta. *And They Didn't Die*. London: Virago Press, 1990.

Odamtten, Vincent O. *The Art of Ama Ata Aidoo: Polylectics and Reading Against Neocolonialism*. Gainesville, FL: University Press of Florida, 1994.

Ogunyemi, Chikwenye Okonjo. "Womanism: The Dynamics of the Black Female Novel in English." *Signs* II (Autumn 1985): 63–80.

Schipper, Mineke. *Source of All Evil: African Proverbs and Sayings on Women*. London: Allison and Busby, 1991.

Taiwo, Oladele. *Female Novelists of Modern Africa*. London: Macmillan, 1984.

Walker, Alice. *In Search of Our Mothers' Gardens*. New York: Harcourt Brace, 1983.

Chapter 2

The Woman Artist in Africa Today: A Critical Commentary

Micere Mugo

A Definitive Introductory Anecdote

Once upon a time, when I was about ten years old, a paternal uncle came to our home one early evening. My father and a teacher colleague of his who was visiting us had gone out. My mother and a paternal aunt, a great friend of hers, were in the house. A group of us children was outside playing. After greeting the children and the women, my uncle proceeded to ask: *Hi! Kai andu matari kuo guuku umuuthi?* Literal translation: "I say! Are people not here today?"

A telling pause followed the question and then, in a matter-of-fact fashion, mother answered, *Moimiite ku? To ng' oombe na mburiici uroona!* Translation: "Where would they (people) come from? There are only the goats and cows that you see."

Not permitted to laugh at grown-ups, we the children simply took to our heels and ran to the back of the house where we rolled on the grass and giggled ourselves silly. We missed the rest of the drama.

This story introduces the underlying concern behind this paper's focus on the woman artist in Africa. The paper is both a statement as well as a restatement of a problem that women continue to pose even as we speak now: Why is it that criticism has paid such scanty attention to our women's artistic productivity? Why the imposed invisibility, in the face of so much harvest all around us?

Intention and Scope

Given the forbidding size of the African continent, the particularity of detail will have to suffer under broad generalizations, even though these should apply without falsifying the former. Similarly, under the constraints of time and space, the myriad of rainbows of artistic expressions produced by African women will have to wait while we narrow ourselves to the concerns of orature and literature.

The paper opens with a reiteration of the question already posed and comes in the form of articulations by a selected group of women artists and critics. The articulations are followed by a review of critics, mostly concerned with the written tradition, who have addressed African women's creativity. The presentation then proceeds to examine women artists creating in the orature tradition. Following this, the paper looks at statements by African women writers, revealing how they view their art and its role in society. Finally, the conclusion attempts to link some of the issues raised by the paper to reflections on the tasks and challenges that face CODESRIA (Council for the Development of Social Science Research in Africa), twenty years since inception.

Gender Discrimination and Women's Artistic Creativity

A number of critical commentaries on African women's writing have identified gender discrimination as the primary problem affecting women's creativity and the nature of discourse surrounding it.

Jessie Sagawa of Malawi argues as follows:

> The discussion of African Literature usually centers on the male writer and character. If the critic is concerned with women, it is mostly her significance to the style of the author that interests him. Rarely has the role of the women in fiction been of serious interest to the critic of African Literature. And the female writer finds herself in similar circumstances. While most of the male African writers have received wide coverage, the female writer has, until recently, tended to be neglected. (Sagawa, 164)

Sagawa goes on to argue that the woman critic has not, on the whole, done much more than her male counterpart to redress the imbalance, pointing to sexist indoctrination as the problem behind the marginalization of and bias against women writers and female depiction in African literature as a whole. She provides overwhelming evidence to support the case she is making and one so often made by other women before as well as after her.

In a similar vein, discussing problems faced by women artists, a paper entitled "Women Writers" (Mugo 1984, 162–205) explores the question of female writing and publishing, posing a related question: "Why is it that the written tradition appears to have pushed the African woman to the backwaters of literary achievement?" To answer the question, the discussion takes us back to the history of writing in the West, where patriarchal tendencies had led to the appropriation of the art by males to the extent that certain women writers were forced to assume masculine names in order to be published at all. The paper then traces African women's creativity through colonization and colonial education to the current oppressive neocolonial realities. All these environments are shown as not only promoting patriarchal subjugation of the African woman, but as actively militating against her potential artistic productivity, while she struggles to remain at the center of the creative process.

Penina Mlama comments on the discriminatory treatment of women artists in Tanzania, further reenforcing the arguments under discussion and thus demonstrating the universality of the experiences encountered by members of her gender. She observes:

> I think there are very good women artists. If you look at the traditional performances, the women are some of the best performers. But when it comes to writing, it is the men who are given prominence. If you look at the village, who are the best storytellers? It is the women. Who are the dancers? It is the women. So I think that, on the one hand, there is a deliberate attempt not to give prominence to women writers. I don't think this trend is confined to Africa alone, because I think this happened in Europe in the past. In many cases men do not like challenge from women. (Mlama, 86)

Ama Ata Aidoo pushes the debate further. In characteristic articulateness, she denounces a whole line of male critics, both African and Western, for negligence, discrimination, and callous condescension towards African women writers, punctuating her extended argument with classic illustrations, including what she terms, "a personal detail." The "personal detail" reveals how Robert Fraser once went as far as accusing her of borrowing the title *No Sweetness Here* from Ayi Kwei Armah's *Two Thousand Seasons*, published in 1973, whereas her short story "No Sweetness Here" had come out as early as 1962, and her collection of stories bearing that title in 1970. Having further detailed the "abuse" of other African women writers by a world of literary criticism dominated by men, Aidoo observes:

> In fact, the whole question of what attention has been paid or not paid to African women is so tragic, sometimes one wonders what desperation keeps us writing. Because for sure, no one cares. To have blundered our way into one more exclusively male sphere of activity can be forgiven. After all, clumsiness is a human failing. We all make mistakes. What is almost pathetic is to have persisted in staying there in the face of such resistance and some times resentment. Some of us believe that for writers and other creative persons any critical attention is better than none at all. (Aidoo, 117)

Beyond the question of negligence, there are other problems. Molara Ogundipe-Leslie, for instance, finds men as critics of women's writing "usually patronizing and legislative," further arguing that "many feel the concerns of women are not serious enough since they are about the area of emotions and the private life." She wonders "how we got the idea in colonized societies that only political themes are respectable" and argues that, in fact, "great literature has always been about emotions and the actions which spring from them," citing from Soviet literature to illustrate the case she is making. (Ogundipe-Leslie, 72)

Under interrogation here is the authenticity of gender-biased criticism that assesses women's writing using patriarchal values, standards, and paradigms. Indeed, Adeola James's book, *In Their Own Voices,* where Ogundipe-Leslie makes these observations, is full of statements like those expressed above. The writers include: Flora Nwapa, Buchi Emecheta, Rebeka Njau, Asenath Odaga, Penina Mlama, and others. Historically then, African women writers have been sidelined not only by the application of patriarchal measurements of what is success and what is failure, but through downright sabotage, viewed by women as a ploy to ensure male domination. Adeola James summarizes the debate as follows:

To say that the creative contribution of African Women writers has not always been recognized is to put the case mildly. In fact, the woman's voice is generally subsumed under the massive humming and bustling of her male counterpart, who has been brought up to take the women for granted. (James, 2)

In *The Collector of Treasures,* Bessie Head blames this male superiority syndrome on erring ancestors:

The ancestors made so many errors and one of the bitter things was that they relegated to men a superior position in the tribe, while women were regarded in a congenital sense as being an inferior form of human life. To this day women still suffer from all the calamities that befall an inferior form of human life. (cited in James, 5)

Clearly, Bessie Head identifies one of the root causes of our problems as being situated in patriarchal false consciousness. In this respect we do well to remind ourselves that even as we respond to Amilcar Cabral's call and "return to the source," our journey must be one of search: a critical retracing of ancestral footsteps, avoiding those that would lead to pitfalls instead of to a celebration of self-knowledge. In other words, the perpetuation of patriarchal values that undermine women's creativity must be addressed with uncompromising frankness. Unless this is done we will be condoning oppressive cultural practices designed for the purposes of creating islands of power in the midst of oceans of powerlessness. One is arguing that societies should nurture creative beings and not slaves of fettering traditions. With this understanding in mind, critics at whose hands women artists suffer should be perceived as undesirable intellectual power brokers whose empires and monopoly enclaves must be challenged. The structures that negate women's creativity are indeed a version of those found at the macrosocietal level. Ama Ata Aidoo makes a graphic representation of this reality when she observes:

Women writers are just receiving the writer's version of the general neglect and disregard that women in the larger society receive. . . . You know that the assessment of a writer's work is in the hands of critics and it is the critics who put people on the pedestals or sweep them under the carpet, or put them in a cupboard, lock the door and throw the key away. I feel that, wittingly or unwittingly, people may be doing this to African women writers. (cited in James, 12)

Of course the whole of the foregoing debate would be incomplete unless contextualized within the societal, cultural, political, and economic formations against which the contradictions highlighted take place. For it is these that shape the consciousness, or false consciousness, that are in a clash as we observe the interplay between the various subjects engaged in the conflict. Indeed, it needs to be argued that the seeming line between males and females, lumped in two generalized opposing camps, cannot stand the rigors of a pointed analysis. Socialization, indoctrination, and internalization of the kind of sexist, patriarchal values that deny the female artist her proper place/role and status in society, often cut across this assumed line. The systems and institutions that breed the unjust conditions, as well as the "myths" and "lies" that reinforce the false constructions under challenge apply to both men and women, even though to men more so than to their sisters. In this respect, of course, African women writers are not the only victims. We hear other women, particularly those from the southern hemisphere, and other oppressed groups complain about similar marginalization and belittlement. Demonstrative cases in point are highlighted in such works as: *Caribbean Women Writers* (Selwyn-Cudjoe); *The Sexual Mountain and Black Women Writers* (Hernton); *Black Feminist Criticism: Perspectives on Black Women Writers* (Christian); *Black Women Writers* (Evans); and others.

Cult of the Giants and Celebrities

Another patriarchal construction that has adversely affected women's writing is what might be described as the "cult of the giants and the celebrities." There is a tendency in literary criticism to exclusively focus on the works of already well established authors (read male writers). Why this "cult of the giants and celebrities"? Can these literary heavyweights be so fascinating that we can see nothing in other writers? Could it be a need, on the part of the critics, to remain on safe grounds, beaten as these might be? Is it fear of the unknown, the unfamiliar, and the unsung? Is it the kind of laziness that shies away from innovation? Is it loyalties to personal friendship, ethnic connections, nationalist bonds, ideological camaraderie? Is it careerist calculations that dictate patronage to celebrities so that they can bring us closer to the limelight in which they bask? Or could it be that we are afraid of touching women writers because of the sensitive gender issues raised by their works? These questions need to be wrestled with, for better or for worse. A celebration of giants is okay, but fascination with them to the point of fixation is wrong. Mesmerization can only lead to a freezing of possible extended action.

One is saying that African literary critics need to immunize themselves from the personality worship syndrome, which is one of the problems in Africa's larger democratization project. In the same way, if the works of women writers are to compete in the book market, as they should, the publishers and their distributors have to rise above the "big buck" syndrome. More than this, the academicians need to convince us that they are more than professional merchants who are only interested in promoting big names for what they can get out of them professionally. This may well be too much to ask in these days of IMF- and World Bank-maladjusted economics.

Worse off under this unfortunate contest of the big and the small, the powerful and the powerless, is the plight of women artists working within the orature tradition. Whereas women writers are correct in demanding the critics' attention and calling "foul" at the way the sexist game is played in criticism, looking at the orature tradition, the class factor becomes just as problematic as the power equation. Women working in this tradition have altogether been ignored as individual artists, being lumped under broad generalizations encompassing orature composers. Of individual talent and creativity, nothing has been really said. Generally, then, the written word boasts weightier currency than the spoken, and, under this equation, the woman writer becomes a "giant" while her sister remains a nonentity.

A Broad Categorization of Critics

At this junction, it is imperative that we focus briefly on the character of critics, because their response to literature can influence creativity either positively or negatively. More than this, they often shape the direction that creativity assumes.

Critics also play a major part in molding the consciousness of the audience at whom creative writing is aimed. Taking into account the debate generated in the previous sections, the first question that we need to ask here is: Are all critics of African women writers as negligent, biased, arrogant, condescending, and sexist as they have been made out to be? Secondly, are female critics of women writers free of these blindspots? The answer to these questions is obvious. Male or female, critics are not a homogeneous fellowship of identicals. They come in all types, shapes, shades, voices, and class positions. At the risk of generalizing, it might be useful to place them in three broad categories: conservative, liberal, and progressive. These categories are neither static nor sealed from interference by all forms of social dynamics and dialectics. The point under discussion, however, is that in discussing the role of critics and their influence on women's writing, we need to move beyond lumping them together if we are to pinpoint the source of the problem before us. In other words, conservative critics are likely to do more damage to women's creativity than liberal critics, for instance. On the other hand, if women writers were to call a round-table conference to discuss the dismemberment of their creative products and imaginative integrity, they would be making the most progress sitting down with the third category of critics. These distinctions are important in differentiating between creative and destructive criticism.

A Review of Selected Criticism

We now move back to a question raised earlier, namely: Has criticism on African women writers been as drastic as articulated? Whereas in the last ten years there have been efforts, some of them more than determined, to address the existing dry land of commentaries, sporting thorn bushes and shriveled shrubs, the situation still leaves a lot to be desired. A condensed survey of the literary scene will have to suffice. What follows is really an abridged review and update of the discourse initiated by Ama Ata Aidoo's paper, "To Be A Woman Writer—An Overview and a Detail," in 1985.

Up until the 1980s, criticism on African women artists appeared by way of book reviews, conference papers, journal articles, and book chapters. Perhaps the most consistent of the journals in soliciting submissions on women's work has been *African Literature Today*, originally edited by Professor Eldred Jones of Fourah Bay College and now co-produced by him with Professor Eustace Palmer and Marjorie Jones as associate editors. *OKIKE*, edited by Chinua Achebe, has had a similar policy and has featured women both as critics and as writers. Hans Zell's *A New Reader's Guide to African Literature* and *Présence Africaine* (Paris) have also included coverage on women. There are also a number of undergraduate and graduate theses out there, inside and outside Africa, a few of which I have personally supervised, devoted to women writers and writing. Indeed, individual critics, both male and female, have been persistent in their insistence that African women's creativity be brought to the fore for serious, extensive discussion.

It was not until the 1980s, however, that full-scale published studies on women's writing started to emerge. In 1984, Oladele Taiwo published the first volume of work devoted to African women writers, under the title *Female Novelists of Modern Africa*. In 1985 the Zimbabwe International Book Fair focused on "Women and Books" and devoted the workshop to discourse on women, creativity, publication, and related issues. The proceedings, including presentations by outstanding African artists such as Ama Ata Aidoo, Nawal El Saadawi, Flora Nwapa, Barbara Makhalisa Nkala, and others, were an overwhelming experience. The year 1987 saw the publication of a whole issue of *African Literature Today* devoted to African women writers. In the meantime, Adeola James was busy compiling her research, embracing fifteen African women writers discussing literature, criticism, and their own creativity. The work came out in 1990 under the title *In Their Own Voices*. A full-scale study of Ama Ata Aidoo's works by Vincent Odamtten has recently appeared. There is, of course, a lot more going on. Still, other than Odamtten's book on Ama Ata Aidoo, we are generally speaking of "small-scale," not "intensive," or "large-scale" criticism.

Hence, dissatisfaction still remains with what is obviously such a tiny drop in the sea of creative productivity on the continent. Perhaps the greater challenge is on women intellectuals themselves to get on with the task of generating criticism, in the interest of self-representation. For, other than Adeola James's *In Their Own Voices* and Rudo Gaidzanwa's *Images of Women in Zimbabwean Literature*, the thinness of women's own publication record of full-blown volumes of criticism is apparent.

This challenge is real and urgent, considering the fact that women writers are obviously not amused by some of the voices of their male critics. This, for instance, is what Ama Ata Aidoo (1985) has to say about Oladele Taiwo's work:

> In 1984, Oladele Taiwo published *Female Novelists of Modern Africa*, a book whose publishers blurbed it [sic] "as an important study" and for which the author himself claimed in the preface that it is a "celebration" of the literary activities of female novelists in modern Africa. For any writing woman, reading that "important study" should be a fairly sobering experience. . . . He virtually treats those African women writers whose novels he discusses (and short stories when the spirit moves him) as though they were his co-wives to whom he dishes out his whimsical favors. He constantly remarks on their intelligence or storytelling capabilities in the best "dancing dog" tradition, or as if they were a bunch of precocious six year olds who had demonstrated some special abilities to the headteacher.

The angered writer leaves Taiwo there, to rest in pieces!

Women Artists in the Orature Tradition

First of all, why orature and not oral literature? During the last three decades, some areas of the African Academy have demonstrated a very productive response to Amilcar Cabral's call for African societies to "return to the source" as part of the agenda for cultural emancipation, which this intellectual freedom fighter rightly perceived as a necessary revolutionary act in the struggle for economic-political independence. Scholarship in African orature has been one such area, the term orature itself being an innovative coinage on the part of the East African School, best articulated by Austin Bukenya and the late Pio Zirimu. The coinage liberated the heritage from the begging posture that the term "oral literature" tends to subject it to as scholars debate whether or not the African creative tradition can be taken as seriously as literature. Orature has achieved much needed independence as a result of this coinage, standing as a defined heritage on its own terms.

So, How Do We Define Orature?

African orature is an art form that uses language to create artistic verbal compositions. The verbal art culminates in dramatized utterance, oration, recitation, and performance. It has its distinct set of ethics, aesthetics, values, and philosophy that distinguish it as a unique heritage that has existed in the African world since time immemorial and that is still appreciated by the majority of Africa's population up to this day. In this respect, it should be understood that African orature continues to be created and consumed, even as we speak now. It also continues to influence creativity in written drama, poetry, fiction, music, song, and other forms of artistic expression. As Africa's indigenous popular art form, it is dynamic and still evolving, continuing to define itself alongside current trends in economic and political development and underdevelopment.

There is, for instance, a difference between the way orature is generated in a rural setting as opposed to an urban setting. There is also a difference in the way the various social classes preserve, attend to, and generate the art, with the affluent hardly having any use for it, except for "decorative" and expedient purposes, while the masses use it on an active basis. Further, it is possible to distinguish between progressive orature and reactionary orature. Orature that celebrates patriarchal values of domination, all forms of injustice and the silencing of the powerless in any society, is negative. On the other hand, orature that affirms life, growth, self-realization, human rights, and self-determination, is progressive.

Women Orature Artists

African women have always dominated the African orature tradition as cultural workers, storytellers, singers, dancers, riddle posers, dramatists, and so on. As creators, educators, guidance counselors, family historians (which is a common arrangement in horizontal social formations), women artists become, so to speak, the collective memory and stream of con-

sciousness that links a specific social unit from one generation to the other. The woman artist combines this role with
those of mother, aunt, grandmother and, at times, big sister.
The woman artist sits at the heart of a community's well-being
and fans the fire at the hearth of its imaginative furnaces, especially those of its youth. But, let us not fall into the trap of
either idealizing or generalizing, for, as intimated, like all other
artists and culturalists, women creators in orature have never
constituted a uniform group.

It is nonetheless safe to generalize and say that, of their own
free will and given a choice, most women artists will belong to
a positive orature tradition. Political coercion and enforcement
under neocolonial military and so-called civilian governments
have, however, exploited the negative aspects of orature to notorious levels, abusing the powerlessness and vulnerability of
women as performing artists in the worst possible manner.
Witness the arrival of African dictators at airports, often following trips during which they have either squandered national
resources through extravagant shopping sprees abroad, or
brought back foreign-aid packages with all kinds of strings at-
tached (once, ironically, mistakenly referred to as "AIDS" by a
peasant woman). On such occasions, women are rounded up,
often in the thousands, to dance and ululate for the returning
"heroes."

Wearing prints overwhelmed by humongous images of these
ugly neocolonial rulers on their backs, on their stomachs, across
their chests and upon their heads, these poor women carry
weighty symbols of Africa's betrayal and oppression. Roasting
in the sun, dancing themselves lame, they sing praise poetry
and ululate to these dictators as they swell with flattery, the
lies caressing their ears. This coerced *waheshimiwa* orature is
part of what may be termed neocolonial "ululation culture"
and not people's authentic orature.

A few years ago, a crowd of such "ululation culture" artists
actually referred to a senile octogenarian dictator as "a man in
his prime, full of youth, vitality and virility"! The subject of
praise waved back his fly whisk in self-appreciation. Now,
whereas one may not be in possession of personal details that
could possibly testify to this octogenarian's "virility," it is clear
that, physically, he could not possibly be so agile. Some days

following this praise song, it became evident that the subject of the song was far too old to even climb down an insignificant flight of stairs. When he tried to do so, the results were disastrous. He went plunging down, causing commotion in a packed conference center.

Another notorious dictator, under whom children and youth have been so impoverished that their plights will leave a telling scar on the future of the land to which they belong due to the extent of their dispossession, thrives as a national father figure. Even after fifteen years of economic mismanagement, repressive rule, and sheer police terrorism, coerced teams of "ululation culture" artists continue to poetize him in song, dance, and orations as *mtukutu raise* (almighty president) and worse still as *baba wa taifa* (father of the nation) and particularly, father of the children. Imagine these economically exploited and socially deprived mothers referring to this man as the father of their children! The creative imagination of Africa's orature tradition is under serious abuse and the result is what East Africans call a *kasuku* (parrot) culture in Kiswahili. The appropriation of orature through state patronage is a very serious cultural coup in the hands of today's African ruling classes.

Luckily, alongside this *waheshimiwa* orature, the resistance tradition of *Mapinduzi* orature is being created in the mines, the factories, the matatus, on the farms, in homes, and other arenas of productive democratic praxis. In this connection, it needs to be noted that it is during peoples' historical struggles that human beings have created positive orature in volumes. In this undertaking a lot of African women combatants and "sheroes" have been active creators. Slave narratives, dramas, protest poetry, and songs were composed as much by men as by women across the middle passage and in the lands of enslavement. These creations conscientized, uplifted, and spurred victims of unspoken atrocities and dehumanization not only to defy oppression but to overthrow it. *Mapinduzi* orature inspired liberation struggles in Algeria, Kenya, Angola, Mozambique, Zimbabwe, Guinea Bissau, Namibia, and other places, producing a body of creative compositions that continues to influence the direction of art in these countries up to this day. *Mapinduzi* orature artists have nurtured the collective memories of their communities. They have exposed and decried the abuse of human rights and have been active participants, mobilizing for democratic change. They have played the role of articulators of the people's collective vision, even as the collective group searches for more humane alternatives of defining who they are. They have created an orature that affirms not only the resiliency of the human being, but one that asserts people's humanity and capacity to defy oppression, while lifting heads high, in order to show the true face of humanity.

It is no wonder that dictatorships have panicked whenever *Mapinduzi* orature has mushroomed amidst oppressed groups in our societies. The panic has worsened when the creators and participants have happened to be women. The example of Kamiriithu, near Limuru in Kenya, demonstrated this. In 1982, after the government had closed the theatre and then demolished it, the Kiambu District Commissioner publicly chastised women for their participation in the work of the theatre, accusing them of neglecting their domestic duties in favor of frivolous dramatic activities.

Clearly, *Mapinduzi* orature women artists are a threat to neo-colonial dictatorships where *kasuku* and "ululation culture" producers are used not only to ensure the validation of the dictators, but to promote escapism, tourist entertainment, and false conscientization. As Laura A. Finke argues, "we must understand utterance as an ideological construct produced through conflict and struggle within a specific historical and social context." (Finke, 3) Utterance by women orature artists, who are a part of the oppressed world, becomes an "ideological construct" that interrogates the agents of enslaving systems and structures which negate their existence, and this is threatening to the status quo.

Paulo Freire argues that utterance of the "authentic word" is a liberating act. This is so because true utterance leads to reflection and possible action. Meaningful action impacts on structures of oppression and threatens to change them. Thus for as long as *Mapinduzi* orature women artists continue to struggle to transform the stifling reality around them, they remain a threat to the systems that create the injustice they fight. Consequently, they become agents of development. One does not need to be a soothsayer to predict that this kind of people-based, people-generated orature will far outlive neocolonial "ululation culture," composed in praise of *waheshimiwas,* their fly whisks, *fimbos,* and guns.

Women Writers Speaking for Themselves

Self-articulation and self-definition are very important processes on the journey of attempted self-determination, which then enables an individual to become a full participant in collective social human development. For this reason, it is crucial to listen to women writers sharing and analyzing their experiences in creativity. As we have seen in previous sections of this paper, most writers are not in the least bit satisfied with what the world of criticism has done with their creativity. In this concluding section, pronouncements by some of the writers will be commented and elaborated upon, in an attempt to show their relevance to African and human development.

So, what do African women writers have to say about their writing? What do they write about? Why do they write? And how do they write?

In August 1985, the Zimbabwe International Book Fair had as its theme, "Women and Books." Among the women writers gathered at the Book Fair were Ama Ata Aidoo, Nawal El Saadawi, Flora Nwapa, Barbara Nkala, Bertha Musora, Freedom Nyamumbaya, Christine Rungano, Asenath Odago, myself, and others. Bessie Head could not attend, at the last moment. In the keynote address, "Women and Books," since then published in a number of sources, I highlighted the concern that "book apartheid" had tended to exclude women from among the masses as creators. Later on in the workshop a hushed audience listened to a sad story from a Zimbabwean primary school teacher who had labored on a manuscript for years and then had suffered the pain of seeing her husband shred it to bits before throwing it into the fire. Reliving a part of the hurt, she had remarked something to this effect: "He had torn up so many years of my life and set them on fire!" At the same forum, Nawal El Saadawi and Flora Nwapa described writing as a part of themselves, arguing that those who shared their lives would have to accept "the writer" in them as a vital part of "the person" to whom they were united. Buchi Emecheta once referred to her books as her children, and she too has a sad tale about another shredded manuscript. Tsitsi Dangarembga has stated, "I write to save myself. . . . I really believe that's the only valid reason for writing." (Wilkinson, 193) What sobering pronouncements!

These writers are speaking about what is obviously a very shared need by women in the profession. Writing and creativity are lifelines, as far as African women writers are concerned. They are means of achieving what Okela Oculi once described as "explosion of silences," a neat poetic conception which I have since expanded on to read, "explosion of negative silences," seeing that silence can be positive or negative. Negative silence is imposed: positive silence is self-willed. Women are indeed sinking under the weight of mountains of negative silences that need to be exploded. Some of the stories over which the woman writer has to explode silence defy narration. The torture that Bessie Head narrates in *A Question of Power* is not just a work of imagination: the harrowing nightmares there are real. Ellen Kuzwayo, similarly, tells of the years of pain and suffering that she carried as heavy baggage until she sat down to write *Call Me Woman.*

In a lot of societies, African women are socialized to believe that suffering in silence is a virtue. Among the Gikuyu of Kenya, a married woman is, in fact, known as *mutimia*, literally meaning, the one who keeps her mouth shut. At marriage ceremonies, almost every woman is reminded that one of the ways of ensuring a lasting marriage is to shut up, to be a *mutumia*. It is a real wonder that mental asylums are not bursting with women! The tragic storyline of silences that needs to be exploded stretches between here and the beginnings of history, under all kinds of terrorizing experiences: patriarchal oppression, slavery, colonization, imperialism, war, etc. Women writers are attempting to break some of these silences. But as Molara Ogundipe-Leslie has argued in her essay, "The Female Writer and Her Commitment" (Jones, Palmer, and Jones, 13), these explosions will have to occur outside the present conventional structures and means of naming women's oppression. Women will have to "invent themselves," as Maya Angelou has argued time and again. Only such self-inventions will release stories and tragedies of rape, abuse, enforced self-bashing, and others that women have been coerced to bury in their subconscious. Women will have to "remember" and "articulate." Luckily, such stories have had beginnings in works such as El Saadawi's *Woman At Point Zero*, Kuzwayo's *Call Me Woman*, Ken Bugul's *The Abandoned Baobab* (its ideologically problematic areas notwithstanding) and others. The shame of humiliation will need to give way to the "utterance of the liberating word" (Finke). In this respect, it is relevant to point out that biographical and autobiographical writing will provide key sources in helping us understand the strength, spirit, and imagination that keep women going in the face of a rejecting world. In this respect, too, it is absolutely essential that African women network with other women of African origin in sharing the proposed forms of action that African women have to turn to in order to ensure a lasting explosion of silences. This is one of the forms of commitment that Ogundipe-Leslie discusses in "The Female Writer and Her Commitment." "The Transformation of Silence into Language and Action," which the late Audre Lorde (18–23) so articulately discussed in an article under that title, is of utmost importance here.

Another discovery that emerges from most of the fifteen women writers interviewed by Adeola James is that creative writing is empowering. In fact this is perhaps the answer to the rhetorical question raised by Ama Ata Aidoo, in a quotation cited earlier, where she wonders what kind of insistence it is that had kept women writing under the trying circumstances that she outlines. Concern with the need for empowerment partly explains why a lot of women writers not only insist on writing, in spite of the great odds that face them; but more than this, the reason why they have created such strong women characters in their writing, an issue that clearly emerges in Adeola James's interviews. Ama Ata Aidoo says at one point:

> If I write about strong women, it means that I see them around. People have always assumed that to be feminine is to be silly and to be sweet. But I disagree. I hope that in being a woman writer, I have been faithful to the image of women as I see them around, strong women, women who are viable in their own right. (James 12)

This compelling need on the part of the woman writer to empower not just herself but other women symbolized by the female fictional characters in her writing, comes out clearly in Ellen Kuzwayo's *Call Me Woman*, which is more than a personal autobiography: It is the life story of a whole line of South African sheroes. She says:

> I was challenged by the lives of so many, many women, who have made such tremendous contributions to the development and growth of our country, in particular to the development of the Black woman. . . . In fact, when the publishing process of the book was coming to an end, I noticed that the publishers had edited so many women out. I had to tell them to push me out of my book and put the women in because those were the people who inspired me to write. (Kuzwayo, 53)

Empowerment must be a key issue here, or we would not be dealing with the kind of violent reactions to women's creativity earlier discussed: the shredding of manuscripts, the imposition of "book apartheid" on women from the masses and the ridiculing of underprivileged women when they participated in artistic creations/productions. Indeed, *In Their Own Voices* reports women asserting that being women writers has enhanced their status both within the family and in society at large. A number of the writers interviewed, for instance, say that their children express special pride in them as writers, over and above everything else that their motherhoods symbolize.

Indeed, on the question of empowerment, Buchi Emecheta makes it categorically clear that to her, writing is power. Describing her young days in the village, she says:

> . . . Some women will sit for hours just peeling egusi (melon seed) or tying the edge of cloth or plaiting hair. Some will be telling stories and not to young children. I saw it and I used to sit with them. I liked the power these women commanded as storytellers. Since then, I thought I would like to be a storyteller myself. (James, 47)

This leads us to the third point consistently made by women writers: the fact that they have been influenced by the mothers, aunts, grandmothers, or older sisters who told them orature stories. (Interestingly, none of them claims to have been influenced by male orature artists). There is, therefore, not just a bond between many women writers and the orature on which they were nurtured. There is no doubt that part of the strength in the voice of the female writer draws from the attributes of what I have earlier identified as positive orature, including the following: the conception of "my story" as "our story": collective s/heroism; refraining from enigmatism; redefinitions of notions such as strength, courage, and achievement; preoccupations with human rights for the powerless; and so on. The concern with human rights is of special relevance when we look at the effects of war, famine, refugee existence, the fate of the African child, and everything else that this paper cannot even begin looking at. In *African Orature and Human Rights* (1991), I tried to touch on some of the ways in which connections with orature might provide us with a set of ethics and aesthetics that we have come to either disregard or belittle, centered as we are in Euro-ethics. The woman writer has an important role to play in all this. Indeed, a lot of women writers are creating their works, drawing from positive orature frameworks of reference.

Another woman writer who defines orature as a major influence upon her and her writing is Tsitsi Dangarembga. She observes:

> Another very significant experience was in fact the 1990 independence celebrations. I heard the most beautiful poem I've ever heard being recited, and of course it was a Shona. It brought back to me that we have an oral language here. It isn't written, it's oral, and when it is reproduced in the medium in which it is meant to be, it is absolutely astounding. (Wilkinson, 195)

Brief as it is, this discussion on the bonding between orature and women writers would be incomplete without a look at the work of Penina Mlama, a playwright who has: (i) created all her ten-plus works in Kiswahili; (ii) deliberately written in Kiswahili in order to address her local audience; (iii) consciously researched in the ethics and creative forms of orature in order to explore her themes, as well as evolve her aesthetics; and (iv) spent a good part of her theatre career operating in the community theatre mode, as a means of applying her art to the reality that her works address. She is a true popular

artist in the Brechtian sense of the term, as well as literally
being extremely popular and admired in Tanzania. How many
people have heard of this artist in the conferences that discuss
language, community theatre and popular culture? What about
this as a case, in illustration, of the "giants-celebrities" syndrome? In the following Penina eloquently states her views:

> I have been using the Tanzanian traditional forms like songs and
> storytelling, dance and recitation, so as to come up with plays which
> will appeal to the Tanzanian cultural identity. . . . We use theatre as
> a means through which people can discuss and analyze their prob-
> lems, put them into a theatrical performance, show it to the audi-
> ence and then discuss what the solution should be. When we first
> started working on the popular theatre movement, we did not de-
> sign it deliberately to engage "the woman issue" as such. But as
> soon as we started working, the woman issue always came up which-
> ever problem we dealt with at the village level. (cited in James, 77, 83)

Above, Penina Mlama demonstrates the way the type of community theatre she engaged in has tapped orature creativity
using performance to provide a people's platform for naming
the problems facing their communities and then dramatizing
them, in an effort to find solutions. She also shows how, over
time, these performances have provided space for addressing
sexism and the woman question in society. On the issue of
women as performing artists, she observes:

> In the area of drama, it is even more serious because many people
> still feel that women should not be performers. It is seen as a profes-
> sion which is despised; therefore respectable women should not be
> performing on the stage. This is a big contradiction because in a
> society like Tanzania, if you go to the village, our mothers are the
> dancers and the storytellers. Why is it that when you come to the
> city and a woman stands on the stage performing she becomes cheap?
> There are all these contradictions which really don't make sense
> and they have all contributed towards making the woman writer re-
> main unrecognized compared to the man. (cited in James, 86)

Mlama's statement takes us back to the debate on the censor-
ship of women as creators, artists, and performers. She demonstrated that in Tanzania, community theatre is an area of
contention for women artists—a regrettable fact, in light of the
potential that performance offers, combining, as it does,

orature and the written tradition. We are once more reminded that women artists are continuously being stifled by patriarchal constrictions and prejudice, even as they struggle to remain creative.

It is not possible to exhaust the discussion on what women see themselves as contributing to society through their art in the limited space allowed by this paper. As intimated, the subject has been quite extensively covered by the sources cited at the beginning of this section and in particular by Ama Ata Aidoo and Omolara Ogundipe-Leslie (1990). The paper's objective was to facilitate access to more voices and to highlight some of the concerns seen as being key to the promotion or negation of women's creativity.

In conclusion, let us summarize the issues raised by this paper in a poetic statement that is both an elaboration of the role of the African woman artist in society and a celebration of her undaunted determination to remain at the center of history and human development:

Prosaic Poem
In commemoration of those moments
when we make prosaic statements
that end up sounding poetic and then
we are reminded that ordinary human
dialogue is often punctuated with poetry.

Refrain: One Day!
One day, we shall rescue our lives from peripheral hanging on and assume the center of historical action. We shall explore every avenue that runs through our lives and create life roads that know no dead ends, extending them to the limits of human destination. We shall put an angry full stop to the negation of our human rights.

One day!
One day, we shall undertake a second journey along the bushy path of denied human development, chasing away the wild beasts that prowl the route of our narrow survival lest they make a complete jungle of our already bes-

tialized lives. We shall then cultivate a huge global garden and plant it with the seed of true humanity.

One day!

One day, we shall emerge from the wings and occupy the
center stage in full visibility, refusing to be observers and
understudies who wait behind the curtain of living drama.
We shall liberate the word and become its utterers, no
longer cheer crowds or ululators who spur on and ap-
plaud the molesters of our affirmative speech.

One day!

One day, we shall explode the negative silences and paralyzing terror imposed upon us by the tyranny of dominating cultures and their languages of conquest. We shall
discover the authentic voices of our self-naming and renaming, reclaiming our role as composers, speaking for
ourselves, because we too have tongues, you know!

One day!

One day, we shall make a bonfire of currently dismantling
and maladjusting economic structural adjustment
programmes, then engage in the restructuring process,
producing coherence around our scattered daily existence
til it is full to bursting. We shall stop at nothing short of
holding the sun to a stand still until the job is complete.

One day!

One day, we shall move the sun of our existence so that it
truly rises from the east of our lives, reaching its noon at
the center of our needs. We shall then release it to set in
the west of our perverted and dominated history, never
to rise again until it learns to shine upon the masses of
global being, not only islands of pirated living.

One day!

One day, we shall exterminate the short distance between
the kitchen and bedroom of our lives, storm out of the
suffocating space between the factory and the overseer

of our exploited creative labour, paving a path that leads to the buried mines of our suppressed human potential. We shall walk it if it stretches unto eternity.

One day!
  One day, we shall celebrate this earth as our home, standing tall and short, boasting of the abundance and multifariousness of our fulfilled human visions. We shall not look to the sky waiting for unfilled prophecies. We shall upturn the very rocks of our enforced stony existence, converting them into fluvial banks of life sustenance.

One day! (Mugo 1994, 83–85)

Works Cited

Aidoo, Ama Ata. "To Be a Woman Writer—An Overview and a Detail." Paper presented at The Writer's Workshop, Zimbabwe International Book Fair, 1985.

Bugul, Ken. *The Abandoned Baobab*. New York: Lawence Hill, 1991.

Bukenya, Austin, and Pio Zirimu. "Oracy as a Skill and as a Tool for African Development." Paper presented at the Colloquium, FESTAC, 1977.

Christian, Barbara. *Black Feminist Criticism: Perspectives on Black Women Writers*. New York: Pengamon Press, 1985.

El Saadawi, Nawal. *Woman at Point Zero*. Totowa, New Jersey: ZED Books, 1975.

Evans, Mari. *Black Women Writers*. New York: Doubleday, 1984.

Finke, Laura A. *Feminist Theory, Women's Writing*. Ithaca, NY: Cornell University Press, 1992.

Gaidzanwa, Rudo. *Images of Women in Zimbabwean Literature*. Harare: College Press, 1985.

Head, Bessie. *A Question of Power*. London: Heinemann, 1974.

Hernton, Calvin C. *The Sexual Mountain and Black Women Writers*. New York: Doubleday, 1987.

James, Adeola, ed. *In Their Own Voices: African Women Writers Talk*. London: James Currey, 1990.

Jones, Eldred Durosimi, Eustace Palmer, and Marjorie Jones, eds. *African Literature Today* (1987).

Kuzwayo, Ellen. *Call Me Woman*. San Francisco: Spinsters, 1980.

Lorde, Audre. "The Transformation of Silence into Language and Action." *The Cancer Journals*. San Francisco: Spinsters, 1980.

Mlama, Penina. Interview in James, ed.

Mugo, Micere Githae. *My Mother's Poem and Other Songs: Songs and Poems*. Nairobi: East African Educational Publishers, 1994.

———. "Women Writers." Paper presented at the New Writing Conference, Commonwealth Institute, London, 1984.

———. *African Orature and Human Rights*. Human and Peoples' Rights Monograph Series, No. 13, ISAS, Lesotho, 1991.

Ogundipe-Leslie, Molara. Interview in James.

Sagawa, Jessie. "The Role of Women in African Literature: Feminism and the African Novel." Undergraduate honors thesis, Department of English, Chancellor College, University of Malawi, 1984.

Selwyn-Cudjoe, R., ed. *Caribbean Women Writers*. Wellesley, Massachusetts: Calaloux Publications, 1990.

Taiwo, Oladele. *Female Novelists of Modern Africa*. New York: St. Martin's, 1985.

Wilkinson, Jane. *Talking with African Writers*. London: James Currey, 1990.

Zell, Hans, ed. *A New Reader's Guide to African Literature*. New York: Africana Publishing Company, 1983.

Chapter 3

The South End of a North-South Writers' Dialogue: Two Letters From A Postcolonial Feminist "Exmatriate"

Micere Mugo

Editorial Note: *The dialogue referred to in the title took place between Micere Mugo and Birgitta Bouch, a minority Swedish poet writing in Finland. As is alluded to in one of the letters, the correspondence arose in conjunction with a UNESCO project on women writers. Here, in keeping with the theme of our collection, we present only the letters of Micere Mugo, who provided them with the suggestion that they be edited to sharpen the focus on the theoretical issues and concepts discussed. However, in accordance with the feminist spirit of the writing, we have decided to include them more or less in their entirety, believing that even (indeed, perhaps especially) in the personal details of the writer's life, there is much to be learned about the major challenges that confront a postcolonial literary figure. In the following letters, Mugo suggests that the hierarchies of colonialism and neocolonialism can be actively challenged through personal actions. Exploring her situation as an exile from Kenya who attempts to keep her voice of protest vital and audible to all who are interested, she pays special attention to the power of sisterhood and the supportive nature of community. In short, while on one level these letters appear simply to chronicle the experiences of one woman, they serve eloquently to demonstrate a broader phenomenon: the making of a contemporary African feminist protest writer and social activist.*

Birgitta Bouch
Mechelingatan 4 B 60
00100 Helsingfors
FINLAND

Dear Birgitta,

I am giving myself the liberty of addressing you by your first name, hoping that you do not mind and also that this will influence you to drop the *Mugo* part of me when addressing me next time. And now, how are you doing at the many fronts of struggle that characterize a woman's life? For, like me, you seem to be all persons in one: head (or is it one of the heads?) of household; mother (and wife); professional; writer; political activist; private and public figure. Well, the Gikuyu language has a proverb that says: *"njogu ndiremagwo ni miguongo yayo"* (an elephant does not give up carrying its tusks), but, frankly, I must admit that my tusks have proven too heavy over the last two years. However, my usual spirit of "never give up!" continues to be one of my anchors. I will explain what I mean by all this in a moment.

For now, let me ask you to please accept my most sincere apologies for the regretted and unintended role I have played in causing the delay of the South/North women's dialogue. More personally, let me apologize for keeping you under suspense during this past year as my partner in correspondence. Believe me, I find this letter very difficult to write because the long gap that stares at me between June 29, 1991 (when you wrote the launching letter) and today, November 3, 1992, is more than embarrassing—making my task most awkward, to say the least. The irony of it all is that under normal circumstances I am such an avowed keeper of promises and strict observer of deadlines that I am sometimes accused of being "neurotic" where honoring these matters is concerned. Furthermore, my political activism has come to convince me that collective efforts are so "sacred" that not even personal problems should be allowed to sabotage them. Yet, here I am, having allowed just that to happen. I feel awful and wish that I had been more firm about withdrawing from the project at the time I had suggested I should last year. Anyhow, it is too late to regret this now and I do want to thank you for your patience as well as insistence that I go on. I will do my best not to break the contact this time.

Having tendered my apologies, let me now take time to explain what went wrong—why I am writing from America and not Zimbabwe. Later on I will have to answer your questions as to why you were writing to me in Zimbabwe and not Kenya. Oh, the stories of my life! Where do I begin now? Oh yes. I think that the last time I communicated with you was when I was in London last year, on my way to the Edinburgh Women's Writing Conference where I was due to give a key note address. At that time, I had hoped that come the end of December I would have responded to your communicative one of several months earlier. I had clearly underestimated what it would take to wind up seven years of active living and working in Zimbabwe, which I needed to do because I was going to be away on sabbatical leave for the entire year in 1992. The whole of December was a nightmare. I needed forty-eight-hour-long days to do all that had to be done. And of course, being a single parent, mother of two "minors" *by law* (in real life they are two very mature and tough women combatants!) amounted to winding up for three people where official business was concerned.

By the end of December, the idea of correspondence had become a dream. The reality was that my fatigue became extreme to the point where I was involuntarily making a public joke of myself. Quite a number of times I found myself driving through red lights, unaware that this was the case and at other times I would be reminded by impatient hooting drivers that I had stopped at a green light—obviously waiting for it to go red in order to move, eh? Dangerous stuff, I tell you! In connection with this, let me encourage you to keep up the tradition you seem to have made a part of your routine: taking off to the countryside during the summer and stealing off to Sweden or some place for a short vacation. If we laboring women do not learn to take time off, cool out and just regroup—emotionally, intellectually, socially, physically, etc., etc.—the responsibilities around us will ensure that our body systems unwind on us, not to mention the possibility of their winding up on us! I am, of course, preaching about the desired ideal. The reality is that most of the time, in order for some of us (and for our children to live), we are forced to remain human bees. When I think how much worse it is for our sisters who are members of the oppressed masses of the world, I become absolutely persuaded that if our feminist struggle does not place the agenda for economic justice at the forefront of the rights we must fight for as women, we will have started the battle from the rear and not the front. If other feminist struggles can afford to do this, those of African women and sisters from the so-called "Third World" will have betrayed the struggle for basic human rights which the majority of their kind are faced with on a day-to-day basis. They will have assumed a simplistic civil rights approach in addressing the problems that deny life itself, to the overwhelming lot of womankind in our stifling econo-socio-political systems today. . . . But let me continue with my narrative.

By the morning of my departure (I had to be at Harare airport around 4 A.M. on Sunday, January 5, for a six o'clock take off), I had not had even a wink of sleep for two full days and nights. Up to four hours before the flight, I honestly did not know that I was going to ever make it to the flight. And I was on the type of ticket that could not be changed in any way. Let me tell you, I only managed to catch that plane due to the love and generosity of some close friends and members of my extended family in Zimbabwe. (My daughters had left two weeks earlier to go through Kenya in order to reconnect with our family as well as relink with their motherland, following almost a decade of separation). These wonderful people took control of a situation that would have been impossible for me to face alone. They packed up my bags, rescued all the vital documents that I needed for travel from piles of engulfing paperwork, made sure that one of them would drive me to the airport and absolutely insisted that what they were doing was only natural! Imagine it being natural to have to go back to my flat the following day (and a few more after that!) to sort out the upside down state of things there! What would we do without friendship and love? Take it from me, some of these people have been sorting out my unfinished personal business up to the present.

You know, Birgitta, self-sufficient as I try to be as a general rule, there are times in my life when I know that I would never survive, let alone manage, without collective networking and group support. My departure from Zimbabwe was clearly one of those situations. My short visit with some very close friends in Addis Ababa and a flying stop-over in London during which my daughters and I spent a healing weekend with a very dear elder sister, Judi and her family, confirmed the same. Njoki's home in Addis and Judi's in London gave me what I could not find in my own home: sleep, peace, and rest. I cannot tell you how much I needed what these two homes gave me as replenishment in order to undertake the final lap of my journey to the United States of America where I was going to spend my sabbatical leave with my daughters, at the Africana Studies Center of Cornell University.

We arrived in Ithaca, New York, in mid-January, under incredible temperatures of around sixty degrees—very odd for north country winter weather. Six hours later there was a mean storm that deposited piles of snow, making the story that was circulating about a green Christmas only some weeks before a bit difficult to buy. The Mugo family decided to make a joke of this whole drama by boasting that they had taken Ithaca by storm! However, the joke did not last us very long because barely a month later I was taken by storm myself by the unexpected diagnosis of an illness that landed me in a local hospital for an operation. Before I had time to recover from the shock—physically and psychologically—I was hit by a vicious virus attack that almost wiped me out and I mean just that. I had never known that a virus attack could be so dramatic and fateful. It was a frightening experience and it left me a wiser survivor. However, up to now I have not quite recovered from the follow-up "expenses" that these hospitalizations occasioned, at the health and financial levels.

Before my hospitalization here, I knew that under capitalism being poor is a "crime," but now I know that given the unaffordable cost of medical treatment, it is an added "crime" for a person with light pockets to be sick in this United States of America. I have had to take up a full teaching load at Cornell University—which I was fortunate enough to secure—in order to pay up my health bills. Since I essentially came here to finish up the compilation of some manuscripts that I wanted to hand in to a publisher early next year, this has meant an enforced double load of work. Once again, my correspondence has had to be shelved and you are one of the unfortunate victims. But, even though I am under siege, especially in so far as unfulfilled deadlines are concerned, I feel sufficiently strong and defiant of the odds before me to promise that I will do my best not to break the process of dialogue that we have set in motion and that needs to continue.

Now let me turn to some of the questions that you asked in your letter.

First of all, congratulations on having hit the half century mark a little ahead of me. I am going to be fifty this year. So, other than the roles that we seem to have in common, here is something else that brings us together—the age circle. By the way, being members of the same generation is quite a big, uniting experience in my indigenous Kenyan culture and in Zimbabwe, my new home.

On the question of gender, unlike you, I have never wanted to be male even as a child. In fact, I have always embraced my femaleness. Part of this self-affirmation came from my parents' attitude towards patriarchal values. Both of them, well-known educationists during the thirties, forties, and fifties in our part of Kenya, fought relentlessly for the rights of women—including the then controversial issue of girls' education. There were seven "girls" and three "boys" in the family before the death of one of my younger sisters, just several years ago. We were all brought up as equals and there was never any demarcation line between what patriarchal society considers work for males and work for females. My father used to do household tasks defined by sexism as "women's work" and also encouraged us girls to cross the artificial boundary line mystifying certain tasks as male and "unfeminine." My parents taught us the discipline of productively engaging in manual labour—using our own hands to take care of our personal business and working around the farm/home—even though there were a lot of domestic and farmhands employed by them. The other influence had to do with my mother's family background. She came from a family of extremely liberated women, led by her mother, Nzisa. My maternal grandmother, whom I still remember with unceasing admiration, was beautiful, extraordinarily intelligent, articulate, forceful, and also one of the most compassionate of human beings that walked this earth. *Guuka* (grandfather), her husband and a famous teacher, also some kind of reverend, was gentle, wise, and charming. He too believed in women being equal achievers with men. This is difficult to believe, isn't it? More so when one remembers that my grandparents would have been born in the 1880s or 1890s. Anyway, with this kind of pro-female family background, one always felt good about being a woman. Ironically, I never traced any contradiction in a statement that my father used repeatedly, addressing the "girls" in my immediate family. He would tell us: "Always remember that you are my boys!" Now that I think about it, I never heard him refer to my brothers as his girls. He must have been loudly debating with the world out there and its hangups about female children.

Perhaps I should tell you a little bit about my place of birth. I was born at a place called Baricho in the Kirinyaga district of Central Kenya, on the slopes of Kirinyaga, that legendary and mythical/mythological mountain, poetized by matriots, patriots, historians, geographers, mountaineers, beauty lovers, and the like. My mother's farm still sits under the majestic grandeur of that awesome mountain with its famed trio peak covered with snow. So, we are quite privileged to be a natural part of a beauty spot that people travel from great distances to see. It is also important to point out that it was in the forests of this historic mountain (among other places), that the Mau Mau combatants waged the armed struggle against British colonialism. Field Marshall Dedan Kimathi operated between Nyandarwa and Kirinyaga mountains, but one of his deputies, later, Field Marshall Muthoni wa Kirima, whom I call my *chimurenga* mother (liberation war mother), had Kirinyaga forests as her regular base. From all this you can see that my life seems to have been surrounded by a series of historic and historical struggles since childhood. I am, to a large extent, a child, a product and an extension of these struggles—a note on which I should now turn to the question of why I am in Zimbabwe and not Kenya, my home of birth.

This is another one of my long stories which I will try and summarize. On the other hand, because the story defines my plight as a woman political activist, struggling against imperialism in a neocolonial situation, a position which consequently unravels the condition of many other women in Kenya under the same conflicts—women whose stories are not in the international press—I will also have to be careful not to mutilate the account; otherwise I will smother its essence. Let me be quite direct and say that I have been in exile from Kenya since August 1982. When I went into exile, I had just won a divorce suit that I had initiated some years earlier and had been given custody of my two daughters, Mumbi and Njeri. Mumbi was just about turning eight and Njeri had just turned six. For the first two years of our exile, we lived in Canton, upstate New York, where I was a visiting professor at St. Lawrence University. Being the first-ever Africana member of the academic staff at that very fine, wealthy, and overwhelmingly white institution, I dedicated my time and energy to the agitation of concerns such as: the hiring of progressive people of color on the faculty, the incorporation of Africana Studies in the curriculum, the strengthening of Africana associations on campus—including the Black Studies' Union—and so on. I was also involved in voluntary community work around the Canton area. I designed and launched a program for African American prisoners at a nearby jail in which I taught Kiswahili, African History from antiquity to the present and held workshops in creative writing. In between my campus and community activities, I jetted back and forth around North America, campaigning for the release of political prisoners in Kenya and conscientizing my audiences on the abuse of human rights by the neocolonial ruling classes in our motherland. Take it from me, it was quite an uphill battle then, given the conspiracy of establishment-controlled media in the West, determined to depict Kenya as the epitome of democracy since the regime was capitalist and anti-"communism." As far as the American government was concerned, of course, its military bases superseded the interests of the Kenyan people, and so in its eyes, the police state that neocolonial Kenya was remained a democracy and the world was actively and deliberately misinformed so. It was a difficult time for us.

During our stay at St. Lawrence University, ideological differences between me and a lot of my colleagues notwithstanding, my daughters and I were really made to feel a part of the campus family life. We experienced hospitality, support, solidarity, and love from many people that I need not mention by name since you do not know them. The most moving support came from a community of East African women students, especially a core of Kenyans, led by two particular ones who literally parented Njeri and Mumbi while I concentrated on political activism. I would not have survived without the support of these young sisters. They were constant and tireless in their solidarity. Students and colleagues at St. Lawrence were also very supportive in signing petitions for the release of political prisoners and in helping with their distribution. The community played quite a significant role in assisting us to expose the hypocrisy and criminality of the Kenya police state. My courses were always fully subscribed and since St. Lawrence University had a Kenya programme, contact with the students who might be a part of this journey provided a very important meeting point. So, St. Lawrence became our first home in exile.

However, much as the St. Lawrence University community in itself made us feel a part of it, my daughters and I were not happy living in America. The girls had a harder time than me. They became targets for attack by some of the children they went to school with and were treated to the worst racism that they could have imagined possible, by children like themselves. However, the most distasteful aspect of it was that the oppression came from bullies who were years older then they were. Their class teachers—both of them tremendous, professional people—did everything they could to protect my daughters in the classroom; but life outside the classroom, especially on the bus and the playing fields, was a perpetual battlefront for them. Not even the headmistress, another wonderful individual and professional, could control that. It is to the credit of the girls that their strength, fighting spirit, and love for each other saw them through all this. But the experience left emotional and psychological scars that have taken time to fade. In fact, it is not possible for these kinds of dents to go away altogether.

Concern over the development of the children thus became the instigating reason behind my decision to return to Africa after two years of exile; but there were other very serious underlying needs for this return. In America I felt very alienated, geographically, historically, and spiritually, from the heart of the political struggle that my comatriots and compatriots were waging at home. I needed to get back to some closer position.

Physical removal from the scene of action can become a seriously alienating factor. One stands in danger of losing hold of the heartbeats that dictate the rhythm and pace of the action on the primary ground. Furthermore, I could not deal with the self-whipping that I constantly put myself through every time I stood up in front of my American students, struck by the guilt of the realization that my skills and services were much more desperately needed by our mother continent than by America. These considerations aside, my daughters were losing both of their indigenous tongues rather fast and I felt that another African locale would at least give them a compensating African language to work with, not to mention a better chance to retain their Kiswahili and Kikuyu which they had spoken fluently before our departure from Kenya. So, two years following our arrival in Canton we set out for Africa.

The University of Zambia had offered me a position as Chairperson and Professor of the English Department, an offer I had accepted immediately. On our way to Zambia, my daughters and I stopped over in London and while there, we received notification from the University of Zambia that the Moi regime had contacted the government of Zambia at state level objecting to my presence there. That was the end of my intended journey to Zambia. I was stranded in London, without a job or home for a few months. This was another stage in life when the support, generosity, and love of friends and caring relations helped me live through a most destabilizing experience. Another generous act—this time from the government of Zimbabwe—brought about a solution to the crisis. They invited me to go and make Zimbabwe my home. When way back in 1970 I had become an active member in solidarity work with—among other struggles—the Zimbabwean liberation struggle, an engagement that I had continued with until Zimbabwe's independence, little did I know that this involvement would end up providing me with a home in a desperate moment. That great African country whose ancient history is a symbolic reminder of the continent's contribution to global civilization has been our second home since November 1984. My base has been the English Unit in the Department of Curriculum and Arts Education, at the University of Zimbabwe.

And now another short story to answer a question that I can already read in your mind: why did I have to go into exile?

At the time I left Kenya in 1982, I was serving a second term as the elected Dean of the Faculty of Arts—then the biggest faculty at the University of Nairobi, comprising departments in the Arts, Humanities and the Social Sciences. Interestingly, the faculty was predominantly male, but a good section of my male colleagues had no hang ups about my academic leadership as a woman and I had a most productive working relationship with the majority of them. The faculty must have been happy with what we had collectively achieved during my first two year term of deanship as well because after it, they had unanimously elected me for a second term—unopposed. Among some of the needs we had tried to address was the challenge of relating theory to practice, beginning with the use of our skills and knowledge to serve the masses of Kenya whom we perceived as victims of extremely oppressive socio-economo-political structures under the pro-imperialism neocolonial dictatorship of the day. I also belonged to the Kenya Writer's Association, the executive committee of which I was a member. The progressive wing of this Association shared the above vision and was challenging writers to use the art of writing and composition in the struggle for economic and social justice, raising an uncompromising voice against the abuse of people's rights at all levels of existence. I was a member of the University Academic Union as well. Among a whole long agenda of the human rights we were fighting for were: the removal of American bases from our country, an end to organized state violence at all levels, and an end to detention and imprisonment of political activitists on account of their views, freedom of expression, etc., etc. These and many other activities that helped me contextualize the struggle that needed to be engaged in if women and other oppressed people in our country were to achieve their liberation became a part of my daily life. Inevitably, I found myself in the circle of people targeted by the police for harassment, arrest, habitual investigation, and torturous interrogations anytime that the police felt like rounding its victims up. But we survived, through sheer obstinacy and a vision of what we saw as the inevitable end of the oppressive regime on the one hand and the sure victory of the people on the other, however long the struggle might take.

Following the attempted coup in August 1982, there were massive arrests all over the country. I was confidentially tipped that I was to be included in a swoop that was meant to net colleagues and students on the university campus. I immediately left with my two daughters, but under a firm promise to myself and the comrades who helped me escape, that I would use all the time and energy possible to internationalize the Kenya struggle. Up to now this is my mission and I will never look back, for, what has happened to awaken the international community to the plight of the Kenyan people, ultimately stripping the lies that this community has been told about imagined democracy under neocolonial capitalism, is important if global struggles are to be linked. With the solidarity of other international struggles, the Kenya masses have pushed the Moi dictatorship into a corner and forced the discredited regime to bow to the democratic political process. Unfortunately, even as I compose this communication, the emerging opposition leadership is busy enacting predictable betrayal of this mass-based collective achievement. The big fish are preoccupied with squabbling over who is to be the president of the country, instead of pushing forward the issues on the people's agenda for real socio-econo-political liberation. It is sad. Still, I have faith in the people of Kenya and if nothing else happens, the experience will have left us more politically mobilized, will have created some space for us to debate a little more freely and will have taught us that true leadership will ultimately have to evolve from the masses themselves, being defined by the form that the struggle takes. The history of elitist leadership, however progressive its claim, will need very systematic proof to correct its betrayals of our history of collective struggle.

You asked about my books. When I published my first three titles: *Daughter of My People, Sing!* (poetry), *The Long Illness of Ex-Chief Kiti and Other Plays*, and *Visions of Africa* (literary criticism), I deliberately chose a local publisher, in the spirit of promoting our local publishing houses. In this particular case, I was dealing with the East African Literature Bureau, a child of the East African Community, which I believed needed to be nurtured as an experiment in regional co-operation. Many of us were saddened by its break-up. With that demise emerged the Kenya Literature Bureau, as a part of the Ministry of Education. Its distribution of books has been very poor, especially internationally. Compound that problem with the fact that according to the government I am a "dissident" and you have a major part of the statement of my problem as far as the books go! Well, I have to do something about getting them re-issued by another publisher. In the meantime, I will try and get some copies for you even though this may take quite some time. By the way, has the copy of *The Trial of Dedan Kimathi* that you were looking for resurfaced? It is the kind of work that should be readily available on inter-library loan, and so I hope that you have managed to secure another copy.

I would very much like to read what you have written as well. You said that *This World Is Ours,* the work you have co-authored with Carita Nystrom, is in English. For some reason, it is not in our library here and I wonder whether you would be kind enough to send me a copy of it at some point, or to give me details about the publisher so that I can do the ordering myself. I would appreciate that. You see, I am engaged in discourse touching on women's liberation and consequently, I have a deep interest in examining aspects of feminist theory and praxis. In fact, right now I am teaching a course on African and African American women's biographical and auto-biographical sketches. So, I would very much like to hear what you and your colleague have to say about these matters.

I was quite fascinated by your language status as a member of the Swedish-speaking minority in Finland. What is the political history behind this? Artificial boundaries? Conflicts resulting in dispersion? Migration? I need some education on this as my knowledge of your part of the world is rather limited—thanks to the British concept of global education that taught its products so little outside its empire! Believe me, I have spent the better part of my life re-educating myself in response to the miseducation that denied us a true knowledge of ourselves, our history, and our culture, while also leaving us rather ignorant of anything that was not British or British-made, as it were. So you see, I need your help and solidarity in this process of self-education.

And while you are at it, please tell me: are you considered a Swedish writer by the Swedes or are the geographical boundaries so firm that you can only be a Finnish writer working in Swedish? I have a feeling that I may seem to be asking the obvious, but I am deliberately provoking the nationalist debate in an effort to suggest that we need to do a remapping of a lot of these boundaries that artificially separate people all over the world. The African case and the frightening carving job of the continent that was done in Berlin during the so-called Scramble for Africa by western imperialist powers, who really proved to be professional civilization butchers, is of course a tragic demonstration of this. Last semester, a Nigerian colleague who was a visiting scholar here told me of an outrageous case in which a boundary between two West African nations cuts through a family farm. Can you imagine the kind of administrative problems this must create?

The other issue in your letter that intrigued me was the statement that you like being a member of a minority group because it sharpens your sensitivity in viewing details that the majority tends to take for granted. Strangely, in terms of logical connections, your argument took me to South Africa (and to the historical contexts under which the tragic drama of colonial and imperialist domination has been enacted by ridiculously small minorities, using the power of the gun, or money) and I simply had to conclude that sensitivity must be completely alien to these invaders' constitutions! Look at the terrorism they have used and continued to use, not only to try and make the overwhelming majority invisible and immaterial, but to condemn them to eternal servitude! But then, we are not really dealing with normal human beings, are we? For, if they had a claim to this they would realize that the act of being human is in the affirmation of others' humanity. Without this we are a mockery of the human essence.

Lastly, let me answer the question you asked regarding my language situation. I speak Gikuyu, Kiswahili, English, and rather inarticulate Chishona. The last is a Zimbabwean language that I need to polish up so that I can learn another major tongue there, known as Sindebele. I am probably being a bit ambitious, but there is no harm in creative ambition! Other than these, I speak and write very poor French which I used to be quite good at. I have done some short unpublished pieces in Gikuyu and Kiswahili that I need to channel into publication at some point. My other ambition, as far as the language of creative composition goes, is to write and publish in Kiswahili which I have had to teach myself mostly as it was not on my colonial high school curriculum. The reason for this future agenda is that Kiswahili cuts across the more than 52 language groups that exist in Kenya and has become the medium of communication among the workers as well as across the rural communities in the country. I am convinced that one of the reasons why Tanzania has been able to define itself as more of a nation (in terms of ethnic non-antagonism) than Kenya has, for instance, is because in its planning and policy-making, the government has given Kiswahili a true national status, allowing it to serve as an important communication link between the various Tanzanian nation groups. But, more on language another time.

For now let me end here, hoping to hear from you before too long if this lengthy and political letter of mine does not put you off altogether. Whatever you do or do not do, please tell me how you spent this summer. Your description of the Finnish summer in last year's letter was so poetic that I look forward to some more of that. And what is the fall or autumn like there? In this part of America, it is beautiful. Some trees have leaves that come out in stunning colors. As for the winter, to be quite honest, the cold tends to freeze my vitality. In fact, I would need an overdose of inspiration to ever do a repeat performance of something that I did in 1969 during my first winter in Canada. I actually poetized snow! Amazing!
Stay well!

Warm regards,

Micere Githae Mugo

P.S. I started this letter two weeks ago and had promised to send it early last week but I became extremely busy just before going to the women's conference in Toronto and could not complete it. Today, November 19, I am off to yet another conference. By the way, the Toronto event is a success story that I must relate to you in detail sometime. Do not let me forget to do this, please, because it is very important.

Very finally, should there be too many errors in this letter, please understand. I am working on it late at night to make sure that I post it before traveling later on today.

Thank you and stay well.

222 Sapsucker Woods Road, #2A
Ithaca, NY 14850

May 28, 1993

Dear Brigitta,

Thank you very much for yours of March 23, 1993 and for the beautiful card that you sent along with it. I was very sorry to learn that the flu had calculated its unwelcome visit in your direction even as history was ushering in the new year. I do hope that you are feeling better by now because the flu bug can last a long time.

Your question: WHY ARE WE DOING THIS? made me laugh, not out of insensitivity, but because you posed it in such an agonized way. Your obvious irritation (I apologize if I misread you) itched through each one of your words with such drama! Let me, by the way, confess that I fully share these feelings with you. There is no doubt that pressure that you and I could have well done without has been created by the need to meet the publisher's deadline which by now, most regrettably, must be more than dead. I think that if there is anything to be learnt from all this, it is that the processes of creativity and dialogue cannot and should not be manipulated, however well-meaning this manipulation is. I also have a feeling that beyond this and, outside the tightness of our individual schedules, the delays in getting back to one another have been due to the fact that we are conscious we are somehow engaged in an abstract exercise. I mean, we are communicating with each other as agents of a publication project rather than as voluntary correspondents. Do you see what I mean? This creates some form of awkwardness and even, to an extent, artificiality in dialogue. For, as you say, complete strangers who have virtually nothing in common (except their humanbeingness and womanhood), do not all of a sudden begin holding intimate debates with each other out of the blue.

For me, quite frankly, the basic incentive has had to do with a need that I have been feeling for quite sometime now, to bridge the big gap between me and my last published creative writing effort. Closely tied to this is the reason I gave in my earlier letter: that I have always been a firm believer in dialogue. Again, especially given the poor distribution of my East African publications abroad, I have looked upon this as an opening for me to address an audience that may not know of my work. Thirdly, I really do believe that the world should be made aware of the way women of African origin view their own gender struggles—which is not to say that there is any homogeneity or consensus based on women's geographical or cultural locations, for, in the final analysis, it is each individual's worldview that illuminates these engagements. The point is that too much speaking has been done on our behalf. I am attracted by the possibility that this exchange will provide a small part of the global platform, and is it not true that all of us seek for this as writers? So, there you are, as far as my reasons for having lasted this far go.

By the time this letter reaches you, you will have started your summer holiday. Well, have a restful time, whatever you do. And, frankly, I am glad that your extended family challenges the construct of "Villa Garbo"! It is true that we need and must create space to be alone, but it is also true that the force of the larger group provides a wonderful validation of our essential selves, and this, too, is something we must seek.

The seriousness and intensity with which you addressed the challenge before all of us to rise and live above mere proclamations spoke to me very clearly. However, unlike you, I do believe in truth—meaning, at the most basic, the historical, materialist reality that confronts us whether we want to acknowledge it or not. This reality either affirms our humanity, or denies it. Because of this, I also feel that it is a human responsibility to make clear proclamations when negation diminishes the human being in any one of us. You may not agree with this, but I believe that refusal to make a proclamation in the face of injustice and oppression of other human beings is evasion of a human responsibility. However, the greater truth is that mere proclamation without concrete action to change the reality under question is another form of irresponsibility too. In this connection, may the practical work you have been engaged in and continue to perform find fruition, however long this takes.

This point reminds me to tell you a little bit about the women's conference in Toronto last year. The occasion brought together such an impressive volume of women (mostly from cultures which have been victims of colonization, imperialism and dictatorship), that the sheer experience of their multitudinous presence became empowering. There must have been at least three thousand at the opening ceremony. I have never had this kind of experience all my life! The other moving thing about the opening and closing sessions in particular was the amount of space and prominence given to first-nations women who have been historically relegated to the background in their own land of origin and birth since the invasion of North America by Christopher Columbus. The opening main speaker was a first-nations woman as was the closing speaker, Menchú, the Nobel Prize winner. Then there was a group of first-nations women singers whose songs were full of fighting spirit and creativity. Similarly, most of the panels featured very strong women voices, who shared living experiences of their struggles for their rights, for the rights of their children and those of their communities. The conference deliberated on the creation of links that would bring women's struggles together in solidarity. The umbrella theme was "creating and making links." As with every conference, there was a lot of talking, but it was the kind of talk that is absolutely necessary if women are to emerge out of the isolation that they often tend to live in as an oppressed community of human beings. In other words, women shared real experiences from their lives, some of them most gruelling. The experiences of women living in North America made it quite clear that racism remains a way of life in the so-called "developed" "first world." I participated on a panel that was discussing "women under political repression and torture" and also read poetry at an open evening session.

The Toronto women's conference was one of the few where I have seen a conscious attempt made to place practical knowledge before theory and academia. I heard ordinary women speak to me with such power and sincerity that I suddenly felt as if there was something fake about the university environment that I was returning to at Cornell. I think there should be more of those kinds of forums.

I am winding up here at Cornell to go to Kenya and Zimbabwe for the summer. I now have a leave of absence from the University of Zimbabwe and will be based at the Department of African American Studies at Syracuse University as of September when I return from home. Right now, I do not know how I am going to emotionally handle the return to Kenya, following a period of nearly eleven years of exile. I have walked through the motions of my arrival in my mind, but I know that the heart, the feelings, and the being in me will do their own live walking. Well, all I can say is that it will be wonderful touching home again. Unfortunately, there is also anxiety in my heart because in dealing with the hawks in neocolonial power at home, one cannot ignore the fact that one is before a ruthless bunch of unprincipled people who thrive on the political harassment of others. Moi's KANU regime is still very angry with those of us who have used their exile experience to expose its abuse of human rights and corrupt squandering of the economy, for, this has all along reinforced the internal struggles by the ordinary people of Kenya. The combined efforts finally brought the government to its knees last year in accepting multiparty politics, a possibility it had not only rejected but dismissed before then. So, I hope that I will be safe.

Winding down at Cornell has ended up being more of a task than I had anticipated. I got involved in a poetry drama production which I was directing, using the community theatre method. The production was a practical component of a course that I was teaching on African theatre and drama. The poetry drama had as its theme: Mother Africa and her children and was actually entitled, "Mother Afrika's Children." I thought it important to focus on the plight of Africa's children and the agony of the mothers who see these little ones die in their arms, even as they are struggling to prevent it. My latest collection of poetry, which is with a publisher right now, focuses quite a bit on this tragic situation, linking it to imperialism and neocolonialism. We performed to a Cornell audience and then took the show to the community in Ithaca. The community performance was a wonderful experience. The audience was so moved by the effort that the students had put into the acting, singing, and dancing that some of them were in tears.

The other activity that has come to mean a lot to me is some voluntary work that I have been doing in a maximum security prison at a place called Elmira, forty-five or so minutes from Ithaca. It is a very large prison, with over two thousand men locked up in there, but guess who constitute the overwhelming

majority? Men of African American origin—a sizable percent-
age of them under twenty-five! The next biggest groups are
Latinos and Hispanics. So, the American system obviously has
ways of criminalizing the poor and powerless in their society,
unless we are to assume, of course, that certain groups of people
are born criminals! What is most painful about it is that the
men in there have some of the sharpest minds that I have ever
dealt with. I had the exact same experience ten years ago, when
I did voluntary work at Ogdensburg maximum security prison
from St. Lawrence University, which I wrote about in my last
letter. I am reminded of what George Jackson once said at the
height of the Black Power struggle in this country: that the
best minds among African American men are wasting in jails.
What I have tried to do is to contribute towards keeping those
minds alive by visiting the men and taking some students with
me on the visits. I think it is important for Cornell students to
confront this reality. Cornell is a very rich and privileged institution, and living here can create all kinds of illusions for
people of African origins, when it does not enforce alienation,
that is. The men identify topics that are of relevance to their
lives and then the students and I facilitate discussion. However, they (the men) do most of the talking and what they have
to say is worth all the listening that one can do. So we engage
in discussion sessions, debates, dialogue, poetry readings, etc.,
etc. I plan to continue with this work from Syracuse, which is
only an hour and a half or so away from Elmira.

Lastly, I had a wonderful experience reading through examination scripts from students at the end of this semester.
The set of answers that I enjoyed reading most were related to
a question through which I was trying to elicit their practical,
personal experience so as to encourage them to apply knowledge to real life situations. The question read something like,
"Discuss the content of three works studied in this course, demonstrating their relevance to your special experience and reality." The course itself was on African women writers, studying
artists such as: Ama Ata Aidoo, Nawal El Saadawi, Flora Nwapa,
Mariama Bâ, Tsitsi Dangarembga, Ellen Kuzwayo, and others.
Oh, you should have read the responses! They were the most
articulate, the most genuine, the most powerful statements I
have ever heard from those students. Some of the stories and

experiences related were at one level frightening. It hurt to read about what some of these young people have been through. At another level, however, it became a celebration of the strength and unmolested beauty of some of this community of the youth that I had taken so much for granted in the class-room. All through the semester, one or two of the male students in the class had expressed discomfort with the fact that most of the books we had read had depicted men in what they saw as a negative light. In fact, two of them insisted that women writers were involved in "male bashing." For me, the stories told through the answers that I am referring to closed this strange debate on "male bashing" once and for all. The narra-tors had relived concrete experiences, which were anything but fictional. Each story was a painful indictment of the oppres-sive systems that humankind has constructed (mainly at the invention of patriarchal males), to institutionalize women's oppression, which is linked to the oppression of the poor and powerless in the world. And on that note I leave my teaching and research experience at Cornell as I move on to new pastures.

I really have to stop now as I have a whole lot of other busi-ness to take care of before I travel in another week. But before I put a full stop to this communication, let me say that in the final analysis, I am glad this dialogue ended up taking place. It is my hope that we will meet before too too long. Perhaps we can ask the publishers of these women's debates to find a way of bringing the debaters together when the book is out. For the time being, stay well and experience productivity in what-ever you undertake.

Sincerely,

Micere Githae Mugo

Chapter 4

The Genesis of "Male-ing Names in the Sun"

Ama Ata Aidoo

In 1990, I found myself in Sydney, Australia, like the year before, in November. I had been and was there again for the Pan-Commonwealth meeting to select the year's winners of the Commonwealth Writers Prize. Among the participants were a number of women from around the Commonwealth, including Anna Rutherford, that tireless "enabler," as Norman Jeffers had earlier described her. We were all there in our official capacities as judges for the Comonwealth Writers Prize. Among this group of women, one felt enveloped in a secure glow as other women writers' names got dropped easily, appreciatively, every now and then. Miriam Tlali, Patricia Grace, Margaret Atwood, Olive Senior. . . .

During one of those times of surprisingly amicable and leisurely group discussions on a rather busy and stressful schedule, it struck about three or four of us that it must have been a quirk of history had brought us together. There we were from Africa, Asia, the Caribbean, Europe, North America, the Pacific: the whole world, really. Or much of it. So, however reluctantly on the part of one or two of us, we all agreed that "the Commonwealth" must be a good notion for something! From that point, it was a quick hop to wondering aloud about English as a major unifying force in an increasingly fractious world, and then on to the irony in the fact that this "unifying"—therefore wholesome(!)—"force" was really, for some of us, a rather potent symbol of our humiliation as a people . . . and finally on to the idea, "Look at us!"—as the current propagators of

English, and therefore upholders of "the Empire," were we not an odd bunch? After all, and we said so ourselves, we could easily fall into any society's traditional—and unfair, of course—classification of "wild women." Think "wayward wolves" and "wicked witches," including our respective own. . . . We could not resist to conclude that if they could see us now, the original Empire builders would surely turn in their far-flung graves. For after all, it was not just the fact that they could never have envisaged Africans and other "sabled-hued" natives as arbiters of who wrote the best prose fiction in the language, but that even the whites among us would not possibly have fit their notion of the kind of individuals they might have selected to play such a role. Beginning with the fact that we were women. . . .

The idea of doing a collection of essays was born for the first time for some us and was fast maturing for Anna Rutherford. According to their introduction to the volume, the idea of the book had occurred to her and Shirley Chew earlier that same year "from a conversation [they] had while attending a conference on postcolonial literature at Lecce in April." Clearly, it was a book waiting to be put together. In our individual ways, we would explore the possibility of each of us looking at ourselves as women from our countries—typical or not—but certainly together, making a strange group of representatives of the British Empire. The volume came out soon enough as *Unbecoming Daughters of the Empire* (Aarhus/Coventry/Sydney: Dangaroo Press, 1993). "Male-ing Names in the Sun" was my contribution to it.

Chapter 5

Male-ing Names in the Sun

Ama Ata Aidoo

Toli[1] Number One

In May 1949, a young girl stood in the blazing sun on the parade grounds of Dominase, the district capital of Abeadze in the southcentral region of a country then known as the Gold Coast. She and her schoolmates had been there for at least two hours, waiting for they-didn't-know-whom-but-the-then District Education Officer to come and inspect them. The inspection was part of the main business of the day. The girl had led her school's contingent—a two-file formation—to march for four kilometers between their village and the parade grounds.

The early morning excitement of dressing up for the occasion had died down, although if you had asked the girl and her companions, they would not have confessed to fatigue, hunger, and thirst. And why should they, when they were the chosen few from the whole district? Earlier, they had stood stiffly at attention. Now they were chattering to one another, now squatting, now straightening up, or just generally fidgeting. One or two bold individuals were testing the teachers' patience by breaking free from their own positions to run between the lines.

It was "Empire Day," the name given to the birthday of a certain English woman called Victoria Alexandrina. The girl was to learn later that this Victoria had been the "Queen of the United Kingdom of Great Britain and Ireland," and strangely, also the "Empress of India." Victoria, alias Mrs. Albert Francis Charles Augustus Emmanuel of Saxe-Coburg-Gotha, had been born over one hundred years before this African child was born, and died in the second year of the twentieth century.

What she was to remember most clearly from the day, though, was that she had wanted to scratch her right palm very badly. She had also been aware that she should not. She had been told that as a hyperactive toddler, she had sustained a big and vicious burn when she stumbled, fell, and put her palm solidly in the middle of a wood fire on which her mother was cooking. This scar, she had been warned, would itch whenever she felt hot and uncomfortable.

I was that child.

It is a fact that in the southcentral region of Ghana, there is a division of the Akan nation known as the Fanti. It is also a fact that until quite recently, Fanti was an entry in nearly all respectable and scholarly dictionaries of the English language, including those reprinted in the 1960s. The user was informed that as an adjective (!) "fanti'" as in *to go fanti* meant to "go native" (sic), "wild," "untamed."

My first language is Fanti.

Nobody spoke well of the Fanti as imperial subjects, including Fantis themselves. While the British lamented that "those damned Fantis" were ungovernable, the Fanti unashamedly boasted of their recalcitrance, their rudeness, their contempt for the imperial set-up and for the white man. Their language became crammed with proverbs and other sayings attesting to this:

> *Aban wotwiw n'zdze, wonsoa n.* [You don't carry a government (on your head). You drag it behind you.] *Kohwinyi na ose e dasefo wo aborokyir.* [It is a liar who claims his only witness is in Europe. (Who wants to go that far to bring such a witness?)]

Fantis called every white man *Kwesi Buronyi*. Kwesi is a Sunday-born male. And why? White men = missionaries = Christians = Sunday's children (or Sunday workers.) *Buronyi* is "corn person." That is, one with cornsilk hair. There was no equivalent nickname for white women. Maybe they did not exist in the imagination of Fantis.

I also grew up knowing that long before I was born, my father's father had been arrested along with other *Nkwakwafo*[2] for "disturbing the King's peace." They had been sent to the castle prison at Elmina, and tortured. The mode of torture was to force the prisoners to pass cannonballs among themselves, as though they were playing volleyball. Within a week, they were dead, each and everyone of them, including my grandfather. No beatings, no bruising. Very gentlemanly, very civilized.

By the way, the fact that these days, our governments are postcolonially (!) torturing and killing Africans does not lessen or justify colonial crimes. It only goes to show how long our people have suffered.

God say, God say, God say, God say, God say, God say, God say . . .
God say, God say,
God say, God say, God say
God say, God say, God say,
God say, God say, God say,
God save the King. . . .

Ghanaians never sang the lyrics of the British Empire anthem as they were taught, instructed, and were expected to. Not if they could help it. Of course, much of the time, most of them could. But why should they sing that anthem correctly? It was too much trouble. "After all, it isn't our mother's anthem," is what they would have probably told anyone if challenged. Nothing concerning the Empire was their mother's or their father's So they took their time to do everything; they did everything halfheartedly or they didn't do anything at all.

Ghanaians have always suspected that Kwame Nkrumah influenced the choice of May 25th as Africa Day (also known as "OAU Day" or "Africa Liberation Day"). The 24th of May had been Empire Day. You do not have to take someone's day over. You only put yours close enough for people to remember "the good old days" without considering the change spiteful.

These days, Empire Day is supposed to be Commonwealth Day. "Commonwealth" day? So you ask yourself what on earth you've got to do with Boris Yeltsin? You wonder if it refers to Yeltsin's or Lenin's birthday? However, you also suspect that if there is a Russian whose birthday ought to be celebrated by someone, it should be Vladimir Ilyich Ulyanov, alias Lenin, because in his heyday, he was revered by as many people as Victoria was in hers. White man's tribal politics. . . All this business of the mind of the African child getting farmed out to different European centers of power was always quite tragic, really. It's like suffering from a permanent migraine. No wonder we are amnesiac. Meanwhile everyone expects us, and we expect ourselves, to solve all our problems instantly. Whew!

So then, was W. E. B. DuBois some malevolent wizard cursing humankind into stupidity and intolerance when he said that the problem of the twentieth century was going to be that of race? Or was he just an honest prophet? One thing is certain. Seventy years after he spoke and with only a few years of the century left, the issue of race is still allowed to assume all forms, subsume all controversies, and consume every little bit of human energy, vision, and imagination. The twenty-first century is almost upon us, and we are still imprisoned in the colors of our skins. How absolutely awful! How humanly pathetic!

When we are going about our normal business, we do not stop to wonder whether we might have experienced the whole imperial/colonial *wahala* differently if we had been white. However, on some idle occasions, we do wonder. Of course the honest answer is a clear "yes." After all, we were "the natives" whose lands and other resources had to be taken and given to the emperor's relatives in Australia, Canada, Kenya, and Zimbabwe, no? Why some of them had to leave their homes became irrelevant once they arrived in our neighborhoods.

> God say, God say, God say
> God save the King . . .

Toli Number Two: A FRAGMENT FROM A LOST NOVEL

Once upon a time, there was a fisherman who lived in Mowure, a seaside village in the Central Region. As everyone who knows the area is aware, Mowure is really within a stone's throw from the town of Oguaa . . . ah-h-h. First, about Oguaa, alias Cape Coast.

Those were the 1920s. Oguaa was the big city of Fantis, who were then congratulating themselves for having used (read "helped") the British to conquer Ashanti, their more aggressive relatives to the north, whom they were always in mortal fear of! The British had "pacified" Ashanti, looting Kumasi, the capital, especially of its legendary gold arts and finally exiling the king and other core members of the royal family.

Another feat the Fantis had recently accomplished included making Oguaa unviable as the seat of the colonial government.

Now Oguaa was settling down to become the self-appointed, self-conscious fashion center of the Gold Coast while its people set about the business of Europeanizing themselves with panache. In dressing, they opted for the clothes of the owners of the Empire, as the latter dressed in their cold country. So under the 88 degree sun, the men wore three-piece woolen suits, complete with top hats. The women wore the equivalent long evening gowns, hats, stockinged feet, gloved arms and hands, and all.

According to the rest of the country, which came to look upon their antics with a mixture of derision and envy, this was also when Fanti wives started the haute cuisine that became so haute, it tipped over into requiring women to light their charcoal and wood fires with butter, and at the end of a cooking session to extinguish the fires with milk. And that in a region of the world where there had never been dairy farming at all. In fact, one cow seen within a 20-kilometer radius was enough for people to name their children after, and for the day to be remembered in historical narratives. So both the milk and the butter were canned and imported from England or the Netherlands.

. . . Maybe it's time to return to the fisherman.

He had been the only surviving child from his mother's six full-term pregnancies. So as an *Equ-ewu, Abiku,* or *Kwasamba,* and in line with custom, his parents had had to give him a name he would not want to return to his spirit mother with. They chose Srako, the local term for One Shilling. Since he was born on a Wednesday, his full name was Kweku Srako, although everybody conveniently forgot the Kweku and just call him Srako.

Srako and his wife had eight children and thereby proved more fertile than his parents. Their fourth-born but first son was Kojo Kuma, named after a revered ancestor of his father's house.

One day, just as Srako was setting out to sea, his wife Esi-Yaa asked him to listen to a thought that had occurred to her. "What is it?" he asked somewhat impatiently, standing. "Sit down," she commanded. Srako could not believe his ears. Was the

woman going out of her mind? As if it was not provocation
enough to bother him with woman thoughts when he should
be on his way. However, he was also thinking that the surest
way to bring bad luck on himself and his mate would be to
quarrel with her now. He sat down. She sat opposite him.

"Y-e-s?"

"We should send Kojo Kuma to school," Esi-Yaa said firmly.

"Nyankopon-above and the Gods of our Fathers!" he exclaimed as he jumped up, fetched his sack, and dashed out to
go and join his mates, who were by then taking the dragnet to
their boat.

Srako could not believe that he had heard Esi-Yaa right. How
could the same idea occur to him and to her? When a few days
earlier, he had realized he should send Kuma to school, he had
postponed discussing it with her because he was not sure of
how she would react. (Meaning, he had not convinced himself
that it is a good idea.) After all, as their oldest son, the child
would be expected to go to sea and, in fact, very soon. He was
about ten years old. Besides, sending him to school would mean
exiling him to go and stay with some of those snobbish and
cruel Cape Coast characters. He had decided to give the matter a think-over while he was at sea on this trip. Now he would
forever have to give the woman the credit of being the first in
bringing up the matter. Ah, ah, ah!

A month later, Srako, his wife Esi-Yaa, and their son Kojo
Kuma were on their way to Oguaa. It had to be a Tuesday,
since that is the sacred day of Nana Bosompo, the god of the
sea, and a day on which no self-respecting fisherman would go
to sea. A hol(y) day.

They set out quite early. By the time the sun was shaking
itself up to be hot, they were on the eastern outskirts of the
town. Around half-past eight, they knocked on the door of Isaac
Goodful, the circuit minister of the Methodist Church.

Going to the priest instead of any other Oguaa resident was
not the result of a random decision made by Srako. Apart from
being the immediate leader of his church, the priest was also
some kind of a distant relative. Meanwhile, not wanting to take
any chances, he had sent a message to the priest to please expect them. Soon Srako, his wife Esi-Yaa, Reverend Goodful and
his wife "Maame Sofo" (Mrs. Goodful) were seated around a
big table. The boy had been deposited with the priest's boys

somewhere in the back of the house. The discussion was short and concluded soon enough. Or almost. It was agreed that Kojo Kuma would stay with Osofo and his wife, as one of about half a dozen youngsters, apart from their own children, who lived in the priestly household, getting properly brought up and educated.

Kojo Kuma was sent for. He came and stood before the priest, with his cloth neatly wrapped around his body, and the upper ends tied behind his neck. The presence of his parents gave him some courage, but he was still shaking. The priest looked completely formidable. Even seated, he was much taller than the boy on his feet.

"What is your name?"

"Kojo."

"Kojo what?"

"Kojo Kuma."

"I hear you want to go to school?" Kojo nearly said that actually, it was his parents' idea. He liked the thought of it anyway. So he nodded. The four grownups jumped on him.

"Hei, that's not done."

"You cannot use your head to answer questions."

"You must open your mouth and say: 'Please, Master, yes.'"

The last was from Srako. As for the boy, all he wanted to open his mouth to do was cry. But if he did, everybody would shout at him that "a man does not cry." "Kojo," the priest began again, kindly, "what is you Christian name?"

"Sofo, we have not baptized him yet," Esi-Yaa cut in.

"So you had not thought of a Christian name."

"Osofo, no."

"I can baptize him even this coming Sunday. But we must find him a Christian name." He paused significantly. Then, "We shall call him George," he said with finality.

As we are all supposed to know, "George" is nowhere in the Bible. It just happened to be one of the names often given to the men who sit on the throne of England.

"Osofo, we thank you," Srako and his wife said in unison.

"Thank you, Osofo," Kojo Kuma piped after his parents.

"Next time, you must say, 'Sir. . . Thank you, Sir.'"

Another pause. "The child must also have a surname," the priest pressed on, addressing the parents.

Hardly finding his voice, Srako asked, "Osofo, what is a surname?"

The man of God chuckled to himself. He cleared his throat, faced the fisherman squarely and explained that "surname" really meant "sire's name, a name which you get from your father."

"Kuma . . . Kojo Kuma," the fisherman timidly intervened.

"Ow," said the priest, "but that is the boy's own name, no?"

"Yes," the mother, the father, and the son had all replied. Then Srako added clearly, "I gave it to him. He was named after his grandfather, my father's father."

The Reverend had tried to be patient, but all this was taking too long, and getting too far. How could he explain the new system brought by the Europeans to them? He knew that his people's naming system defined each individual clearly, with no ambiguities. However. . . but then . . . yes, he had to admit it to himself, it was based on some. . . eh . . . unfortunately primitive matrilineal notions. Whereas the European system of naming people against one singular male line was . . . eh . . . more . . . sensible, Christian and civilized.

His guests watched his face with anxiety. He would have to explain it to them some other time. Maybe, he could even build a sermon around it, since the question was probably cropping up all over, as people took advantage of the new order and enrolled their children in the white man's schools. This morning though, he didn't have much time. So, barely able to conceal his impatience, he told them that the law from the Europeans said that when children go to school, they must have their father's names as their surnames. So the boy's surname was Srako. He would be registered in school as George Srako.

Another pause. Something had occurred to the priest. Srako is Shilling! He exclaimed into the air: "Kojo, your name is George Shilling! . . . No, since it's your father's name, and you are the son of Shilling! . . . Kojo, your name is Shillingson. George Shillingson. George Kojo Shillingson . . . G. K. Shillingson!"

G. K . . . G. K. G. K. . . . . The priest was very excited. How could he help it? He had just remembered that he had heard there was a distinguished Englishman called G. K. Chesterton. What he was not sure of was what this other G. K. was distinguished for.

In time, G. K. Shillingson became a distinguished lawyer. He had many children with his lawful Christian wife, Mrs. Docia Shillingson, as well as other women, including his receptionists, a young girl from the "hinterland" who was a servant in his house, and at least one hawker he had lured to his offices. That was to half explain the different kinds of spellings of the name that were passed down over the years.

People also point out that over the years as an educated, westernized, civilized, and a self-consciously developing patriarchy, the Shillingsons spread their male seeds in the countries of Europe, where, failing to blend their skins into their new environments no matter how hard they tried, they laboured to at least get the family name to conform to the different tribal ways of spelling it.

And so, in time, apart from the original SHILLINGSON, there were SHILLINSONS, SHELLINSONS, and SHILINSTONS, SHILLINSINS, SHILLINSSONS, SHILLINSSENS, SCHILLENSOHNS, SCHIELLINSOHNS, SCHILLENSENS, SCHILLINGSENS, SCHILLENSTEINS, and ZWILENSENS. They even say that when some got behind the then Iron Curtain—of course, some did!—they became either ZEILLENVITZ, ZVILENSKY, or CZVILLENYEV.

Toli Number Three

This is May,1992. We hear that a couple of days ago something interesting happened in Oguaa. A young woman called Achinba was getting married to Dr. Kwesi Shillingson. They even say that she was the daughter of one of the schoolmates of the little girl who stood in the sun on Empire Day. We hear that when everything was ready for the wedding, her future mother-in-law called her to her inner chamber to talk to her, woman to woman. Mrs. Bessie Shillingson had made the mistake of opening the meeting with, "My Lady, as a future Mrs. Shillingson. . . ."

"Maa, I shall not call myself Mrs. Shillingson," Achinba declared.

"Ei." Mrs. Bessie thought she had not heard right. "You mean you are not going to marry my son?"

"I am." Achinba giggled and then continued, "I am marrying Kwesi. But I want to keep my own name . . . I like my name. Besides, you know that as a professional woman, an architect, everybody knows me as Achinba."

They say that Achinba need not have bitten back what she was about to say next but had thought better of. Which was that she loved her man, but not his name . . . because she had always thought Shillingson sounded funny, and silly. They say that, in fact, Achinba could have said all that and more to Mrs. Bessie. No one would have heard her. Because Mrs. Bessie had decided to faint a long time ago. You know that kind of fainting that only certain women suffer when they do not want to hear, or otherwise deal with, anything unpleasant? This kind of fainting, her own son, the doctor, was later to admit privately to himself, was an art: an art perfected in Europe by the mothers and the wives of the men who built the Empire.

Notes

1   Toli is pidjin for a story. The term is often used to mean "a tall tale."

2   The term means "Youngmen" and refers to a specific group within the Akan socio-political structure.

Chapter 6

Beside Every Good Woman Was a Good Man

Vincent O. Odamtten

In general, discussion of the role of women in African society and its creative reproduction—African literature—has sought to underscore the proposition that women's present marginal status is the result of precolonial traditions of patriarchy. However, recent criticism has begun to explore more complex causes for the relative disempowerment of women, as depicted in the literature of contemporary Africa. These recent explorations do not accept narrow notions which place the blame for women's conditions on the door step of an a priori African patriarchy. The assignment of such blame is not only facile, but paternalistic. These new explorations demand that we examine with more sophisticated tools of analysis the problematic which gives rise to the relative marginalization of African women. Through the polylectic examination of some short narratives by Ama Ata Aidoo, we will demonstrate that the condition of women at the present time owes more to the legacy of tendencies "imported" during the colonial era, than to holdovers from precolonial African social relations.

The matrilineal nature of Akan society in particular, and many other African societies in general, makes it immediately apparent that the imposition of a causal patriarchal precolonial factor precipitating the marginalization of women is fraught with ambiguities. In part, Aidoo's authorial project has been to more completely contextualize the historical phenomena that have led to the present condition of African women. She notes that

on the whole, African traditional societies seemed to have been at
odds with themselves as to exactly what to do with women. For although some of them appeared to doubt gender and biology as bases
for judging women, in the end, they all used gender and biology to
judge women's capabilities. (Aidoo 1992, 323)

This conflict is brilliantly depicted in her second drama, *Anowa*.
The titular heroine of that play marries Kofi Ako, a young man
who, at first, is looked upon with disfavor by her parents, particularly her mother. Anowa's motives for marrying such a man
are multifaceted, indeed contradictory. She is driven by a desire to make her mark, to reproduce *her self* on her own terms,
and a love which allows her to see the potential for good in this
"watery male." Ironically, Anowa's success in realizing her goals
precipitates the very conditions that are detrimental to the
healthful articulation and reproduction of *her self*. Thus we see
the linkages between the young couple's increasing prosperity,
the rising economic and ideological influence of the British
merchants, and the growing marginalization of African women,
exemplified by the character of Anowa. Her consequent re-
gression from confident, sane, and hard-working woman to an
uninspired marital ornament on the brink of insanity and suicide, is graphically linked to Kofi Ako's internalization of European attitudes about women, matrimony, and the acquisition of wealth and power. (Odamtten, 71–74)

It is against such a background of love, greed, and betrayal,
that an examination of various male roles and relationships in
some of Aidoo's narratives becomes crucial in revealing Aidoo's
radical interrogation of the received notion of "the battle of
the sexes." In very general terms, we may agree that

men in Miss Aidoo's fiction are mere shadows or voices or just "fill-
ers." Somewhere, quietly, they seem to be manipulating the women's
life or negatively controlling it or simply having a good time, knowing
that they are assured of something like a divine top-dog position in
life. (Mphahlele, xix)

However, a closer examination of such storytelling events (narratives) as "For Whom Things Did Not Change," "Certain
Winds from the South," and "Something to Talk About on the
Way to the Funeral," points to the possibility of non-colonizing, mutually supportive gender relationships, even as some

of Aidoo's other works underscore the consequences of the impact of colonialism on a dynamic African terrain.

In "Everything Counts," the opening story of Aidoo's *No Sweetness Here*, the experiences of Sissie, the protagonist, clearly demonstrate that in the new dispensation gender relationships between African men and women are frighteningly transformed. The men react in new and strange ways:

> They looked terrible, their eyes changing, turning red and warning her that if she wasn't careful, they would destroy her. Ah, they frightened her a lot, quite often too. Especially when she thought of what filled them with that kind of hatred. (Aidoo 1990, 2)

It is, perhaps, a western turn of mind, a tendency to place things, issues, and people in hierarchical categories, coupled with the privileging of patriarchy, which is at the root of this new association. Sissie remarks that, "if there had been any [war of the sexes] at all in the old days . . . [it] could not possibly have been on such a scale." (Aidoo 1990, 2)

It is in the second narrative of the collection, "For Whom Things Did Not Change," that we are given a clearer indication of the nature of gender relationships that are less combative. Elsewhere, I have discussed the ties between Kobina, the young medical doctor, and Zirigu, the caretaker of a government resthouse in northern Ghana. (Odamtten, 84–92) Significantly, this relationship is not just a master-servant one, because around the issue of food preparation Zirigu's identity as a man is called into question. The division of labor between Zirigu and his wife, Setu, is clearly defined; however, the colonial legacy demands that Zirigu contravene those definitions by being a cook for Kobina. Zirigu's discomfort is alleviated by the intervention of Setu, who asserts her role as traditional cook and provides the evening meal for Kobina.

Although Setu's voice is somewhat muted in this narrative, this does not mean that she is peripheral to that action or Zirigu. Indeed, we hear of her role and importance from the story that Zirigu tells Kobina as they drink "pito." Although Setu was a widow when Zirigu met her, he echoes her brother's words:

> She is a good woman. Like most of our women, she always believes in a woman having her own little money, so that she does not have to go

> to her husband for everything. On the coast, she mostly sold roasted plantains and ground-nuts. Here she makes kafa. (Aidoo 1990, 25)

Setu's "goodness" is measured by her economic independence, rather than her biology or abilities in the domestic arena of cooking. Setu's brother had asked Zirigu, a non-believer, to marry Setu because, against Islamic custom, the brother recognized that Zirigu was "a cool one . . . a sober man . . . a good man and she is a good woman." Setu becomes the center in Zirigu's life, preventing him from doing harm, to himself or others:

> For a long time, I was drinking. I wanted to go away. I wanted to kill somebody. Any time I went to the office in town to get my pay and give my reports about the place, I felt like spitting into their eyes. Those scholars. But Setu talked to me. She said I was behaving like a child. That it is nothing. We should never forget who we are, that's all. (Aidoo 1990, 29)

Setu's advice echoes the comment by the Old Man at the end of *Anowa* when he observes that, in spite of all the adversity and betrayals, Anowa was "true to herself." So Zirigu, who does not want "to be like them [civil servants] . . . or like you" deserves our respect and admiration—as does Setu, who, for different reasons, also wishes to be herself.

Setu understands that in this new world, which is so like the old colonial one (Aidoo 1990, 11), only more corrupt, women are at a disadvantage. Earlier in the narrative, their conversation turns to their own economic and social plight. For the indignant Setu, prostitution and concubinage symbolize *the complicity of both "big men," and the numerous "fathers and mothers,"* who benefit from the continued rape of both persons and property after the formal end of colonialism. (Aidoo 1990, 9–13) Setu's identification of those who must share the guilt, for doing "shameful acts" (Aidoo 1990, 11), is fueled by a vexation that propels her toward a more radical position vis-à-vis injustice and oppression. In many ways she is like Anowa, who acknowledges the need for change, especially if we are to avoid being slaves to our histories. Zirigu, on the other hand, is somewhat like the Old Man, although more pessimistic than the latter. Beyond the generalized outbursts of rage and frustration, or enigmatic interjections such as "Ah . . ." and "Mmm . . ."

(Aidoo 1990, 12–13), their resistance to and anger against oppression is hardly heard, let alone effective. Yet they are able to survive the horrors and disappointment of colonial and postindependence life because they listen to each other and their relationship is based on mutual respect. Aidoo's depiction of the relationship may appear idealized to some, but it is firmly rooted in a tradition that more often than not rejects gender and biology as bases for judging women.

Despite the impoverished life of Setu and Zirigu, Aidoo affirms the possibility for a *non-colonizing gender relationship*. However, we should not see this as a valorization of poverty as the only site for such relationships. Aidoo avoids such simplistic suggestions. In another story, also located in the North, we meet an equally impoverished family in which things do not always turn out for the best, even if there is "a good man" for the "good woman." In "Certain Winds from the South," we are forced to recognize that despite the best intentions and, perhaps, because of the attraction of the perceived wealth of the South, many young men leave their families in search of work that cannot be found in the North. Issa, the somewhat innocent son-in-law of M'ma Asana, is willingly seduced by the idea that the government would pay him for cutting grass in the big city to the South. He has dreams of amassing a fortune, which he would triumphantly bring back for his child, Fuseni, and Hawa, his wife. Yet M'ma knows from experience that this will not be. (Aidoo 1990, 49–52) The same independence that makes Setu "a good woman" is exhibited in these unlucky women who have and will survive despite the poverty of their environment and the absence of "good" men. In this regard, Mphahlele's observation is pertinent:

> Given this premise the woman, without worrying about her traditional place, simply gets up on her feet and asserts not her importance in relation to the male, but her motherhood. . . . (Mphahlele, xx)

However, it is perhaps more accurate to say that the issue is not exclusively "*motherhood*," but humanity in the face of these constraining neocolonial arrangements.

"In the Cutting of a Drink," Aidoo explores the subsequent effects of the absence of a "good man" in the urban environment. The girl-woman, Mansa, is subject to the predatory hunger of the city and its "big men," while her brother, potentially a "good man," has yet to learn the true nature of a society in which all people are commodities for exchange. In such a world, the "good man" who would be beside the "good woman" is hard to find, and the values or scruples that mediate village life are inadequate. Although it is intimated that life in the village is more conducive to the development of meaningful, mutually supportive gender relationships, albeit somewhat conservative, Aidoo rejects such a prelapsarian retreat.

The central narrative in her collection, "No Sweetness Here," effectively challenges and dispels such a possibility. The story centers on a failed marriage, the consequences of the divorce proceedings, and the struggle for custody of Maami Ama's son Kwesi, whose untimely death due to a snake bite put a tragic end to the sorry episode.

The narrator, Chicha, is a young western-educated woman who is fond of Kwesi and whose relationship to his mother is very complex, revealing an interesting perspective on the issues of women's opportunities and choices in a world of apparently unchallenged male privilege:

> The irony is that the progressive, liberated and sophisticated image of the Western-educated woman is really a mask: underneath, there is the familiar vulnerability to the power of the male, and the new insecurity bred by the conflict between two cultural traditions. This is implied by the narrator's uneasy sense of kinship with the isolated and victimized mother. . . . (Brown, 117)

Brown's observations point to an important aspect of Aidoo's central story, namely, the narrator's subject-position in the work. Chicha, whose profession as educator seems to exemplify the "new woman," is seen as projecting onto Kwesi what she desires in "a good man." (Aidoo 1990, 72–73) All the while she ignores or downplays the determinate factors that had so transformed the society, even in the village, that such "selfish and bullying" men as Kojo Fi, Kwesi's father, could neglect their parental responsibilities with impunity. (68) Maami Ama's divorce proceedings are to take place on the very day that celebrates the sacrifice of one individual for the welfare of the larger community. We also learn that Maami Ama is a Methodist, and that she had had her son baptized to protect him from the machinations of Kojo Fi and his family. (61) Maami Ama's deep religious faith and the fact that the divorce proceedings take place during *Ahobaada* help to explain why, in the final analysis, she does not contest the divorce; despite the fact that she is legally the wronged party. (62–63) Maami Ama's stoicism, in the face of such loss, reflects the spirit of resistance found in such *good women* as Setu, M'ma, and her daughter, Hawa.

Lest we be persuaded that the marginalization of African women today leaves them with only the "choice" of being relatively impotent resisters to the neocolonially enhanced power of patriarchy, "Two Sisters" demonstrates that the hegemonic sway of patriarchy has dubious *benefits for women as well as men*. (Odamtten, 106–110) In this narrative, Mercy, one of the two sisters of the title, exemplifies how some of the worst aspects of the dominant ideology are so internalized by an individual, that she cannot see how she contributes to her own victimization. Further, the narrative demonstrates how ideology represents itself to the individual as *natural*, as an incontestable given of one's life. For Mercy in particular, and the other characters in general, the *prostitution of oneself is the only means of survival and avenue to success*. Despite this depressing thought, Aidoo returns to the assertion that it is indeed possible, even in this neocolonial society and in opposition to the dominant ideology of patriarchy to find "a good man" beside "a good woman," without having to accept a vow of poverty.

In the penultimate story, "Something to Talk about on the Way to a Funeral," Aidoo presents us with Auntie Araba and her husband, Egya Nyaako, the cocoa farmer. Like Setu in "For Whom Things Did Not Change," Egya Nyaako is a muted presence, but nevertheless, "a good man" because, although Auntie Araba had a son "out of wedlock," he still married her:

> I used to be one of those he hired regularly during the cocoa harvest. He never insisted that we press down cocoa as most of those farmers do. No, he never tried to cheat us out of our fair pay. (Aidoo 1990, 118)

In addition, he accepted Auntie Araba's son, Ato, as his own, until his biological father, "that lawyer-or-doctor-or-something-like-that," came with the trappings of privilege to claim Ato as his own and send him to college. (119) Even though Egya Nyaako's presence is minimal and he dies well before the story's conclusion, his positive presence is felt throughout the narrative. He represents the male figure who is *not* corrupted by the intrinsic privilege of patriarchal society and stands in contradistinction to the irresponsible behaviors of Ato and his biological father.

If Aidoo's assessment of traditional African societies, and by extension the colonial and neocolonial versions, is that women's status has been at once marginal and contradictory, she insists that this is not only the fault of preexisting patriarchal practices; but, more important the complex articulation of subsequent historical interventions with that less overt ideology. Her stories demonstrate that if we look honestly enough, we will find that beside every good woman was a good man.

Works Cited

Aidoo, Ama Ata. "The African Woman Today." *Dissent* (Summer 1992): 319–325.

———. *The Dilemma of a Ghost and Anowa*. Harlow, UK: Longman, 1985.

———. *No Sweetness Here*. Harlow, UK: Longman, 1990.

Brown, Lloyd W. *Women Writers in Black Africa*. Westport, CT: Greenwood, 1981.

Mphahlele, Ezekiel. "Introduction." In Ama Ata Aidoo. *No Sweetness Here*. Garden City, NY: Doubleday, 1971.

Odamtten, Vincent O. *The Art of Ama Ata Aidoo: Polylectics and Reading Against Neocolonialism*. Gainesville, FL: University Press of Florida, 1994.

II

A CRITICAL DEBATE ON ACHEBE'S DEPICTION OF WOMEN

The three essays in this section all examine the controversial issue of whether or not Chinua Achebe's portrayal of women characters may be considered sexist or patriarchal. Certainly if there is a contemporary African writer whose work has eroded the exclusivity of the western literary canon, it is Achebe, whose *Things Fall Apart* is sufficently read and taught to be considered by many as a canonical work in its own right. And of Achebe's challenge to the hierarchies of imperial hegemony and neocolonialism there is little doubt. However, what some readers have questioned is the way in which (to use Mugo's phrase) this "giant and celebrity" author has depicted women in his fiction.

As we will see, although the general perception exists that Achebe has in some sense defaulted in the matter of challenging the oppression of women, these three articles indicate that the issue is in fact complex and more highly nuanced.

The opening article, "From Stereotype to Individuality: Womanhood in Chinua Achebe's Novels," by Chioma Opara, effectively represents the tenor of the critical commentary that has swirled around Achebe's treatment of women characters. In the essay, Opara surveys Achebe's novels with specific regard to the fairness of his portrayal of women, and, overall, she finds that the news is not good. In particular, for his work in *Things Fall Apart, No Longer at Ease, Arrow of God,* and *A Man of the People,* Opara awards Achebe low marks. In these

novels, she observes, "Women are cast either as dumb appendages of overbearing male protagonists or as bed-hopping wives
and courtesans." With the publication of *Anthills of the Savannah*, however, Opara sees the depiction of "new women infused
with dynamism and selfhood." Even though Achebe's more
feminist approach in *Anthills* is to be applauded, however, Opara
regrets that his depiction of women falls short in that, unlike
the male protagonists, who are "all poets," the women are still
denied the power of the pen. So, while Achebe has made strides
to shed his chauvinism, he still has a considerable way to go.

Catherine Bicknell, in "Achebe's Women: Mothers, Priestesses and Young Urban Professionals," offers a view consonant
with that of Opara, asserting that *Anthills of the Savannah* represents in large measure a reversal of Achebe's earlier portrayal
of women characters. Like Opara, she sees Beatrice as a much
stronger and more positive figure than her predecessors in
Achebe's novels. Also like Opara, she finds that even Beatrice,
however, fails to measure up to the stature of the male characters, at least in the earlier parts of the novel. Whereas Opara
laments Beatrice's being denied the power of the pen, Bicknell
finds it unfortunate that Beatrice is represented only as an abstract or symbolic figure, not a "realistic" character (such as
Sam, Chris, or Ikem) who takes specific and decisive actions
within the society. Even so, Bicknell concludes on a positive
note, observing that Beatrice's behavior following the death
of the three male characters distinguishes her as a woman who
can fulfill the role of a man.

The final selection in this section, Obioma Nnaemeka's "Gender Relations and Critical Mediation: From *Things Fall Apart*
to *Anthills of the Savannah*," takes issue with prior critical assessments of Achebe's depiction of women. Essentially,
Nnaemeka rehabilitates Achebe's reputation with regard to the
charges of sexism leveled against *Things Fall Apart*. When read
within the context of the Igbo worldview, she says, Achebe's
first novel can be seen to represent women in a fair and realistic way. Citing such previous critical oversights as the failure
"to take into account gendered division and sharing of work"
and Igbo views on *silence* versus *being silenced*, she concludes
that earlier critical analyses are "problematic." While acknowledging that "the . . . juxtaposition of women with objects . . .

is troubling," Nnaemeka nevertheless asserts that "Women are marginal in the novel primarily because they are peripheral to the male space on which the novel focuses"—not because Achebe's approach is sexist.

Nnaemeka further pursues her critical revisionism in examining the degree to which Beatrice may be considered "feminist" in *Anthills of the Savannah*. Taking a position counter to most of the criticism, she debunks the notion that Beatrice is a strong, exemplary female character. Beatrice, she maintains, is "lightweight and superficial," representing not feminism but "what went wrong with feminism—arrogance, elitism, intolerance of difference, [and] struggle to be like 'one of the boys.'" Indeed, Nnaemeka argues that much of *Things Fall Apart* contains a more feminist approach than can be seen in the actions of Beatrice, the putative feminist. In Nnaemeka's reading of *Anthills of the Savannah*, Beatrice's pseudofeminism does not reflect badly on Achebe's depiction of women, for there are more genuine feminists in the novel, such as Elewa. Rather, she is concerned to show that the general critical wisdom about Beatrice's role as a positive woman character is seriously flawed.

Chapter 7

From Stereotype to Individuality: Womanhood in Chinua Achebe's Novels

Chioma Opara

There has been a proclivity in literature to portray women in a negative light. Strong portraiture of women by male writers has been a rarity in African writing. Vilified or muted women have peopled the fictional world of early male-authored works. One reads about Cyprian Ekwensi's urban prostitutes, Wole Soyinka's lustful heroines, and Chinua Achebe's urban sluts or rural dummies. Commenting on this distorted image of the African female stereotypes, Charles Larson posits:

> In many early West African novels, the female characters play almost no significant part; if they are present, they are mere objects performing a function. (Larson, 149)

There can be no doubt that reification is, in the main, a function of characterization in Achebe's early novels, which manifest flagrant sexism. Women are cast either as dumb appendages of overbearing male protagonists or as bed-hopping wives and courtesans. One is, however, relieved that the lull of about a quarter of a century in the author's creative production has proved to be the gestation of Achebe's new women infused with dynamism and selfhood.

Achebe's *Things Fall Apart* and *Arrow of God* focus on the debilitating consequences of colonialism in the traditional African society with the sacrosanct male protagonists at the center of that society. Since the woman's voice is, as it were, muted and the man's accented, many a feminist reader, nettled by such gross marginalization of the female gender, has relent-

lessly flayed Achebe's masculinist bigotry. Chikwenye Okonjo
Ogunyemi has rightly observed that:

> Achebe's macho spirit with its disdain for women robs him of the
> symbolic insight into the nurturant possibilities of women's vital role.
> Things fall apart also because of misogyny. (Ogunyemi, 9)

Indeed, things fall apart because women have not been recognized as a potential dynamic force. Consider, for example, that
when a daughter of Umuofia was killed in Mbaino and
Ikemefuna was brought into Okonkwo's household as a
propitiary sacrifice, none of Okonkwo's wives was consulted.
When the most senior wife dared ask the roaring lion, Okonkwo
"thundered": "Do what you are told, woman." (cited in
Ogunyemi, 10) The meek lamb of a wife is not in the least
thunder-struck, for she has gone through a socialization process that has almost proclaimed man a law unto himself.

Achebe makes no bones about delineating a woman as a slave
rather than a partner to her spouse. A woman set in this cultural milieu, such as Nwakibie's wife, accepts a horn of wine
from her husband and goes down on her knees before drink-
ing it. One could argue that Achebe is simply portraying African tradition, but the authorial voice seems to condone such
sexist mores. Again when Okonkwo beats his second wife, "Neither of the other wives dared to interfere beyond an occasional
and tentative, 'it is enough, Okonkwo,' pleaded from a reasonable distance." (Achebe 1958, 27)

Throughout the novel, the female gender is derided. In the
wake of the murder of Ikemefuna, Okonkwo asks himself:
"When did you became a shivering old woman . . . Okonkwo,
you have become a woman indeed." (Achebe 1958, 45) The
new converts are described as "effeminate men clucking like
old hens." (Achebe 1958, 108) Yam, the king of crops, stands
for manliness, while the less important crops such as coco-yams,
beans, and cassava are grown by women. At Ezeudu's funeral,
Okonkwo commits manslaughter, culturally termed female
murder, and is exiled from Umuofia. In Okonkwo's opinion,
his place of exile, Mbainta, his motherland, is considered
"female." Okonkwo continuously regrets that his favorite child,
Ezinma, is not a boy. Surely the roaring flame that is Okonkwo
is fatally doused partly because of his contempt for
womanhood.

Clearly Okonkwo's obduracy and bigotry are reincarnated in Ezeulu, the Chief Priest in *Arrow of God*. In the vein of Okonkwo, Ezeulu is depicted as the patriarchal head of the household and his wives as dumb servants scurrying around like rabbits at his every command. He "normally took no interest in women's shouting." (Achebe 1964, 43) Achebe is nonetheless more realistic in his depiction of a polygamous household in this novel than he is in *Things Fall Apart,* where wives seem to have risen above the squabbles arising from polygyny. The *esprit de corps* which exists between Okonkwo's wives is obviously lacking in Ezeulu's compound, where the bickering wives Ugoye and Matefi exude rank malevolence and pettiness.

While the women in *Things Fall Apart* are practically invisible, we can only remember the female characters in *Arrow of God* by their manifestations of jealousy. We, in fact, get a picture of "women bantering scandals in the market place." (Dathorne, 73) The women in these novels seem to have accepted the status quo with complacence as they remain passive and contented. Kirsten Holst Petersen sees Achebe's traditional women as:

> happy, harmonious members of the community, even when they are repeatedly beaten and banned from any say in the communal decision-making process and constantly reviled in sayings and proverbs. It would appear that in the traditional wisdom, behaving like a woman is to behave like an inferior being. . . . The obvious inequality of sexes seems to be the subject of mild amusement for Achebe. (Petersen, 38)

Achebe has treated female subjects in these novels with such gross levity that women's reactions to colonialism and Christianity are hardly documented. Women are as muted as their men are made vocal.

The shift to the urban milieu in *No Longer at Ease* and *A Man of the People* does not improve the author's negative depiction of women. The fractious, strong female character, Clara, in *No Longer At Ease* has a chink in her armor. Tainted with the *osu* caste, Clara is implicitly depicted as the force that drags Obi Okonkwo to his doom. Obi's relationship with Clara alienates the former from his clansmen. And as Achebe has pointed out in *Arrow of God*, "No man however great was greater than his people . . . no one ever won judgement against his clan." (Achebe 1964, 230) It is fairly certain that Obi's dissension with the Umuofia Progressive Union over Clara is the genesis of his precipitous fall. This grim fact is anticipated when Clara drags Obi, an inhabitant of Ikoyi, to the Lagos slum areas where her seamstress lives. The drive from Ikoyi to the shantytown is analogous to the plunge from grace occasioned by the social intercourse with an outcaste.

Clearly *No Longer At Ease* is riddled with unsavory urban white and black women. Achebe descends upon the hypocritical white reverend sisters and mothers who foment racism. The vivacious Marie Tomlinson is as loquacious as she is prying. Christopher's girl friends are in the main urban sluts. One has to go back to Umuofia to pick out the sole unblemished female character in the novel—Hannah Okonkwo. Isaac Okonkwo, who "is not really a man of action but of thought" (Achebe 1960, 150), acts as a foil to his more practical wife. We are told that when faced with problems "he relied heavily on his wife." (Achebe 1960, 150) We are surprised to be filled in on this fact towards the end of the novel because Hannah has hitherto fitted the image of a very docile wife of a catechist; she is an epitome of wifehood and motherhood, for she trains girls in housekeeping. Achebe destroys her and drops her from the plot probably because she does not fit in the mold of the urban licentious women.

Such women glut the world of *A Man of the People,* a novel set in postindependence Nigerian society. Odili travels from the village to the capital city Bori to take a peep at national hedonism. The author's negative delineation of women is more pungent in this novel than in *No Longer At Ease.* It would appear that, in Achebe's vision, urbanization is synonymous with corruption. Much as *A Man of the People* is a mordant satire against society, women in particular seem to be at the receiving end of Achebe's reproof. Both the white and black women make cuckolds of their husbands. In the case of Barrister Mrs. Akilo she was paid like a prostitute by Nanga. The first person narrator intimates that John was "cowed by his beautiful and bumptious wife" (Achebe 1966, 50), Jean, who slept with incontinent Odili, a man with whom she only had a bowing acquaintance, much to the chagrin of another American lady, Elsie Jackson. Again Elsie, betrothed to a medical student in Edinburgh, feels no qualms about hopping into bed with total strangers. The energies of most of these urban women are directed towards partisan politics, in which women like Mrs. Eleanor John and Mrs. Koko revel. Some of them, incidentally, end up being exploited during elections.

It is interesting to note that when Achebe tries to create a positive female character in the city, Eunice, he does it with half-measure. Her character lacks complexity as she is presented to us only through snippets. A member of the Common People's Convention, she is only thrown into action the moment she avenges Max's death. But Achebe undermines this noble act of heroism by remarking sardonically that she fell down on Max's body and began "to weep like a woman." (Achebe 1966, 160)

As in *No Longer At Ease*, Achebe takes us back to the rural area where his ideal woman is ensconced. Achebe's oblique fixation for rural verdant women could be linked with his penchant for tradition. Chief Nanga's rustic wife has to be sent back to the village to preempt any further interactions and attendant baseness emanating from sophistication. Nanga's "parlor wife," Edna, fits the image of feminine fulfillment—self-effacement and docility. She is practically forced into this marriage by her avaricious father. Edna allows her selfhood to be bought by Nanga, a man old enough to be her father, and she can only set herself free in the wake of the coup. No doubt Edna is not the feminist ideal new woman. Achebe's three E's—Edna, Eunice, and Elsie—lack the vigor and complexities of Sembene's or Ngugi wa Thiong'o's female heroes. They are rather redolent of black Eve, and, like the biblical Eve, they constitute a vitiating force that drives their men out of their wonderland. Elsie the temptress not only lures Odili to Bori but also sets in motion the rancorous rift between Nanga and Odili. Edna becomes the bait that almost launches Odili into Hades. Eunice's initial inertia and stoicism rubs off on Max, and when he is felled, she is stunned before the spur of the moment decision to avenge his death.

In the main, Achebe's female stereotypes are sex objects, and their choice of unchallenging professions is predicated on their passivity. Aside from the armchair lawyers, Eunice and Barrister Mrs. Akilo, who are not even portrayed in this role, most of the female characters are either dumb housewives, teachers, nurses, or secretaries. Like Liza in Cyprian Ekwensi's

Jagua Nana's Daughter, the female lawyers are never seen prac-
ticing the legal profession. This profession seems to be a half-
hearted concession granted women by paternalistic African
male writers. Kenneth Little has rightly noted that there is a
dearth of female professionals and high-ranking female civil
servants in the works of African men. Says he: "Until it is done,
the charge to male chauvinism may be difficult effectively to
rebut." (Little, 157)

It is possibly in an effort to counter this observation that
Achebe casts a character like Beatrice Okoh in *Anthills of the
Savannah.* Unlike his other works, which are replete with women
confined to low occupational status, *Anthills* makes its principal woman character, Beatrice, a senior assistant secretary in
the Ministry of Finance. Endowed with beauty, brains, and
brawn, Beatrice is introduced by Sam as

> the only person in the service, male or female, with a first-class honours
> in English. And not from a local university but from Queen Mary
> College, University of London. Our Beatrice beat the English to their
> game. (Achebe 1988, 75)

On coming back to Africa with a wealth of experience, the
female hero Beatrice tries to beat Sam, the Kangan head of
state, to his own game. Like most African neocolonial leaders,
Sam is crass and corrupt. Silhouetted against this background,
Beatrice is poised for a revolt that she modestly describes as
puny and likens to "the rebellion of a mouse in the cage." (72)
Achebe's imagery is, indeed, apt. The ideal African woman is
culturally a mouse. Since timidity denotes subservience, the
mouse is caged in marriage by a patriarchal head of the household. The rebellion of a mouse in a cage is ineffective as
Beatrice's proves to be when she is marched out of the presi-
dential retreat the worse for it.

It would seem that Beatrice's family background occasioned
her rebellious disposition. Brought up by a bigoted, stern father and a battered mother, "terrorized as she was by her
woman's lot" (Achebe 1988, 109), Beatrice Nwanyibuife has
always been conscious of the lot of womankind in her society.
The fifth in a row of daughters, Beatrice was named
Nwanyibuife ("A female is something"). Beatrice was neither
close to her father nor to her mother, who she believes bore

her a grudge because she was a girl. Having had four daughters, Beatrice's mother had longed for a son and had been utterly disappointed when the fifth child turned out to be a girl—Beatrice. Both Beatrice and her mother are victims of a patriarchal society that holds a son at a premium. To quote Eustace Palmer, "The preoccupation in African societies with continuity of the line means not just a desire for children, but a preference for sons." (Palmer, 41) Feeling like the rejected cornerstone, Beatrice felt alone in her father's house, where she claimed she experienced enough male chauvinism "to last her seven reincarnations." Not only did her cowed mother resent her, her father "deplored the soldier-girl who fell out of trees." (Achebe 1988, 105)

The dynamism of the military runs through her being, and she turns out to be both a controversial and radical figure. Patently immune to malicious gossip about her personality, she expresses her reservations about marriage, which most girls see as a *sine qua non*:

> I was determined from the very beginning to put my career first and, if need be last. That every woman wants a man to complete her is a piece of male chauvinist bullshit I had completely rejected before I knew there was anything like Women's Lib. (Achebe 1988, 88)

The interior monologue employed by Achebe here enables us to probe the female individual's feminist consciousness.

The complexity of this individual is lucid. We see in her characterization a mélange of the qualities of other female characters in Achebe's earlier novels. The willfulness of Clara in *No Longer At Ease*, the defiance of Eunice in *A Man of the People*, and the mythical stature of Ezinma in *Things Fall Apart*, are all visible in Beatrice. A mythical, willful, and defiant figure, Beatrice stands out as an enigma in her capacity as a diviner, priestess, and prophetess. She is a daughter of Idemili—pillar of water: "Such is Idemili's contempt for man's unquenchable thirst to sit in authority on his fellows." (Achebe 1988, 104) Little wonder Beatrice spurns the despotic head of state, Sam, "a soldier-turned politician." Note that when Sam nestles up to Beatrice, Achebe resorts to serpentine imagery: "The big snake, the royal python of a gigantic erection began to stir in the shrubbery of my shrine. . . ." (81) But this is a mundane python, a phallic symbol. The mystical royal python—Eke-Idemili—sends out an arrow that renders Sam's lust stillborn. The irate Sam, who could be likened to the lecherous widow's lover that earned the wrath of Idemili, roaring like a wounded lion, humiliates the priestess of Idemili: a faux pas that serves as a prelude to his ineluctable destruction.

True, the numinous figure of Beatrice pervades the novel. The aura of "goddessy" about her is so distinct that she feels it. In her own words: "As a matter of fact I do sometimes feel like Chielo in the novel, the priestess and prophetess of the Hills of the Caves." (Achebe 1988, 114) Beatrice struck Chris "like the maiden Spirit Mask." (199) Even in lovemaking she manifested "power and authority." It would appear that the aquatic imagery Achebe employs at the zenith of her passion is predicated on her rapport with The Pillar of Water; we are told that:

> Chris saw the quiet demure damsel whose still waters nonetheless could conceal deep over powering eddies of passion that always almost sucked him into fatal depths. (Achebe 1988, 105)

Again:

> And as he did she uttered a strangled cry that was not just a cry but also a command or a password into her temple. From there she took charge of him leading him by hand silently through heaving groves mottled in subdued yellow sunlight, treading dry leaves underfoot till they came to streams of clear blue water. (114)

Her womanhood, is, no doubt, her temple—a receptacle of supramundane water that can destroy or nurture.

It must be pointed out that Beatrice's ethereal stature does not in the least preclude her from nurturance. On one occasion she stood aloof, "immobile as a goddess in her shrine, her arms across her breasts." (Achebe 1988, 196) Folding one's arms across one's breasts, which is a mannerism of Achebe's women, denotes nurturance. This nurturant quality facilitates her role as the pivot of the two other female protagonists—Elewa and Agatha—as well as the trinity—Sam, Chris, and Ikem. The insight into women she gives Ikem changes the latter's vision of the female gender in his works.

It would seem that the revision of Achebe's persona's chauvinistic stance marks the beginning of the author's positive

attitude towards women. Ikem is, as it were, the author's spokesman. The writer Ikem notes that "a novelist must listen to his
characters who after all are created to wear the shoe and point
the writer where it pinches." (Achebe 1988, 97) It is only logical to presume that Achebe has listened to his character Ikem,
who knows where the shoe pinches and where the sun scorches.
It is Ikem's view—a priori Achebe's—that

> women are, of course, the biggest single group of oppressed people
> in the world and, if we are to believe the Book of Genesis, the very
> oldest. But they are not the only ones. There are others—rural peas-
> ants in every land, the urban poor in industrialized countries. Black
> people everywhere including their own continent, ethnic and religious
> minorities and castes in all countries. (Achebe 1988, 98)

Achebe would seem to agree with Carole Boyce Davies that
there is an "inextricable link between an African feminist consciousness and a Socialist orientation—both committed to total
freedom of all people." (Davies, 11) Identifying with the down-
trodden in society and infused with Marxist feminist consciousness, Ikem picks a girlfriend not from his own social class but
from the masses. Elewa is a half-literate salesgirl who lives in
the slums of Bassa with her mother, a petty trader at Gelegele
market. She is, however, diametrically opposed to Achebe's female stereotypes. She in fact radiates "warmth and attraction
and self-respect and confidence." (Achebe 1988, 184) A spirited individual, she bears heroically the tragedy that besets her.

Clearly Achebe plays unequivocal sexual politics by revers-
ing roles and custom at the naming of Elewa's baby. Of significance is the fact that the sex of the baby is female, not male.
Besides, she is named by a woman, Beatrice. In the manipulation of the plot the father, who should have named the baby,
has been fatally struck. Asks Beatrice, the embodiment of feminism: "What does a man know about a child anyway that he
should presume to give it a name?" (Achebe 1988, 222)

The proponent of tradition, Elewa's uncle, is inadvertently
late for the ceremony. That the baby is given a boy's name,
Amaechina, establishes the author's advocacy for the
complementarity of gender roles and molds. Besides, the ceremony provides a forum for "ecumenical fraternization"—Aina,
representing Islam; Beatrice, traditional religion; and Agatha,

Christianity. Straitlaced Agatha, whose individuality has hitherto been vitiated by Christian dogmatism, now begins to thaw. The rapprochement of the different groups anticipates a formidable female solidarity that is indispensable to the reformation of Kangan society.

Society is well represented by the motley party: soldier, student, high-ranking civil servant, housewife, driver, maid, salesgirl, and aged custodians of tradition. The party unanimously declares Chris the hero of the reformation. A martyr, Chris dies gallantly for the cause of the people. Both Emmanuel and Adamma, the student nurse he was trying to protect, testify that he died with dignity. Although the last of the green bottles has been smashed, female dreams have not in the least been shattered. The spate of tragedies is closely followed by the propagation of the seed of reform. The birth of Amaechina ("May the path never close") is metaphorical. "The Shining Path" of Ikem—the vanguard of "new radicalism"—remains wide and open. That woman embodies this path proffers an authorial vision of relentless quest for female autonomy.

In sum, Achebe has made a *volte face* in *Anthills of the Savannah,* in that female individuals are substituted for the stereotypes that glut his early novels. Self-actualization of prime women becomes axial in this book. The flaw in Achebe's ideology, however, lies in the fact that he has, in the vein of the biblical and traditional myth, elevated woman from under man's foot and placed her "reverently to a nice corner pedestal." (Achebe 1988, 98) Differently put, Achebe's male protagonists are all poets. Women have been excluded from this noble station and rather given the subordinate role of moonlight storytellers. Not even the British-trained English graduate, Beatrice, is armed with the pen. She is invariably given an ethereal status and thus kept at bay while men delve into artistic creations with political undertones. This blatant omission notwithstanding, Achebe has advanced from a chauvinistic posture to that of empathy for womankind.

Works Cited

Achebe, Chinua. *Anthills of the Savannah*. Nigeria: Heinemann, 1988.

————. *Arrow of God*. London: Heinemann, 1964.

————. *A Man of the People*. London: Heinemann, 1966.

————. *No Longer At Ease*. London: Heinemann, 1960.

————. *Things Fall Apart*. London: Heinemann, 1958.

Dathorne, O. R. *African Literature in the Twentieth Century*. London: Heinemann, 1976.

Davies, Carole Boyce. "Introduction: Feminist Consciousness and African Literary Criticism." In *Ngambika: Studies of Women in African Literature*, edited by Carole Boyce Davies and Anne Adams Graves. Trenton, NJ: Africa World Press, 1986.

Larson, Charles. *The Emergence of African Fiction*. London: Macmillan, 1971.

Little, Kenneth. *A Sociology of Urban Women's Image in African Literature*. London: Macmillan, 1980.

Ogunyemi, Chikwenye Okonjo. "Women and Nigerian Literature." *The Guardian*, 25 May 1985: 9–10.

Palmer, Eustace. "The Feminine Point of View: Buchi Emecheta's *The Joys of Motherhood*." *African Literature Today* 13 (1983): 38–55.

Petersen, Kirsten Holst. "First Things First: Problems of a Feminist Approach to African Literature." *Kunapipi* 6 (1984): 35–47.

Chapter 8

Achebe's Women:
Mothers, Priestesses, and
Young Urban Professionals

Catherine Bicknell

Anthills of the Savannah represents a new point of departure for Chinua Achebe, because in it he creates for the first time a main character who is a woman. The stories in each of his first four novels are told in terms of the struggles of a male protagonist with the impact of colonialism. This study will look at the treatment of women in the early novels and examine to what extent Beatrice is a continuation of earlier themes and in what ways her characterization offers the possibility of new roles for women.

Achebe concentrates on women in his first and last novels, particularly. In *Things Fall Apart*, he examines the role of women symbolically, in terms of the female principle. Women in Achebe's traditional society derive their authority from two powerful sources: as mothers, they are in touch with the earth's fertility; and as priestesses, they form a bridge between the visible and invisible worlds. The two major symbols of the maternal principle in *Things Fall Apart* are Ani, the earth goddess, and the concept of Nneka, or Mother is Supreme. Ani renews life, and acts as a restraint on the male principle by punishing crimes of aggression. Mother is Supreme stresses the idea of woman as the one who can be counted on for comfort, sustenance, and protection when all other resources have failed. Chielo embodies the role of woman as implacable representative of the will of the gods. When she is possessed by the Oracle of the Hills and the Caves, no man in the community, no matter what his status, can dispute her authority.

But such symbols of the preeminent authority of the female principle are misleading. In the words of Nigerian feminist Obioma Nnaemeka: "Through the process of idealization, [woman] is elevated to a superior position which conflicts with the subordinate position she occupies in reality."[1] This fundamental ambiguity is illustrated by a common motif in West African sculpture. The stool, supported on the head and hands of a crouching woman, symbolizes that woman supports the world by creating and sustaining life. But the symbolism can be read another way: man is raised up while the woman who supports him is kept in a subordinate position.

In Achebe's "traditional" novels, *Things Fall Apart* and *Arrow of God,* there is a great deal of realistic description of how things worked in Igbo village society. But most of these passages relate to how decisions were made for the community in meetings of elders and at gatherings of the clan, where only men spoke. In these novels, except for the priestess Chielo, women had no voice outside of their family. Merun Nasser observes that "the social scientists, through their research, have elucidated a sphere of women's activities in the African society quite unlike and unparalleled by Achebe in his novels."[2]

In actual fact, women's political subordination was counterbalanced by a certain amount of economic independence, as they could dispose as they saw fit of the profits of their farming and trading activities. In addition, women were able to exercise authority through their own social institutions, analogous to those of the men. According to articles by Kamene Okonjo and Judith Van Allen,[3] there existed a dual-authority system among the Igbo, which gave women control over their own affairs through market associations and secret and titled societies. At the family, village, and intervillage levels, they exercised a corporate influence through associations such as the daughters of the lineage and the wives of the lineage.

In *Things Fall Apart* and *Arrow of God*, the two incidents of wife abuse which occur are punished by men, either by the wife's brothers, or at a trial conducted by elders representing the ancestors. At the trial in *Things Fall Apart*, "there were many women, but they looked on from the fringe like outsiders."[4] Judith Van Allen's research shows, however, that husbands who mistreated their wives were often dealt with by a delegation of women, whose tactics ranged from insulting songs to tearing down the man's obi, or living quarters.[5]

One of the effects of colonization by the British, in whose own late Victorian culture women's status was clearly subordinate, was to compromise the complementarity of the roles that men and women played in Igbo society by refusing to recognize that women had any authority at all.

Achebe has said in interviews that he sees the role of the African novelist as being that of educator as well as artist, and that he feels that African societies were misrepresented in their depictions by European writers. But by limiting himself to descriptions of how men were organized and exercised power, and leaving out how women were organized—socially, economically, and politically—he in fact distorts the reader's perception of how traditional Igbo society functioned.

In *No Longer at Ease* and *A Man of the People*, novels that take place just before and after independence, the traditional social hierarchy is in the process of change, as a result of the impact of colonialism. The authority of the elders and titled men is beginning to be superceded by that of young men who have acquired a Western education and found a place for themselves in the government. Women have not benefited from the changes, because it is education that determines who finds a job, and with few exceptions, the resources required for school are allocated to men. Those women who manage to receive an education generally become teachers or, like Clara and Elsie, nurses.

In the new urban environment, single women, unrestrained by family and tradition, have greater freedom. But because women are economically subordinate, and often have to rely on their relationships with men for economic support, they are vulnerable to sexual exploitation. Sometimes it is the women themselves who choose to exploit their sexuality as a means of economic survival. Miss Marks offers herself to Obi in the hope of preferential treatment in obtaining a government scholarship, and Edna feels she has to marry Chief Nanga in order to pay for her education and rescue her parents from poverty.

Eunice, a lawyer in *A Man of the People*, interacts with the male characters on equal terms as a member of the revolutionary party being formed by her fiancé, Max. At the end of the novel, she shoots Chief Koko, who is responsible for Max's murder. Eunice is barely sketched as a character, but in her ability to speak her mind and take action, Achebe has said that she anticipates Beatrice.[6]

The urban society in which Beatrice lives resembles that depicted in *A Man of the People*, except that the civilian government has been replaced by a military government, and she is moving among the very top rulers of the country. Beatrice is different from the female characters who have preceded her because she is not in a subordinate position, economically or socially, and does not, therefore, have to rely on relationships with men to survive. She has been an outstanding student (Sam introduces her as "the only person in the service, male or female, with a first-class honours in English"),[7] and like her male counterparts, she has used her education to acquire a high-level job in the Senior Civil Service.

Despite the fact that Achebe places Beatrice in a position of equality with the male characters, he tends, as in *Things Fall Apart,* to treat her symbolically, while the men's roles are described in more realistic terms. Consistent with this symbolic treatment of Beatrice is the lack of concrete details we are given about her life. As in *No Longer at Ease* and *A Man of the People,* this is particularly true in the areas of work and of her associations with other women. Beatrice has been appointed senior assistant secretary in the Ministry of Finance. She says: "I was determined from the very beginning to put my career first and, if need be, last."[8] Such a statement would suggest she is deeply involved in her work, but we never see her in her office, and, consequently, we don't know what she actually does at the ministry, or how she interacts with her male and female colleagues. The only reference Beatrice ever makes to her work is to signing "daft letters."[9] Her job is not used to reveal other dimensions of her character, in the way that Ikem's job as the crusading editor of the *National Gazette* is. The fact that with an honors degree in English, she has been assigned to a high-level position in the Ministry of Finance in the first place seems to indicate that the importance of Beatrice's job is primarily symbolic.

In regard to Beatrice's relationships with other women, it is interesting to compare her with another of what Juliet Okonkwo would call "talented" women in African literature,[10] Flora

Nwapa's Efuru. Like Beatrice, Efuru is exceptional in terms of intellect, resourcefulness, and success. But Efuru's immediate response to other women is one of solidarity and helpfulness. Beatrice, on the other hand, demonstrates a surprising lack of identification with the problems of other women. Until the events of the coup, which bring Elewa into her life as a kind of dependent, we never see Beatrice with other women, with the exception of her somewhat abusive relationship with her maid, Agatha. As far as we know, she doesn't communicate with her mother and sisters, she doesn't belong to any women's organizations, and she doesn't have any female friends that she regularly calls or gets together with. She has not, like Efuru, adopted any surrogate mothers to take the place of her own mother, nor is she acting as a mentor to any younger women.

A key to Beatrice's isolation from other women may be found in the anecdote she tells about Comfort, the only woman friend she mentions. At the age of twenty-six, Comfort goes home with her fiancé to his village to meet his family. There she is insulted by an old aunt who makes an indirect attack on her age by saying that "if *ogili* was such a valuable condiment no one would leave it lying around for rats to stumble upon and dig into."[11] The point is that by putting off marriage and children, in order to acquire an education and establish themselves in careers, women like Beatrice have alienated themselves from their mothers' generation, for whom the only honorable roles in life are those of wife and mother. And because career women are a new phenomenon in post-independence society, they also find themselves without role models to follow.

What distinguishes Beatrice most from the women who have preceded her in Achebe's fiction is her self-awareness and her ability to direct her own life. Beatrice is the first of Achebe's characters to engage in self-analysis. There were other characters, most notably Okonkwo, whose personalities were formed to some extent by their childhood experiences and relationships to their parents. But Okonkwo was not conscious of what motivated his behavior. As she pulls together the different strands of the story of the coup, Beatrice considers her own life, from her childhood at the Protestant mission, to her university days in London, to her life in Bassa. What she discovers is that she has been the victim of two kinds of oppression:

subordination of women in African society, and subordination of Africans in colonial and post-independence society. In the other novels, Achebe has explored the effects of colonialism on his characters, but in Beatrice, he examines for the first time the impact of patriarchal values on the psychology of a woman.

Beatrice's father, a Protestant catechist, kept order at home and at school by not sparing the rod. Her mother was so intent on pleasing and appeasing her husband that she neglected her daughters. Beatrice says: "I didn't realize until much later that my mother bore me a huge grudge because I was a girl . . . and that when I was born she had so desperately prayed for a boy to give my father."[12] The experience of male domination as a child leads Beatrice to establish her independence from men as an adult. She declares: "That every woman wants a man to complete her is a piece of male chauvinist bullshit I had completely rejected before I knew there was anything like Women's Lib."[13]

Her wariness in regard to men is reinforced by a realistic appraisal of the position of a single, educated woman in modern, urban society. The Nigerian feminist Molara Ogundipe-Leslie has described this situation in grim terms:

> A childless woman is considered a monstrosity—as is an unmarried woman (spinster or divorcee), who becomes the butt of jokes and scandal and the quarry of every passing man, married or not. She is often seen by males as an unclaimed and degenerating commodity to be exploited in all ways, including emotionally and sexually, financially and intellectually.[14]

Beatrice's desire to avoid both her mother's unhappy life, and the exploitation of women she witnesses in the city, explains why, although she and Chris have apparently discussed marriage, Beatrice never reveals any impatience either to marry or to have children.

If this were all there were to Beatrice—a high-achieving, ambitious young woman whose unhappy childhood with a male chauvinist father has discouraged her from marrying—then Beatrice's story could be set in the capital city of any country in the world. But Achebe's intention here is not just to reply to feminists with a version of the New Woman. Beatrice is set firmly within the context of a specifically African system of values that Achebe has consistently reiterated in articles and interviews, and her meaning ultimately comes not from her independence, but from the nature of her attachments.

In Achebe's world, no one stands alone. He often speaks of the "duality" that is an essential ingredient of Igbo thinking, the proverbial idea that "where something stands, something else will stand beside it." Part of the drama of *Anthills of the Savannah* has to do with Beatrice's integration into the order of things, both through her relationship to the goddess Idemili, and through her relationship to the other survivors of the coup.

Beatrice's relationship to the goddess is suggested by the etymology of her name, which means "beatified" or "sanctified." Like Chielo, she has been chosen by the gods to serve them. She is the priestess of Idemili, an Igbo river goddess, whose function in this novel recalls that of Ani, the earth goddess in *Things Fall Apart*. Idemili's mission is to balance the male principle with the female principle, or aggression with restraint. Like Ani, she punishes those who offend her by overstepping the bounds of their prerogatives. Beatrice reflects the two faces of the goddess, nurturing and punishing, in her relationships with the other characters. With Chris and Ikem, she is life-giving and inspires love and creativity. But with Sam, who is abusing the power that has been entrusted to him, she speaks and behaves like an angry prophetess.

Beatrice's role as priestess to Idemili makes her not only a bridge between the material and spiritual worlds, but a link with African traditions. Achebe has often pointed out the importance of understanding the past. As storyteller, Beatrice tries to unravel the different elements that have led to the breakdown of the government. After the coup, she asks: "What must a people do to appease an embittered history?"[15] The idea that the people of Kangan are being punished by the gods has already been suggested by Ikem in his "Hymn to the Sun" when he asks what abomination his people have committed to be punished by the drought that is decimating the country.[16] These questions echo Ali Mazrui's statement in *The Africans* that the ancestors are angry. Observing that things are not working in Africa, he concludes that it is because of the unequal terms of the pact made between Africa and the twentieth century, in which, in their attempt to "modernize," Africans have turned their backs on "cultural continuities."[17]

There are two critical scenes in *Anthills of the Savannah* that deal with this need to establish "continuities": the party at Sam's, and the naming ceremony of Elewa's baby, in both of which Beatrice plays a major role.

When Beatrice is invited to the party at the head of state's lakeside residence, she assumes it is to patch things up between Sam and his estranged friends, Ikem and Chris. It soon becomes clear, however, that she is there to provide the "woman's angle" for a visiting American reporter. Beatrice later analyzes her violent reactions at the party. On the one hand, the fact that this rather insignificant American woman is able to monopolize the attention of the head of state brings back a painful experience from her London schooldays, when her African boyfriend left her at a dance for a barely articulate Cockney girl. As an African woman, she is infuriated to feel that she is once again playing second fiddle to a white woman as a result of what she calls the "Desdemona complex" in African men.

She is also aware of the dangerous implications of the royal treatment being given to the American woman by the head of state and his military leaders simply because she represents the Western news media. The sinister connections between Sam's government and the West are personified in Alhaji Abdul Mahmoud, Chairman of the Kangan/American Chamber of Commerce, who has become a millionaire through government monopolies and smuggling operations.

The massive abuse of power by the leaders of Kangan is confirmed for Beatrice at the party. And it is their arrogant refusal to recognize any restraint on their greed or authority that stirs the wrath of Idemili. As Beatrice reflects later: "Something . . . was imparting to my casual words the sharp urgency of incantation,"[18] and "Something possessed me. . . ."[19] The American reporter, seen through the eyes of Beatrice/Idemili, appears as a "violent idol,"[20] a rival claimant to the loyalties of the dictator and his political cronies. Idemili delivers a last warning to Sam through Beatrice, who tries to win him away from the influence of the American. But Sam ignores the warning. As a result, the party at Sam's represents a turning point in the action. Beatrice definitively destroys her ties to the ruling caste. Sam soon steps up the silencing of dissident voices, and reaction to the repression eventually culminates in a coup.

In a 1988 interview, Achebe said: "The survivors of the tragedy have learned a few things. They have learned that they need to make a journey back into themselves, to make this connection with their roots and to include in their planning the real center of our concern, the real owners of the land."[21] It will be through the agency of Beatrice and Elewa at the end of the story that these links to the past and to the people will be reformed.

In the wake of the deaths of Ikem and Chris and Sam, Achebe reinvokes the principle of Nneka, or Mother is Supreme. The women have picked up where the men left off and now form the core of a group of survivors who represent all the different factions of Kangan society. Beatrice has become the "captain" of the group.[22] Earlier in the novel, her capacity for assuming the male role was suggested on the occasions when she was referred to as a "soldier."[23] In the last scene, when they gather together for the naming ceremony of Ikem's and Elewa's child, Beatrice claims the traditional male role in presiding over the ceremony and choosing a name for the child, and the name she gives the baby girl is a boy's name.

In Beatrice's assumption of male roles, Achebe may be going back to an old tradition in Igbo society. In *Male Daughters, Female Husbands*,[24] Ifi Amadiume describes how in Igbo society women could assume male roles when there was a specific need. A woman might exercise power as a son or husband, for example, when there was no male to fill that role. Beatrice exercises the traditional male role of leadership, but goes beyond tradition by assuming this role not as a borrowed male function, but by recuperating it as an appropriate role for women.

The fact that at the end of *Anthills of the Savannah*, women have come into their own does not mean that Achebe has a millennial attitude toward women in power. In a 1988 interview, he said that such a turn of events would not necessarily usher in a Golden Age.[25] He is also realistic about the limitations of the power that Beatrice and Elewa exercise at the end of the novel. The women and the other survivors may represent a new day, but it is a new day that has not yet dawned. In the meantime the dictator, Sam, has fallen, but it is still his cronies who are running the government. The naming ceremony at Beatrice's represents a hope and a possibility for a national society that will incorporate and rework traditional values, and in which people of all religions, classes, and ethnic groups will collaborate.

With Beatrice, in *Anthills of the Savannah*, Achebe has created a character who is connected to her personal past through her self-awareness; who is connected to her African traditions through her priestly vocation; and who is connected to her people through her adaptability in the face of violent historical events. Although she continues, like all of Achebe's female characters, to be treated on a symbolic rather than a realistic level, the range of symbols has in this novel been expanded to include the possibilities of personal autonomy and political power.

Notes

1   Obioma Nnaemeka, "Towards a Feminist Criticism of Nigerian Literature," *Feminist Issues* 9 (1989), p. 73.

2   Merun Nasser, "Achebe and his Women: A Social Science Perspective," *Africa Today* 27 (1980), p. 27.

3   Kamene Okonjo, "The Dual-Sex Political System in Operation: Igbo Women and Community Politics in Midwestern Nigeria," and Judith Van Allen, "'Aba Riots' or 'Igbo Women's War': Ideology, Stratification, and the Invisibility of Women," in *Women in Africa*, ed. by Nancy J. Hafkin and Edna G. Bay (Palo Alto: Stanford University Press, 1976).

4   Chinua Achebe, *Things Fall Apart* (London: Heinemann, 1976), p. 62.

5   Van Allen, p. 61.

6   Kay Bonetti, "Interview with Chinua Achebe" (Columbia, MO: American Audio Prose Library, 1988). Taped interview.

7   Chinua Achebe, *Anthills of the Savannah* (New York: Anchor, 1988), p. 68.

8   Ibid., p. 80.

9   Ibid., p. 165.

10 Juliet Okonkwo, "The Talented Woman in African Literature," *Africa Quarterly* 15, 1975.

11 *Anthills,* p. 81.

12 Ibid., p. 79.

13 Ibid., pp. 80–81.

14 Molara Ogundipe-Leslie, "Nigeria: Not Spinning on the Axis of Maleness," in *Sisterhood is Global,* ed. Robin Morgan (Garden City, New York: Anchor, 1984), p. 501.

15 *Anthills*, p. 204.

16 Ibid., pp. 28–30.

17 Ali Mazrui, *The Africans* (Boston: Little, Brown, 1986), p. 11.

18 *Anthills*, p 69.

19 Ibid., p. 74.

20 Ibid., p. 97.

21 Sally Baker, "The Conscience of the Muse," *Africa News*, May 2, 1988, p. 6.

22 *Anthills*, p. 213.

23 Ibid., pp. 80 and 97.

24 Ifi Amadiume, *Male Daughters, Female Husbands: Gender and Sex in an African Society* (London and New Jersey: Zed Books, 1987).

25 Bonetti, "Interview."

Chapter 9

Gender Relations and Critical Mediation: From *Things Fall Apart* to *Anthills of the Savannah*

Obioma Nnaemeka

A good woman does not have a brain or a mouth.
                              Ama Ata Aidoo

Igbo women have their spaces and even if you
do not see them, they are there.
                              Chimalum Nwankwo

Chinua Achebe's *Anthills of the Savannah* inscribes simultaneously the storyteller and the critic. On the one hand, it focuses on the centrality of the writer/storyteller as knowledge-builder, disseminator, historian, and survivor who brings the past to the present and fashions from it lessons for the future. On the other hand, it sketches the critic as provider of (new) meanings and creator of new mythologies. In many respects, *Anthills of the Savannah* is a retrospection; in its rearticulation of gender relations, it simultaneously looks back at and moves away from *Things Fall Apart*. The shift in the naming and renaming of female characters in the two novels is radical: from *Nneka* ("Mother is Supreme" in *Things Fall Apart*) to *Nwanyibuife*, *Nkolika*, and *Amaechina* ("woman is something," "Recalling-Is-Greatest," and "May-the-path-never-close" in *Anthills of the Savannah*). This radical change leads one to wonder to what extent the repositioning, renaming, "rehabilitation," and revalorization of "woman" (to the point of ascribing a man's name, Amaechina, to her) are related to some criticisms of

Things Fall Apart, particularly in its depiction of gender relations.

This paper aims at rereading *Anthills of the Savannah* against the backdrop of *Things Fall Apart* in order to examine the possible mediation of literary criticism (feminist criticism, in particular) in the rearticulations of the woman question and gender relations in Achebe's latest novel. I shall examine some analyses of *Things Fall Apart*, engage their criticisms of gender relations in the novel, and study the reworking of the woman question in *Anthills of the Savannah*. Feminist criticism of *Things Fall Apart* remains, for the most part, unequivocal, unyielding, and strident[1] in its objection to the depiction of women in the novel. In some respects, *Anthills of the Savannah* stands as a counterdiscourse to this criticism, particularly in light of the centrality of the writer/critic relationship as well as the demands, responsibility, and expectations placed on the writer as elaborated in the address given by Ikem, the poet, at the University of Bassa:

> The charge of elitism never fails to amaze me because the same people who make it will also criticize you for not prescribing their brand of revolution to the masses. A writer wants to ask questions. These damn fellows want him to give answers. Now tell me, can anything be more elitist, more *offensively* elitist, than someone presuming to answer questions that have not even been raised, for Christ's sake? . . . . As a writer I aspire only to widen the scope of that self-examination. I don't want to foreclose it with a catchy, half-baked orthodoxy. My critics say: There is no time for your beautiful educational programme. . . . And they quote Fanon on the sin of betraying the revolution. They do not realize that revolutions are betrayed just as much by stupidity, incompetence, impatience and precipitate action as by doing nothing at all. (Achebe 1987, 145–146)

It was again Ikem, writer/poet, who returned earlier in the novel to thank Beatrice for giving him some insight "into the world of women." He went on to offer a feminist critique of women's oppression of women and concluded by revisiting and interrogating the *Nneka* phenomenon that was first introduced in *Things Fall Apart:*

> The original oppression of Woman was based on crude denigration. She caused Man to fall. So she became a scapegoat. No not a scapegoat which might be blameless but a culprit richly deserving of what-

ever suffering Man chose thereafter to heap on her. That is Woman in the Book of Genesis. . . . The New Testament required a more enlightened, more refined, more loving even, strategy—ostensibly, that is. So the idea came to Man to turn his spouse into the very Mother of God, to pick her up from right under his foot where she'd been since Creation and carry her reverently to a nice, corner pedestal. Up there, her feet completely off the ground she will be just as irrelevant. . . .

Meanwhile our ancestors out here, unaware of the New Testament, were working out independently a parallel subterfuge of their own. *Nneka*, they said. Mother is supreme. Let us keep her in reserve until the ultimate crisis arrives and the waist is broken and hung over the fire, and the palm bears its fruit at the tail of its leaf. Then, as the world crashes around Man's ears, Woman in her supremacy will descend and sweep the shards.

Do I make sense? (Achebe 1987, 89)

Of course, Ikem makes sense. What is not clear is the intention and, therefore, the appropriate interpretation of his "feminist" arguments. Is this a *genuine* feminist critique of women's oppression or is it a parody of feminist critique of women's oppression across time and cultures? It is difficult to say. Whatever is the case, the engagement with feminist thinking is apparent here.

In order to fully assess existing feminist analyses of *Things Fall Apart,* it will be useful to examine the cultural context in which the novel is rooted, particularly the place of women in Igbo culture. In a paper on women's leadership in Africa, Martin Ijere identified two opposing "schools of thought" on the African woman: "At one end is the school of thought that sees the African woman as a great achiever, leader and counselor. At the other end is a school of thought that sees her as a helpless, gullible being in the hands of plotting men. There is no dearth of examples of the two schools, some coming from across America and Europe." (Ijere, 69)

Crucial to an assessment of the Igbo environment is an understanding of gendered spaces and the division of labor that Ijere also addresses: "There is a clear division of functions between male and female. Each in his or her own domain attains efficiency and satisfaction. To an outsider, this division of labor is regarded as discrimination." (71) A misunderstanding of the internal dynamics of and the relationship between the gendered spaces and functions can lead to a misdiagnosis of the status of women in Igbo society. Unfortunately, some of the feminist analyses of *Things Fall Apart* are rooted in this misdiagnosis.

Igbo worldview is rooted in notions of balance, give and take, live and let live that are often encapsulated in proverbs: *egbe belu ugo belu* ("let the eagle perch, let the kite perch"), *aka nni kwo aka ekpe, aka ekpe akwo aka nni* ("the right hand washes the left hand and the left washes the right"), *ife kwulu ife akwudebie* ("when something stands, something stands beside it"). Not too long after the publication of *Anthills of the Savannah*, Chinua Achebe was one of "a number of remarkable men and women" interviewed by Bill Moyers for a PBS television series called "A World of Ideas." In the opening discussion on the concept of dualism in Igboland, Achebe elaborated on the Igbo proverb, *ife kwulu ife akwudebie*: "It means that there is no one way to anything. The Ibo people who made that proverb are very insistent on this—there is no absolute anything. They are against excess—their world is a world of dualities. It is good to be brave, they say, but also remember that the coward survives." (cited in Moyers, 333) But *Things Fall Apart* is also the story of excess and transgression. Okonkwo's story of excess, intolerance, and violence is a thread woven into a world that is rooted in balance, tolerance, and complementarity. On many levels, Okonkwo epitomizes the Igbo multiperspectivist view of the world—*adiro akwu ofu ebe ekili nmanwu* ("one does not stand in one place to watch the masquerade")—that insists on "no one way to anything" and "no absolute anything." Okonkwo is a complex man, indeed; he stands for what his people admire (hard work), and also stands for what they disapprove of (intolerance, arrogance, and violence)—*ogbu nma nana na nma* ("he who lives by the sword dies by the sword"); he is both normative and marginal. More importantly, Okonkwo epitomizes the capacity of the Igbo world to absorb contradictions and complexity: the normative and the marginal, the positive and the negative. The Igbo world is a world of "this *and* that" and not a world of "this *or* that." Any meaningful analysis (feminist or otherwise) of *Things Fall Apart* must recognize the imperatives of the Igbo world—balance, complementarity, sharing, and tolerance. In fact, the Igbo see the world not only in terms of the multiplicity of functions and endowments but also, and more importantly, in terms of the interrelationship and interdependence of functions, "in terms of storytelling":

If you look at the world in terms of storytelling, you have, first of all, the man who agitates, the man who drums up the people—I call him the drummer. Then you have the warrior, who goes forward and fights. But you also have the storyteller who recounts the event—and this is one who survives, who outlives all the others. It is the storyteller, in fact, who makes us what we are, who creates history. The storyteller creates the memory that the survivors must have—otherwise their surviving would have no meaning. (Moyers, 337)

It will be useful to examine the ways in which the issues noted above—dualism, storytelling/storyteller and language/speech— are linked to the central concerns in existing critical analyses of Achebe's works, such as the representation of women, sexism, silence, power, and marginality. Most critical analyses of *Things Fall Apart* agree on the sexism or even misogyny that pervades the novel although they do not seem to agree on to whom or to what the sexism ought to be ascribed. Some put the blame on sexist Igbo society, others lay the blame at the feet of the sexist author himself. In my view, any reading of sexism in the novel must be interpreted in the context of the Igbo world view as contained in the Igbo proverbs and Achebe's elaboration noted above. Such a reading will direct the charge of sexism where it duly belongs—Okonkwo (*a character in a novel* conceived by Achebe). Contrary to prevailing notions, Okonkwo is not the "ideal" Igbo man (for one thing, his cultural reality is not grounded in absolutes). Okonkwo represents what his people admire and also what they frown upon: "Indeed he respected him for his industry and success. But he was struck, as most people were, by Okonkwo's brusqueness in dealing with less successful men." (Achebe 1959, 19) Culturally, Okonkwo is a flawed man, a marginal character, because he is excessive—excess is an aberration that his culture relegates to the margins of society. Instances of Okonkwo's excess and accompanying censure from his kinsmen abound in the novel:

Only a week ago a man had contradicted him at a kindred meeting which they held to discuss the next ancestral feast. Without looking at the man Okonkwo had said: 'this meeting is for men.' The man who had contradicted him had no titles. . . .
Everybody at the kindred meeting took sides with Osugo when Okonkwo called him a woman. The oldest man present said sternly that those whose palm-kernels were cracked for them by a benevolent spirit should not forget to be humble. Okonkwo said he was sorry for what he had said, and the meeting continued. (Achebe 1959, 28)

> And that was the year Okonkwo broke the peace, and was pun-
> ished, as was the custom, by Ezeani, the priest of the earth goddess.
> (30)

The existing critical analyses of the representation of women in Achebe's novels range from a total acceptance of the author's portrayal of female characters as cultural/sociological truth, to a mild nod of "acceptance with reservations," to vehement rejection and even accusations of misrepresentation of the "true" status of women in Igbo society.[2] Some of these positions are problematic. First, *Things Fall Apart* is a novel and not a piece of anthropological or sociological research on Igboland. The novel evolved from a specific cultural and historical context to which it refers, but that does not mean that it is a mimesis of Igboland; the novel tells its truth differently. Second, some of the criticisms are misplaced because they fail to pay adequate attention to what the text says. Third, some of the arguments are flawed because they are based on interpretations of the novel in light of other cultural realities that do not speak to the cultural specificity of Achebe's work. Objections to some of these analyses notwithstanding, one thing is certain—the *repeated* (three times in ten pages) juxtaposition of women with objects—barns of yams and titles—in *Things Fall Apart* is troubling:

> Okonkwo was clearly cut out for great things. . . . He was a wealthy farmer and had two barns full of yams, and had just married his third wife. To crown it all he had taken two titles. (Achebe 1959, 11–12)

> Each of his three wives had her own hut, which together formed a half moon behind the *obi*. The barn was built against one end of the red walls, and long stacks of yam stood out prosperously in it. (17–18)

> There was a wealthy man in Okonkwo's village who had three huge barns, nine wives and thirty children. His name was Nwakibie and he had taken the highest but one title which a man could take in the clan. (21)

I shall examine some of the specific objections to the depiction of women in *Things Fall Apart* to see how they relate to the novel as well as the reality of Igboland. Juliet Okonkwo includes Achebe's works in her general critique of works by African male writers:

Through the pages of *Things Fall Apart, Arrow of God, Danda, The Only Son, The Concubine,* women come and go with mounds of foo-foo, pots of water, market baskets; fetching kola, being scolded and beaten before they disappear behind the huts of the compounds. (36)

Olney agrees with and elaborates on Juliet Okonkwo's position:

The most obvious instance would be the wives who claim none of the novelist's attention as people interesting in themselves; in fact, they are not people at all but devices used (by Achebe *and* Okonkwo) to define the central male. None of the women is particularized beyond being numerically 1, 2, and 3. We never learn the name of Wife No. 1; we only hear of her as "Nwoye's mother," a designation of considerable significance when one considers the role of women in this book and in the society it describes. There is nothing in *Things Fall Apart* resembling a physical or mental description of these adjuncts to Okonkwo's masculinity: they seem simply to represent "woman," that useful creature who fetches water, bears children, plants female crops (coco-yam and cassava), cooks, and keeps her personality (if, indeed, she has one) very much to herself. These three women are in no sense and never individuals but rather generic representatives of Ibo wives and abstractions from Ibo womanhood. (Olney, 122)

The criticisms by Juliet Okonkwo and Olney fail to take into account gendered division and sharing of work (including house chores) that appear several times in the novel. A more careful examination of tasks and functions in *Things Fall Apart* shows that females are not singled out for discrimination and exploitation. Boys and girls fetch water: "[T]he children filed in, carrying on their heads various sizes of pots suitable to their years. Ikemefuna came first with the biggest pot, closely followed by Nwoye and his two younger brothers. Obiageli brought up the rear." (Achebe 1959, 43–44) Males are also responsible for certain types of domestic duties: "Nothing pleased Nwoye now more than to be sent for by his mother or another of his father's wives to do one of those difficult and masculine tasks in the home, like splitting wood, or pounding food. . . ." (51) "Almost immediately the woman came in with a big bowl of foo-foo. Obierika's second wife followed with a pot of soup, and Maduka [male] brought in a pot of palm-wine." (70) "Some of the Women cooked the yams and the cassava, and others prepared vegetable soup. Young men pounded the foo-foo or split firewood. The children made endless trips to the stream." (106)

"Okonkwo's wives and children and those who came to help them with the cooking began to bring the food. His sons brought out the pots of palm-wine." (154) Furthermore, Olney's argument that Nwoye's mother lacks individuality because she is not assigned her own name is based on notions of individuation that are not applicable to the world of Okonkwo and his kinsmen. These women have names, but each one of them, as a mother, would be called the mother of so and so. This manner of naming is not a sexist invention on the part of the author; it is rather a way of capturing realistically the people's manner of being and speaking. The mothers themselves do not feel less their individuality because of this manner of identification. Ackley rightly notes the importance of cultural literacy for any meaningful interpretation of Achebe's work: Achebe has in fact created a recurrent pattern of allusion and imagery which is manifested in the associations various characters attach to masculinity and femininity, which is made meaningful not through appeal to any external pattern but through a carefully developed examination *of the male and female roles as conceived by traditional Igbo thought.* (Ackley, 1)

Much of the feminist critique of gender relations in *Things Fall Apart* rests on the voicelessness of the women characters. Central to feminist theorizing is the relationship between language (speech) and power on the one hand, and between silence and disempowerment on the other hand. However, any meaningful analysis of voice, silence, and power/disempowerment in the novel must take into cognizance the Umuofia people's notion of silence, particularly the way in which it is elaborated in the story of Mother Kite. In Umuofia, the speech act is a very complex art that categorizes not only speakers but manners and moments of speaking as well, thus creating shifting realities of and possibilities for speakers and listeners. Man (Okonkwo) does not speak when a god speaks but at other times Okonkwo assumes the position of the speaking subject, imposing silence around him. As the priestess aptly warns Okonkwo, "Beware of exchanging words with Agbala. Does a man speak when a god speaks? Beware!" (Achebe 1959, 95) Silence per se is not necessarily an index of subordination and powerlessness; what is disempowering is the intrusion, transgression, and boundary crossings that appropriate the space of the speaker or listener. The story of Mother Kite is instructive:

> "Never kill a man who says nothing". . . . He ground his teeth again and told a story to illustrate his point. "Mother Kite once sent her daughter to bring food. She went, and brought back a duckling. 'You have done very well,' said Mother Kite to her daughter, 'but tell me, what did the mother of this duckling say when you swooped and carried its child away?' 'It said nothing,' replied the young kite. 'It just walked away.' 'You must return the duckling,' said Mother Kite. 'There is something ominous behind the silence.' And so Daughter Kite returned the duckling and took a chick instead. 'What did the mother of the chick do?' asked the old kite. 'It cried and raved and cursed me,' said the young kite. 'Then we can eat the chick,' said her mother. 'There is nothing to fear from someone who shouts.'" (Achebe 1959, 129–130)

Silence can hide power, but *to be silenced* is an imposition that takes away power and agency. Okonkwo knew how to take away (threaten to take away, at least) power and agency by silencing *both men and women*. Although feminist criticism of *Things Fall Apart* limits its condemnation of Okonkwo to his treatment of women, it is important to note that Okonkwo's "victims" cut across gender lines. Some males, such as Osugo, Ikemefuna, and Nwoye, do not escape Okonkwo's harshness and arrogance in the same way that his wives are subordinated to his high-handedness. In his typical way, he silences Nwoye's mother:

> So when the daughter of Umuofia was killed in Mbaino, Ikemefuna came into Okonkwo's household. When Okonkwo brought him home that day he called his most senior wife and handed him over to her.
> "He belongs to the clan," he told her. "So look after him."
> "Is he staying long with us?" she asked.
> "Do what you are told, woman," Okonkwo thundered, and stammered. "When did you become one of the *ndichie* of Umuofia?"
> And so Nwoye's mother took Ikemefuna to her hut and asked no more questions. (Achebe 1959, 18)

Not too long after this clash with his first wife, Okonkwo confronts Ojiugo, one of his wives. Nwoye's mother provoked Okonkwo's anger by asking a question; Ojiugo earned Okonkwo's wrath by her murmur:

His anger thus satisfied, Okonkwo decided to go out hunting. He had an old rusty gun made by a clever blacksmith who had come to live in Umuofia long ago. But although Okonkwo was a great man whose prowess was universally acknowledged, he was not a hunter. In fact he had not killed a rat with his gun. And so when he called Ikemefuna to fetch his gun, the wife who had just been beaten murmured something about guns that never shot. Unfortunately for her, Okonkwo heard it and ran madly into his room for the loaded gun, ran out again and aimed at her as she clambered over the dwarf wall of the barn. (Achebe 1959, 39)

The relationship between power and speech/voice is not lost to the Igbo. Among them, abject poverty and total disempowerment are often expressed in terms of the lack of the two most desirable possessions—people and voice: *enwerọm nmadu* ("I do not have people") and *enwerọm ọnu okwu* ("I do not have the mouth to speak [voice]"). The Igbo feel violated when someone arrogates to himself/herself the right or power to speak *for* them. Okonkwo's encounter with Ojiugo is instructive. Ojiugo does not remain silent; she speaks (albeit a murmur). As an Igbo woman, she exercises her right to speak, to talk back. But fully aware of the limitation placed on her by her husband's temper and high-handedness, she chooses an appropriate manner to exercise her right to speak—murmur. Thus, as far as the critique of the silence/silencing of Okonkwo's wives goes, the issue should be more about Okonkwo's intolerance and abrupt manner, and less about the so-called sexism of Igbo society.

Many researchers have documented the centrality, relevance, and power of African women across time and cultures.[3] Niara Sudarkasa's account of her research findings differs markedly from the depiction of women in *Things Fall Apart:*

From my own readings on Africa and my research among the Yoruba in Nigeria and other parts of West Africa, it appears that except for the highly Islamized societies in Sub-Saharan Africa, in this part of the world more than any other, in precolonial times women were conspicuous in "high places." They were queen-mothers; queen-sisters; princesses, chiefs, and holders of other offices in towns and villages; occasional warriors; and, in one well-known case, that of the Lovedu, the supreme monarch. Furthermore, it was almost invariably the case that African women were conspicuous in the economic life of their societies, being involved in farming, trade, or craft production. (Sudarkasa, 91)

In view of Sudarkasa's work and similar research findings on African women, some critics of Achebe's works have accused Achebe of distorting Igbo reality. Merun Nasser's comparative analysis of women in Achebe's novels and research findings on African women is a case in point. While giving Achebe credit for "presenting his readers with an array of cultural, social, historical, political settings in his writings . . . an achievement [that] is hardly unsurpassed by any other African writer," Nasser argues that Achebe's novels, which cover different periods of Igbo history—*Things Fall Apart* (early twentieth century); *No Longer at Ease* (mid-twentieth century and pre-independence times); *Arrow of God* (colonial times) and *A Man of the People* (postindependence period)—show disregard for women and their contributions:

> If indeed Achebe must act as an anthropologist, an artist, and an historian, then why has he chosen to disregard women and their contributions during the various periods in his major works? Is it by mere accident that Achebe does not give the full picture of the women's contributions, or is it that the women were passive and subservient and in fact made no outstanding contributions in the society? For answers to these questions, we must turn to social science research which establishes the fact that women have indeed made positive contributions to the history of the region under consideration. (Nasser, 25)

After a detailed analysis of the activism and contributions of African women from the "Igbo Women's War" of 1929 to the 1958 uprising of Kom women of Bamenda Province, Nasser arrives at the following conclusion:

> With these two examples, we find that the social scientists, through their research, have elucidated a sphere of women's activities in the African society quite unlike and unparalleled by Achebe in his novels. The women, who reacted against the colonialists, using traditional organizations to make their grievances known, were heroines in real life. Achebe's novels, it appears, have no room for the woman who does not conform to the role he has chosen for her. It is this state of benign neglect of an important aspect of the woman on the part of Africa's best known and leading novelist which forces the following conclusion: Chinua Achebe has not presented a realistic portfolio of the woman, both in the traditional and modern settings in African society. (Nasser, 27–28)

An important issue that is worth investigating is the extent to which sexist attitudes towards women in the novels are traceable to the author's personal views, the views of his protagonists, or both (as Olney suggests). It seems to me that what needs thorough examination is some of the misplaced criticisms that have plagued *Things Fall Apart* since its publication. For example, Nasser's criticism of Achebe's works for their inability to depict Igbo women as they appear in social science research is not justified. As I mentioned earlier, spaces are gendered and complementary in Okonkwo's world. Boundaries are marked and respected, although Okonkwo transgresses those boundaries even when he is asleep!: "He breathed heavily, and it was said that, when he slept, his wives and children in their out-houses could hear him breathe." (Achebe 1959, 7) *Things Fall Apart* focuses on telling the story of the male space—ceremonies, wrestling, masquerades, war. A specific female space that is identified in the novel is the *uri* of Obierika's daughter: "But it was really a woman's ceremony and the central figures were the bride and her mother." (104) Women are marginal in the novel primarily because they are peripheral to the male space on which the novel focuses: "It was very clear from the way the crowd stood or sat that the ceremony was for men. There were many women, but they looked on from the fringe like outsiders." (83) Often, Okonkwo's high-handedness and abuse of the people around him (male and female) are naturalized, essentialized, and generalized in literary criticism as an Igbo flaw in spite of the fact that, unlike Okonkwo and Uzowulu, most Umuofia men neither abuse their wives nor treat their fellow men disrespectfully.

In light of the above examination of women's status and gender relations in *Things Fall Apart* and criticism of the novel, I shall examine gender relations in *Anthills of the Savannah* to see in what ways the female characters are different from one novel to the other. Obviously, reminders of *Things Fall Apart* resonate in *Anthills of the Savannah*. Issues, such as gendered spaces, voice, and the deity, names (Nwakibie, Chielo), stories (Mosquito and the Ear), and the *Nneka* phenomenon that appeared in Achebe's first novel are revisited in his latest novel. Through Ikem's "strange love-letter," the oppression of women is simultaneously reconsidered within the framework of Judaeo-Christian thought and Igbo cosmology where, according to the

earth/sky story and the *Nneka* phenomenon, woman is objec-
tified and fetishized, condemned and revered, marginal and
central:

> The original oppression of Woman was based on crude denigration.
> She caused Man to fall. So she became a scapegoat. No, not a scape-
> goat which might be blameless but a culprit richly deserving of what-
> ever suffering Man chose thereafter to heap on her. That is Woman in
> the Book of Genesis. Out here, our ancestors, without the benefit of
> hearing about the Old Testament, made the very same story differing
> only in local colour. At first the Sky was very close to the Earth. But
> every evening Woman cut off a piece of the Sky to put in her soup pot
> or, as in another version, she repeatedly banged the top end of her
> pestle carelessly against the Sky whenever she pounded the millet or,
> as in yet another rendering—so prodigious is Man's inventiveness—
> she wiped her kitchen hands on the Sky's face. Whatever the detail of
> Woman's provocation, the Sky finally moved away in anger, and God
> with it. (Achebe 1987, 89)

Now comes the New Testament with "new" ideas. Eve resur-
faces but is installed on a pedestal and christened "Mother of
God"; simultaneously, the millet pounder/cook reemerges as
Nneka/Mother is Supreme. (89) The naming and renaming of
Woman in both traditions expose Man's unwillingness to accept responsibility for the oppression of women. As Eve, woman
is evil and deserves her fate; as Mother of God/*Nneka*, she is
to be grateful for the "honor" conferred on her by installing
her in a space of irrelevance in terms of changing the course
of history. As the Mother of God/*Nneka,* woman is out of touch;
as Eve/millet pounder/cook, she is there to clean up everyone
else's mess. In both instances, her position of subordination
remains unmitigated. Thus, confined to a "space," woman is
denied the power and agency to be an active participant in
becoming/history.

From a feminist perspective, the "strange love-letter" is important not so much because of what it says but because of
who wrote and articulated it—Ikem. The feminist arguments in
the letter are the ideas of the much touted "feminist" in the
novel, Beatrice, but unfortunately, she is silenced in the novel's
most feminist moment. According to Ikem,

> I've come to thank you for the greatest present one human being can
> give another. The gift of insight. . . . You told me a couple of years
> ago, do you remember, that my thoughts were unclear and reaction-

ary on the role of the modern woman in our society. Do you remember?. . . . But I resisted. Vehemently. But the amazing thing was that the more I read your charge sheet . . . the less impressive my plea became. My suspension from the *Gazette* has done wonders for me. I have been able to sit and think things through. I now realize you were right and I was wrong. (Achebe 1987, 88)

Ikem's "love-letter" is made up of two "movements"—the first, which raises feminist issues, is attributed to Beatrice's insight. The second part, which is made up of Ikem's own ideas, goes beyond a gender analysis to show how other factors such as race and class play a role in oppressive situations of unequal power relations. Ikem's love-letter urges, among other things, a feminist revision of the *Nneka* phenomenon. Unfortunately, Beatrice, the originator of that idea, is silenced. Ikem reads for us what Beatrice had already formulated and articulated off-stage; the reader does not hear this very important message from the "horse's mouth" (to borrow Beatrice's favorite phrase). From a feminist perspective, it is troubling that the dissemination of Beatrice's ideas is mediated by a male presence that dwarfs Beatrice at the moment when she should have stood tall.

Ikem, the writer, explains the basis on which the novelist makes adjustments in terms of characterization: "It simply dawned on me two mornings ago that a novelist must listen to his characters who after all are created to wear the shoe and point the writer where it pinches." (Achebe 1987, 88) Ikem's observation and Beatrice's response—"Are you suggesting I am a character in your novel?"—point to the attempt in *Anthills of the Savannah* to create the "modern woman" in the person of Beatrice herself. Beatrice, the latter-day "Madame Pompadour," has been generally hailed as "the most important female character that Achebe has created." (Sparrow, 58) The pervasive assertions that Beatrice is "the most important female character" and *the* feminist in Achebe's oeuvre need to be brought up for a close scrutiny. Beatrice's name, *Nwanyibuife*/woman is something, proclaims the importance of woman; Beatrice epitomizes that importance. But in what ways is she "something"? The clearly demarcated gender spaces in *Things Fall Apart* are disrupted in *Anthills of the Savannah*. Beatrice is inscribed in the male space of the three green bottles—HE, Chris, and Ikem—but to what extent does she *actually* share the space? This arrogant, egotistical, superficial, self-serving so-called "feminist" walks the corridors of power without sharing power, except to be kissed and made love to; she writes her feminist "charge sheet" but hands it over to Ikem who articulates it, thereby silencing and marginalizing her.

In my view, Beatrice is the antithesis of the feminist ideal of female solidarity that is crucial for engineering social change. In fact, one can say that Beatrice represents what went wrong with feminism—arrogance, elitism, intolerance of difference, struggle to be like "one of the boys." Who is Beatrice? Mad Medico introduces her as having taken "a walloping honours degree in English from London University." (Achebe 1987, 57) Even more effusive is His Excellency's introduction later in the novel:

> Meanwhile His Excellency was literally reciting my CV. "Lou, this is one of the most brilliant daughters of this country, Beatrice Okoh. She is a Senior Assistant Secretary in the Ministry of Finance—the only person in the service, male or female, with a first-class honours in English. And not from a local university but from Queen Mary College, University of London. Our Beatrice beat the English to their game. We're very proud of her." (Achebe 1987, 68)

Beatrice rushes off with the ubiquitous "three green bottles" without the honor of being anointed green bottle number four. In spite of her marginalization, her illusion of grandeur is so great that she treats the other women—Lou, Agatha, and Elewa—with disrespect and condescension. Elewa's condemnation of sexism in the society and her subsequent call for sisterhood meet with an uncalled-for snobbish, "erudite" interjection from our learned lady, Beatrice:

> "But woman done suffer for dis world-o," says Elewa.
> "A modern Desdemona, I see. Did she cheer him up?"
> asked Beatrice totally ignoring Elewa's more basic solidarity call. (Achebe 1987, 55)

When Ikem is suspended, Elewa is similarly treated with measured condescension when she asks Beatrice what "suspend" means. Beatrice ignores her question as in her previous "conversations" with Elewa.

"Oh come on, Elewa. I am only suspended not sacked". . . .
"You say no be sack them sack you na . . . weting you call am?"
"Na suspend they suspend me."
"Weting be suspend?. . . I beg, BB weting be suspend?"
"My sister, make you no worry yourself. As we de alive so, na that one better pass all." (Achebe 1987, 138)

Lou, the American journalist, does not fare any better:

As soon as the introductions were over the American journalist came rushing to me to say she hoped that besides getting acquainted this evening we would be able to sit down somewhere in the next seven days over a meal or something and talk about things in general. Especially the woman's angle, you know. To which I replied rather sharply that I couldn't see what a reporter who could stroll in any time and get it all direct from the horse's mouth could want to hear from the likes of me. Involuntarily perhaps her eyes narrowed into a fighting squint for the briefest moment and then just as swiftly changed tactics back to friendliness. (Achebe 1987, 69)

Lou is there ostensibly to find out things from "especially the woman's angle." Beatrice, "the feminist," overtly pleads incompetence in discussing feminist issues. Where, may I ask, is the "horse's mouth" from which Lou would get the information she needs? Furthermore, by the time Beatrice concluded her short comment, she has condescendingly reduced Lou from "the American journalist" to "a reporter."

Beatrice's maid, Agatha, also suffers indignities in the hands of her "feminist" mistress. However, the persistent intrusion of the narrator's voice keeps reminding Beatrice of Agatha's humanity and relevance, and eventually leads to *"the* feminist's" transformation at the end of the novel: *"It is now up to you to tell us what has to be done. And Agatha is surely one of you."* (Achebe 1987, 169, emphasis in the original) Beatrice sees and treats Agatha differently; she no longer ignores Agatha the way she had ignored her and Elewa in the past:

It was Agatha's habit to cry for hours whenever Beatrice said as much as boo to her; and Beatrice's practice to completely ignore her. But today, after she had deposited the used plates in the sink, Beatrice turned to where Agatha sat with her face buried in her hands on the kitchen-table and placed her hand on her heaving shoulder. She immediately raised her head and stared at her mistress in unbelief.

'I am sorry Agatha.' The unbelief turned first to shock and then, through the mist of her tears, a sunrise of smiles. (Achebe 1987, 169–170)

In Beatrice's gesture and Agatha's smile lie the possibility of the sisterhood and mutual respect that drive the engine of true feminist engagement.

Fiona Sparrow's argument that Beatrice's power resides in her ability to influence the action of the trio—HE, Ikem, and Chris—sounds more like the "behind every successful man is a woman" syndrome: "Her power is greater because it works in the minds of the three men who are her concern. Everything that happens in the novel has its natural cause and effect, but beneath it all Beatrice's mystic power is at work." (Sparrow, 61) I am not sure that I would attribute that much agency to Beatrice since all the action, all the wheeling and dealing in the novel are orchestrated by the three green bottles who at times appear to be all that there is in Kangan. Beatrice herself admits that these three men, not herself, constitute the core of her country.

Beatrice is lightweight and superficial primarily because she lacks the power and balance that come from rootedness in the soil:

> BEATRICE NWANYIBUIFE did not know these traditions and legends of her people because they played but little part in her upbringing. She was born as we have seen in a world apart; was baptized and sent to schools which made much about the English and the Jews and the Hindu and practically everybody else but hardly put in a word for her forebears and the divinities with whom they had evolved. So she came to barely knowing who she was. (Achebe 1987, 96)

Daughters (and sons, for that matter) who barely know who they are cannot truly lead a revolution. Quite unlike Beatrice, Elewa is considerably aware; she is aware of the exploitation of women and the need for bonding, solidarity, and sisterhood. Elewa's feminist consciousness/conscience of sisterhood and solidarity is arrogantly dismissed by the "educated" Beatrice, who is obviously irritated by her pidgin English babble and the lack of sophistication with which her ideas are articulated. As Juliet Okonkwo argues, illiteracy undermines the effectiveness of hard-working, respectable, freethinking, independent female characters such as Anowa and Efuru who know who they are and to a great extent know where they are going. How then can one explain Beatrice's low level of effectiveness given her intellectual background? The cultural handicap that undermines Beatrice and the linguistic handicap that marginalizes

Elewa lead me to the conclusion that in the new realities, *the erudite daughter of the soil* is best suited to contribute meaningfully to social change.

Oftentimes, it is assumed that the African village is the locus where the oppression of women was invented and is perpetuated, and that the shift from rural to urban setting automatically guarantees liberation, empowerment, and legitimacy. The history of feminist activism in Africa challenges, the view that an urban setting and "a whopping honours degree" are synonymous with empowerment and relevance. In assessing the general acclaim of Beatrice as *the* feminist and "most important female character" of Achebe's literary career, we must keep in mind the other female characters we met in Achebe's earlier novels. I will limit my examples to some of the women we saw in the village of Umuofia (*Things Fall Apart*). Anasi walks onto a page of the novel with an unforgettable presence:

> Anasi was a middle-aged woman, tall and strongly built. There was authority in her bearing and she looked every inch the ruler of the womenfolk in a large and prosperous family. She wore the anklet of her husband's titles, which the first wife alone could wear. (Achebe 1959, 22–23)

Although Achebe has been constantly criticized for not giving "Nwoye's mother" a name, this so-called nameless woman takes the initiative and covers up for another woman in the spirit of sisterhood:

> "Where is Ojiugo?" he asked his second wife. . . .
> "She has gone to plait her hair."
> Okonkwo bit his lips as anger welled up within him.
> "Where are her children? Did she take them?" he asked with unusual coolness and restraint.
> "They are here," answered his first wife, Nwoye's mother. Okonkwo bent down and looked into her hut. Ojiugo's children were eating with the children of his first wife.
> "Did she ask you to feed them before she went?"
> "Yes," lied Nwoye's mother, trying to minimise Ojiugo's thoughtlessness. (Achebe 1959, 31)

Chielo, the powerful priestess of the Oracle of the Hills, "screams" at Okonkwo: "Beware, Okonkwo! . . . Beware of exchanging words with Agbala. Does a man speak when a god speaks? Beware!" When I think of women in Achebe's work who stand out as strong, relevant, powerful, and with true feminist spirit, I think of the confidence and power in Anasi's footsteps; I think of Nwoye's mother, who lied to protect another woman; Chielo, who dared to scream at almighty Okonkwo; Ekwefi, who ran away from her first husband in order to live with Okonkwo, the man she loves. In terms of stature and relevance, Beatrice pales in comparison to these women. These women are sustained and protected by what holds their land. For example, wife battery occurs in *Things Fall Apart* and *Anthills of the Savannah* but is handled differently in the two environments.

When Okonkwo beat his second wife, his other wives intervened with "'It is enough, Okonkwo,' pleaded from a reasonable distance." (Achebe 1959, 39) The first time Okonkwo beat his wife,

> Okonkwo's neighbours heard his wife crying and sent their voices over the compound walls to ask what was the matter. Some of them came to see for themselves. . . .
> Before it was dusk, Ezeani, who was the priest of the earth goddess, Ani, called on Okonkwo in his *obi*. Okonkwo brought out kola nut and placed it before the priest.
> "Take away your kola nut. I shall not eat in the house of a man who has no respect for our gods and ancestors. . . . Your wife was at fault, but even if you came into your *obi* and found her lover on top of her, you would still have committed a great evil to beat her. . . . You will bring to the shrine of Ani tomorrow one she-goat, one hen, a length of cloth and a hundred cowries." (Achebe 1959, 31–32)

Some feminist critics such as Florence Stratton have argued that the restitution is for the offense against the earth goddess for the violation of the week of peace. However, it must be noted that Okonkwo's beating of his wife is a crime against the land for which restitution is required.

The case of Uzowulu is even more dramatic. When he beat his wife, Mgbafo, his brothers-in-law went to his house, beat him up, and took away their sister and her children. The village is summoned to the *ilo* (village square) to settle the dispute. Odukwe articulates the law of the land and the modality of its application; Evil Forest then states the necessary restitution that comes with infringement:

"The law of Umuofia is that if a woman runs away from her husband her bride-price is returned. But in this case she ran away to save her life. Her two children belong to Uzowulu. We do not dispute it, but they are too young to leave their mother. If, on the other hand, Uzowulu should recover from his madness and come in the proper way to beg his wife to return she will do so on the understanding that if he ever beats her again we shall cut off his genitals for him. . . . Our duty is not to blame this man or praise that, but to settle the dispute. . . . Go to your in-laws with a pot of wine and beg your wife to return to you. It is not bravery when a man fights with a woman." (Achebe 1959, 87–89)

There are recurrent features in these three instances of wife battery in *Things Fall Apart:* individual and collective intervention to halt the abuse, community condemnation, and censure of the recalcitrant, "mad" husband. Women are strengthened and sustained by the protection and support that come with such individual and collective interventions.

In *Anthills of the Savannah*, Ikem's neighbor also beats his wife. However, there is a marked difference between the responses to wife battery in *Things Fall Apart* and attitudes towards wife abuse in *Anthills of the Savannah:*

Mr. So Therefore, the notorious Posts and Telegraphs man in the next flat. . . . Perhaps he will beat his beautiful wife tonight; he hasn't done it now in months. Do you miss it then? Confess, you disgusting brute, that indeed you do! Well, why not? There is an extraordinary surrealistic quality about the whole thing that is almost satisfyingly cathartic. . . . Later I hear how a concerned neighbour once called the police station—this was before I came to live here—and reported that a man was battering his wife and the Desk Sergeant asked sleepily: "So Therefore?" (Achebe 1987, 32)

There is not much difference between the revolutionary, Ikem, who revels in his female neighbor's pain, and Sergeant "So Therefore," who does not want to be bothered. The revolutionary and the sergeant had the opportunity and power to do something but chose not to. Men in Umuofia would have intervened to bring the Posts and Telegraphs man's madness to a screeching halt.

Anthills of the Savannah is a very important work in the sense that it provides the space for introspection and retrospection as they relate to Adrienne Rich's idea of "re-vision" or Michel Foucault's notion of "archaeology." Fundamentally, the novel is about storytelling and the storyteller as rhetorician/linguistic craftsman and orator/historian. More importantly, it is about the storyteller as a survivor; he/she must survive the story in order to engage in its telling:

> The trees had become hydra-headed bronze statues so ancient that only blunt residual features remained on their faces, like anthills surviving to tell the new grass of the savannah about last year's brush fires. (Achebe 1987, 28)

The pervasive intrusion of heights and elevations in *Anthills of the Savannah* is very symbolic and significant. It is by standing tall above the story that the storyteller assesses, articulates, and possibly controls history. The anthills or the high elevation of HE's retreat at Abichi village symbolize vantage positions from which history is narrated and/or written; this intellectual space is similar to what Richard Wright (*Blueprint*) calls "perspective." These heights are *loci* of language and power from which women are banished. To a certain extent, *Anthills of the Savannah* is a failed attempt to install a woman on those heights. As a candidate for installation, Beatrice falls short. The night that Beatrice was invited to Abichi village, she succumbed to the ecstasy of feeling the "gigantic erection" of the "royal python" in "the shrubbery of [her] shrine," discovering that HE, "fully aroused clung desperately to [her]." Consequently, both of them step over to the balcony:

> And I took him then boldly by the hand and led him to the balcony railings to the breathtaking view of the dark lake from the pinnacle of the hill. And there told him of my story of Desdemona. (Achebe 1987, 74)

If Beatrice had known how to worship before the shrine of her powerful African foremothers, she could have avoided the stranglehold of the "royal python," thereby forestalling the "gigantic erection" and narrating not the story of Desdemona but the type of story that fashions history. Like the storyteller, she would have survived "like an anthill surviving to tell the new grass of the savannah about last year's brush fires." (Achebe 1987, 28)

Notes

1   The most strident is probably Florence Stratton's book, *Contemporary African Literature and the Politics of Gender* (London: Routledge, 1994).

2   Gerhard Grohs's article, "Women and Politicians in the Modern African Novel," focuses on, among other works, Chinua Achebe's *Things Fall Apart, No Longer at Ease, Arrow of God,* and *A Man of the People.* Other works examined by Grohs include Cyprian Ekwensi's *Jagua Nana,* Ousmane Sembène's *Les bouts de bois de Dieu,* V. Y. Mudimbe's *Le bel immonde,* Ngugi wa Thiong'o's *Petals of Blood,* Cheikh Hamidou Kane's *L'aventure ambiguë,* and V. Henri Lopes's *La novelle romance.* Juliet Okonkwo's "The Talented Woman in African Literature" examines the problems which independent women, such as Anowa in Ama Ata Aidoo's *Anowa* and Efuru in Flora Nwapa's *Efuru,* confront in a patriarchal society. Phanuel Egejuru, using *Things Fall Apart* and the writings of other authors, argues that in African literature, the fundamental need for the establishment of male/female relationship is not "passionate love" but procreation. Donald G. Ackley, "The Male-Female Motif in *Things Fall Apart,*" sees Achebe's portrayal of women as a faithful depiction of women and "female roles in traditional Igbo thought." Chapter IV of James Olney's book, *Tell Me Africa,* looks at some of the issues discussed by Egejuru. Merun Nasser's paper, "Achebe and his Women: A Social Science Perspective," is an analysis of the discrepancies between the depiction of women in Achebe's novels and research findings on Igbo women in the social sciences.

3   The following scholars have discussed the empowerment/disempowerment of women in precolonial, colonial and postcolonial African societies: Nina Emma Mba, *Nigerian Women Mobilized: Women's Political Activities in Southern Nigeria, 1900-1965* (Berkeley: University of California Press, 1982); Jean F. O'Barr, "Making the Invisible Visible: African Women in Politics and Policy," *African Studies Review* 5 (1975): 19-28; Jean F. O'Barr, ed. *Perspectives on Power: Women in Africa, Asia, and Latin America* (Durham: Duke University Center for International Studies, 1982); Ifi Amadiume, *Male Daughters, Female Husbands: Gender and Sex in an African Society* (London: Zed Press, 1987); Stephanie Urdang, *Fighting Two Colonialisms: Women in Guinea-Bissau* (New York: Monthly Review Press, 1979); Judith Van Allen, "'Sitting on a Man': Colonialism and the Lost Political Institutions of Igbo Women," in *Canadian Journal of African Studies* 6 (1972): 65-81.

Works Cited

Achebe, Chinua. *Anthills of the Savannah*. New York: Anchor/Doubleday, 1987.

———. *Things Fall Apart*. Greenwich, CT: Fawcett Crest, 1959.

Ackley, Donald G. "The Male-Female Motif in *Things Fall Apart*." *Studies in Black Literature* 4 (1974): 1–6.

Eagleton, Mary, ed. *Feminist Literary Theory: A Reader*. New York: Basil Blackwell, 1986.

Egejuru, Phanuel. "The Absence of the Passionate Love Theme in African Literature." In *Design and Intent in African Literature*, edited by David F. Dorsey, Phanuel A. Egejuru, and Stephen H. Arnold, pp. 83–90. Washington: Three Continents Press, 1982.

Foucault, Michel. "The Subject and Power." In *The Foucault Reader*, edited by Paul Rabinow, pp. 101–120. New York: Pantheon, 1984.

Grohs, Gerhard. "Women and Politicians in the Modern African Novel." In *Jaws-Bones and Umbilical Cords*, edited by Ulla Schild, pp. 119–126. Berlin: Dietrich Reimer Verlag, 1985.

Ijere, Martin. "The Imperative of Women's Leadership in the Socio-economic Life of a Nation." Nsukka: *Proceedings of the First International Conference on Women in Africa and the African Diaspora: Bridges Across Activism and the Academy*, Vol. 1 (July 13–18, 1992): 69–79.

Mba, Nina Emma. *Nigerian Women Mobilized: Women's Political Activities in Southern Nigeria, 1900–1965*. Berkeley: University of California Press, 1982.

Moi, Toril, ed. *The Kristeva Reader*. New York: Columbia University Press, 1986.

Moyers, Bill. *A World of Ideas*. Edited by Betty Sue Flowers. New York: Doubleday, 1989.

Mulvey, Laura. "Visual Pleasure and Narrative Cinema." *Screen* 16 (1975): 6–18.

Nasser, Merun. "Achebe and his Women: A Social Science Perspective." *Africa Today* 27 (1980): 21–28.

O'Barr, Jean F. "Making the Invisible Visible: African Women in Politics and Policy." *African Studies Review* 5 (1975): 19–28.

————, ed. *Perspectives on Power: Women in Africa, Asia, and Latin America.* Durham: Duke University Center for International Studies, 1982.

Okonkwo, Juliet I. "The Talented Woman in African Literature." *Africa Quarterly* 15 (1975): 35–47.

Olney, James. *Tell Me Africa: An Approach to African Literature.* New York: Africana Publishing, 1972.

Rich, Adrienne. *Of Woman Born: Motherhood as Experience and Institution.* New York: Norton, 1986.

Sparrow, Fiona. "*Anthills of the Savannah.* Review." *World Literature Written in English* 28 (1988): 58–63.

Sudarkasa, Niara. "The Status of Women in Indigenous African Societies." *Feminist Review* 12 (1986): 91–103.

Urdang, Stephanie. *Fighting Two Colonialisms: Women in Guinea-Bissau.* New York: Monthly Review Press, 1979.

Van Allen, Judith. "'Sitting on a Man': Colonialism and the Lost Political Institutions of Igbo Women." *Canadian Journal of African Studies* 6 (1972): 65–81.

Wright, Richard. "Blueprint for Negro Writing." In *The Black Aesthetics*, edited by Addison Gayle, pp. 315–326. New York: Doubleday, 1971.

EUROCENTRIC CHALLENGES TO COLONIALISM:
REEXAMINING THE ROLE OF IMPERIALIST LITERATURE

This section examines the challenge to hierarchies embodied not in postcolonial African works, but in British fiction of the era of high imperialism. In the first essay, Olusegun Adekoya indeed reminds us that Joseph Conrad's *Heart of Darkness*, despite forceful criticisms raised by Chinua Achebe in "An Image of Africa," did attempt to a significant extent to undermine some of the more overt and pernicious aspects of the imperial order. By revealing the corruption, emptiness, and evil of the European colonizers, Conrad challenged the premises of imperialism.

At the same time, however, Adekoya's essay strongly reaffirms the traditional Eurocentric hierarchy that Achebe decried and which, for all Adekoya's protestations to the contrary, Conrad's celebrated novella appears to uphold. In defending *Heart of Darkness* against Achebe's charges, Adekoya accepts the view that the Africans whom Marlow saw "howling and leaping" on the shore were indeed a "crude and low form of existence." While correctly observing that Conrad also leveled a brutal (and justified) critique at the European colonial establishment, Adekoka fails to note that the critique he leveled at the Africans for being "primitive," "primordial," and "low," was simply unwarranted. In Achebe's view (which we feel compelled to uphold against Adekoya's counter-revisionism), Conrad erred in that his Eurocentrism (or "racism") led him to misinterpret African behavior, which was *different* from European behavior, as being *inferior*. Thus when Adekoya chastizes Achebe for failing to appreciate the ambivalence and just criticism in Conrad's depiction of the "bestial vitality and barbaric frenzy" of the Africans, Adekoya himself buys into the late-nineteenth-century Eurocentric view that considered African behavior as revealing privitivism, not as possibly signifying any well-developed cultural activity of the type that Achebe so compellingly re-created in *Things Fall Apart*.

In short, in sanctioning Conrad's view that Africa represents a "mindless frenzy of the first beginnings," Adekoya shows, with Conrad, an inability to imagine that what the Africans were doing at the time of Marlow's visit might have possessed its own form of sophistication and order. While the "first beginnings" of human life on earth may indeed have been characterized by "mindless frenzy," it is unclear why the nineteenth-century Europeans, Joseph Conrad, and Olusegun Adekoya should conclude that the behavior of Africans in the conduct of their lives should be construed as the representation of that frenzy.

Ultimately, in addition to challenging Achebe, Adekoya is concerned to argue for a universalist view of literature and cultural understanding. Conrad's work, he asserts, probes the deepest recesses of the human spirit and finds it sadly wanting. For Adekoya, Conrad's depiction of the Africans as being "animalized" by the "jungle" is perfectly excusable because Conrad goes on to show that the Europeans also get animalized by the jungle. Thus, for Adekoya, such critiques of *Heart of Darkness* as that offered by Achebe are "uncharitable" and small-minded, failing to appreciate Conrad's supposed ability to transcend the constraints of time and culture in order to fathom the depths of what Adekoya calls the "totality of humanity." That the Africans had in fact *not* been animalized by the jungle is never considered as a possibility.

By contrast, the other essay in this section, Leonard A. Podis's "Narrative Distancing and the (De)Construction of Imperialist Consciousness in 'The Man Who Would Be King' and *Heart of Darkness,"* attempts to view Conrad's famous novella and Rudyard Kipling's paradigmatic story of imperial conquest not as expressions of univeralism, but as creatures that are best seen to dwell within the Eurocentric value systems that produced them. Exploring the ways in which Conrad and Kipling, as "kindred authors of empire," employed five similar devices of narrative distancing, Podis argues that both tales express a powerful ambivalence or "approach/avoidance" towards the whole imperial subject, an ambivalence which undermines the Eurocentric vision that permeates the stories and prevents their authors from viewing the colonized people as "full-ranking" human beings.

While acknowledging that Conrad was indeed writing an anti-imperialist work, Podis notes that Conrad's effort at critiquing colonialism was seriously hampered by his inability to break out of the conventional discourse of imperialism that cast the remote regions of empire as inhospitable settings against which the imperial conquerors and their trials and tribulations became the true focus of interest. The significance of these British colonial works for the production and study of postcolonial literature is great, Podis asserts, because they can be seen as early attempts to problematize Eurocentric discourse, an enterprise that postcolonial literature later makes in earnest.

Chapter 10

Criticizing the Critic: Achebe on Conrad

Olusegun Adekoya

To the criticism by a distinguished and lettered lady—name not given—that the "literature which preys on strange people and prowls in far-off countries . . . decivilized the tales, the strange people and the far-off countries," Conrad gave the following reply:

> The picture of life, there as here, is drawn with the same elaboration of detail, coloured with the same tints, only in the cruel serenity of the sky, under the merciless brilliance of the sun, the dazzled eye misses the delicate detail, sees only the strong outlines. . . . Nevertheless it is the same picture. . . . And there is a bond between us and that humanity so far away. . . . Their hearts—like ours—must endure the load of the gifts from Heaven: the curse of facts and the blessing of illusions, the bitterness of our wisdom and the deceptive consolation of our folly. (Conrad 1895, vii–viii)

Surely, the voice does not sound like that of "a thoroughgoing racist." (Achebe 1988, 8) One trembles at the thought of what the reply of a V. S. Naipaul would have been to the woman's question. I take issue with Chinua Achebe in this essay on some of the serious but largely erroneous allegations made against Joseph Conrad in "An Image of Africa: Racism in Conrad's *Heart of Darkness*." In the revised version (Achebe 1978, 1–15), Achebe grudgingy acknowledges Conrad's negative criticism of imperialism, perhaps in reaction to Wilson Harris' remark that "At no point in his essay does Achebe turn upon the crucial parody of the proprieties of established order that mask corruption in all societies." (Harris, 88–89) However, Achebe has yet to accept the full implications of the parody. My argument is that Conrad's consciousness in *Heart of Darkness* is rooted in primal nature and quickened by the oneness of humanity. His central concern is the moral and spiritual blindness that leads human beings to engage nature in the strife for conquest. Confronted by the immense stillness of primeval forest in a moonlight night in Central Africa, Marlow ponders: "Could we handle that dumb thing, or would it handle us?" (Conrad 1973, 38) Through a symbolic exploration of the Christian myth of Creation, Conrad affirms in the novel that, in the relentless struggle between people and nature, it is people— the questers, the adventurers—who are bound to lose in the end. It detracts enormously from Conrad's creative imagination to reduce his thematic preoccupation in *Heart of Darkness* to the ranking of cultures.

Achebe interprets the novella as "a story in which the very humanity of black people is called in question." (Achebe 1988, 10) I, on the contrary, perceive it as an examination of the totality of humanity. It holds up a mirror—not of distortion, but of reflection and refraction—to nature and erodes the surface in order to expose the bitter truth hidden underneath. Civilized or primitive, humankind is stood naked before the mirror. "The expectations the reader brings to the text," Elizabeth Wright theorizes about reader-text relation, "are challenged by the encounter." (Wright, 117–118)

Conrad challenges our settled ideas of civilization, as represented by industrialized Europe, and of primitivism, as represented by precolonial Africa. He removes the illusion of reality from both "primitive culture" and "modern culture" in order to reveal the bitter truth that, although Africans and Europeans can technologically be centuries apart in *Heart of Darkness,* they share emotionally, physically, and spiritually a common ancestry. Marlow affirms the oneness of humanity thus:

> The earth seemed unearthly. We are accustomed to look upon the shackled form of a conquered monster, but there—there you could look at a thing monstrous and free. . . . They howled and leaped, and spun, and made horrid faces; but what thrilled you was just the thought of their humanity—like yours—the thought of your remote kinship with this wild and passionate uproar. . . . Ugly. Yes, it was ugly enough; but if you were man enough you would admit to yourself that there was in you just the faintest trace of a response to the ter-

rible frankness of that noise, a dim suspicion of there being a meaning in it which you—you so remote from the night of first ages—could
comprehend. And why not? The mind of man is capable of anything—
because everything is in it, all the past as well as all the future. What
was there after all? Joy, fear, sorrow, devotion, valour, rage who can
tell?—but truth—truth stripped of its cloak of time. (Conrad 1973,
51–52)

In *Heart of Darkness* the truth takes the form of man's ac-
quisitive drive, especially for power over other people and
for property. Even though analytic consciousness can catego-
rize a set of emotions in one culture as civilized and refined
and condemn the same in another as crude, barbaric, and inferior, human emotions are basically the same throughout the
ages.

The universality of these emotions—under the general ru-
bric of human nature—makes a mockery of any attempt to rank
the cultures of the world. The builders of technological culture have succeeded to a large extent in mastering matter, but
have failed woefully in dispelling the darkness in the human
heart. It is as if material nature employed passion to take vengeance on humanity for all its acts of hubris.

In the passage cited above, the "shackled form of a conquered
monster" refers to industrialized Europe that has lost its simplicity, innocence, and animal freedom, while the "thing monstrous and free" is primitive, materially undernourished Africa in which it was still possible to live intuitively and establish
a kinship and a sympathetic relationship with nature. The bestial vitality and barbaric frenzy, which unsettle Achebe and
incur his wrath, are perceived by Conrad as positive but
unsavoury qualities of primitive society, the absence of which
makes all mechanized societies appear dead and sterile. The
irony is that industrial civilization hampers the free expression of feelings, depersonalizes people, and tends to reduce
the human being to a mindless robot, while primitive, uncon-
scious subjection to the vagaries of nature, arising from powerlessness, stifles intellectual creativity, animalizes people, and
limits human efficiency. The paradox of human nature is reflected in every aspect of all the cultures of the world. Neither
a mechanized society nor a primitive society is whole, but the
ascendancy of materialism over spritualism makes the former

attractive and irresistible. Nevertheless, it would be deceptive and ludicrous to place Africa and Europe on the same level of socioeconomic development.

That Africa is technologically backward is a fact. Conrad, however, does not celebrate facts. For him, there is nothing to choose between the blind man that is the mechanical man and the mute that is the primitive man. Neither does he create a new vision of human possibility: of being. Hence Wilson Harris concluded that although Conrad reached the furthest limit of imagination, he did not cross it, because he did not go beyond despair. The problem is that a world ontology without strife is inconceivable. What humanity really needs but cannot come by is perfect love and genuine cooperation.

Moreover, consciousness, the tool of culture and scientific analysis, breeds division and, therefore, is evil. In the Christian myth of Creation, it is the acquisition of consciousness, consequent upon the eating of the forbidden fruit, the fruit of knowledge, that separates man from the paradisiac state of the beginning. It is, as hinted at by Conrad in his reply to the lettered lady, one of the dazzling but deceptive gifts that fall on the human race and weigh it down.

The charge that *Heart of Darkness* serves the need "in Western psychology to set Africa up as a foil to Europe, as a place of negations at once remote and vaguely familiar, in comparison with which Europe's own state of spiritual grace will be manifest" (Achebe 1988, 2), is challenged by the enormous evidence supplied in the text, for example, by the paintings by Kurtz of "a woman, draped and blindfolded, carrying a lighted torch." (Conrad 1973, 36) A mordant self-criticism by an evil genius, the painting questions the possibility of a blind man leading another blind man, without the two of them falling into a perilous pit. Rather than make manifest "Europe's own state of spiritual grace," Conrad doubts or denies outright its existence in *Heart of Darkness*.

Bestiality is manifested in the novel by both Africans and Europeans. If anything, the European bestiality is more savage. Whereas material impoverishment imposes a low form of existence on Africans, moral and spiritual impoverishment reduces the European pilgrims to beasts and savages. The bestiality on the part of Europeans can be traced to the factor of human depravity: the animal compulsion that drives the powerful to prey upon the weak. The most politically powerful and the most economically developed states in the world today are constructed on the philosophy of social Darwinism: the theory of survival of the fittest. What is parodied in *Heart of Darkness* is not the stamping of feet or the rolling of eyes by the blacks, but the imperialist's practical realization of this despicable theory of survival that reduces human beings to beasts and savages. To overlook this important dimension of Conrad's vision is to miss the message of the novel. Dennis Lee avers in *Savage Fields* that "Strife is amoral." (Lee, 44)

The amorality of strife forms the basis of Conrad's condemnation of imperialism. He sees the whole colonial enterprise as "robbery with violence, aggravated murder on a great scale, and men going at it blind—as is very proper for those who tackle a darkness. The conquest of the earth, which mostly means the taking it away from those who have a different complexion or slightly flatter noses than ourselves, is not a pretty thing when you look into it too much. What redeems it is the idea only." (Conrad 1973, 10) Conrad is not only indignant at the deceit in the gratuitous and self-serving idea of civilizing the savages that is used to justify the rape and subjugation of Africa, but he also does not believe in the colonial administration. He, therefore, cannot be accused of exhibiting a condescending, paternalistic attitude towards Africans.

Even then, the "ultimate question of equality between white people and black people" (Achebe 1988, 7), with which Achebe is primarily concerned, can neither be raised nor answered in a coherent way outside of Conrad's cogent critique of imperialism. Otherwise the subject of racism would become a mere abstraction, as it in fact tends to do in Achebe's essay. Let us face it, not until Africa can clothe, educate, feed, heal, and house herself will she be accorded equal respect in a world that is becoming more and more materialistic. The imperialist exploiters employ psychological terrorism as a weapon of conquest. There are political and economic motives behind the myth of white superiority.

Situating Conrad's moral vision in its proper context of the particular greed that breaks out in the form of imperial exploitation reduces to the barest minimum, if it does not remove entirely, what racism there is in the novel and its author. It is this profound moral vision, apart from the superb artistry, that makes *Heart of Darkness* a great novel. Hence, in spite of Achebe's rebuttal, the novel continues to appeal to all hearts who yearn for moral improvement and spiritual health of man.

In "The Method of Nature," an oration delivered before the Society of Adelphi, in 1841, Emerson declared: "Let there be worse cotton and better men." (Emerson, 40) In Conrad's understanding of the multidimensionality of cultures and civilization, equal emphasis is placed in *Heart of Darkness* on the moral, spiritual, and material aspects. It is even possible to argue that the moral and spiritual dimensions are given greater emphasis in the novel. Therefore, using a cultural artifact as evidence of black civilization, as Achebe does with the Fang carving, is a waste of time. White racists base their myth of racial superiority on nothing other than the higher level of material development in the West. Affected by the same attitude of using material progress as the determinant of human civilization, Kurtz writes in his report for the International Society for the Suppression of Savage Customs, "we whites, from the point of development we had arrived at, 'must necessarily appear to them [savages] in the nature of supernatural beings— we approach them with the might as of a deity.'" (Conrad 1973, 71–72) It is no exaggeration to claim that Conrad calls in the novel for a total re-examination of our definitions of terms like civilization, humanity, progress, and truth.

Achebe misses in its entirety the ironic and sardonic thrust of the novella. He writes of the Thames and the Congo: "[The Thames] conquered its darkness, of course, and is now in daylight and at peace. But if it were to visit its primordial relative, the Congo, it would run the terrible risk of hearing grotesque echoes of its own forgotten darkness, and falling victim to an avenging recrudescence of the mindless frenzy of the first beginnings." (Achebe 1988, 3) Another hermeneutic explication of the text shows that the Thames has conquered its darkness in certain respects, while in others it has merely replaced darkness with darkness. The picture of Europe presented in the novel is far from being peaceful. A vast graveyard, it is more frightening than the picture of Dorian Gray. London, we are told, "has been one of the dark places of the earth." Marlow meditates on this monstrous town, which is represented as "a brooding gloom in sunshine, a lurid glare under the stars" (Conrad 1973, 7), from which the sparks of the fire of civilization were taken to light the dark corners of the world. The "running blaze" has dwindled to a "flicker"—a Conradian metaphor for decadence and degeneration. The metaphor holds up to ridicule his sardonic wish: "We live in the flicker—may it last as long as the old earth keeps rolling!" (Conrad 1973, 6) It is not a mere coincidence, then, that the novel begins at sunset, a metaphor for the fall of the British Empire. The arrogant, short-sighted slogan that "The Sun Never Set on British Soil" has had its day.

Marlow's description of the conquest of Britain by the Romans parallels the subjugation of Africa by the European emissaries of death. Marlow projects history as cyclic progression. When power left the hands of the Romans, they ceased referring to the British as barbarians. Today, Britain seeks protection under the powerful arms of her Big Brother: the United States of America. Who knows, tomorrow, as the wheel of history continues in its circuitous path, America might turn out to be a loser in the power game. Conrad wrestles with the wheel of history in *Heart of Darkness*, but does not succeed in breaking it. Aided by the cyclic method of nature that informs his cyclic vision of history, he would readily agree with Frantz Fanon that "the man who adores the Negro is as 'sick' as the man who abominates him . . . and truly what is to be done is to set man free." (Fanon, 10–11) To overcome that sickness, Conrad presents Africa as he saw it: a primitive land that was further underdeveloped by Europe; and searching for that freedom, he presents the story of Kurtz as an archetypal example of how not to live and love. Is it not ironical that Kurtz, who killed Africans recklessly in his heyday to satisfy his lust for ivory, can, towards the close of his life, "want no more than justice!" (Conrad 1973, 106) His fall is not effected by the Africans, or through his participation in any unspeakable rites, but by the moral law of nature. The "wilderness . . . had taken on him a terrible vengeance for the fantastic invasion." (Conrad 1973, 83)

Achebe is embittered by the description of Africans as "rudimentary souls," but is silent on the description of the European pilgrims in the very next line as "small souls." (Conrad 1973, 72) Is Conrad's worldview also antihumanist? By rudimentary souls, Conrad means simple souls that have not been cluttered up with debilitating details and bewildering complexities, primordial hearts that have not been befuddled with false, meretricious sophistication. There is a subtle suggestion in the expression of a form of childlike innocence that is shielded from corruption, especially the corruption of facts. However, since simplicity has come to be regarded as a mark of underdevelopment, the expression may be taken as utterly negative: as racial abuse. The expression reveals Conrad's ambiguous attitude to Africa. He is enamored of the people's vitality and harmonious existence with nature, but is appalled by the ugliness in this particular way of life, the strength of which ironically is its weakness. Conrad's paradoxical apprehension of life in its totality reminds one of the romantic irony that there is loftiness in lowliness, and vice-versa. Indeed, there is an undercurrent of a distinctively romantic temperament running through *Heart of Darkness*. It was probably the force that propelled Conrad to the Congo.

One may even be tempted to take umbrage at Conrad's idea that the "savages" have no "clear idea of time." (Conrad 1973, 58) However, the adjective "clear" absolves Conrad, for the primitive conception of time as cyclic and mythical sharply contradicts the scientific conception of it as linear and transparent. The mechanical fragmentation of time by science is such that it has led to the refutation of time. One can then understand why a European who has got accustomed to relying on the wristwatch for time precision would perceive the African idea of time as foggy. The remark does not stem from the author's racism, but from sheer bewilderment, which, of course, is bred by culture shock. A little sympathetic understanding is required in explicating a work like *Heart of Darkness*. It would, for example, reveal that the statement that the "amazing words" of Kurtz's adorers "resembled no sounds of human language" (Conrad 1973, 96) does not place the language of the Africans on Saussure's "indefinite plane of jumbled ideas," that is, in a prelinguistic stage, what Lacan calls "the mirror stage." (cited by Wright, 119) Rather, it is a frank assessment that issues out of a spontaneous reaction to a foreign tongue. Every foreign language, to a non-speaker, sounds ghostly and weird.

"For Conrad," Achebe writes in a satirical vein, "things being in their place is of the utmost importance." (Achebe 1988, 5) Conrad certainly was painfully aware of the enormous damage done by Europeans' violent transplantation of peoples. Among the tragic consequences of the great explorations are death on a massive scale, identity crises, psychic disorientation, racial hatred, loss of faith, rootlessness, and slavery. Europeans went beyond transplantation and almost wiped off the surface of the earth the entire population of the Caribs, the Arawaks, and the Amerindians. The body of Africa was battered with weapons of war and the mind of Europe was bruised by fear and guilt. The point is that the psychosocial problems engendered by colonization, especially the loss by black Africans of confidence and faith in themselves, far outweigh any salutary material effects. Psychological problems are the most pathetic. The moving description of miserable Africans who have been uprooted from their homes, "lost in uncongenial surroundings, fed on unfamiliar food," overworked, reduced by "disease and starvation" (Conrad 1973, 24) to mere skeletons and horrid shapes and, after becoming inefficient and totally useless, abandoned on the coast, like waste matter, to despair, pain, and slow death, is a graphic representation of the evil in the forceful transplantation of people. A sardonic commentary on the so-called Western Civilization, the description contrasts sharply with that of the jolly black fellows with "a wild vitality, an intense energy of movement, that was as natural and true as the surf along their coast," who are having a rollicking time, as they paddle their boat gracefully and with tremendous confidence amidst shouts and songs; for they want "no excuse for being there."

Also sardonic are the passages parodying European Civilization, the destructive power of the invading man-of-war shelling the bush, the rapacious greed and crass materialism of the Eldorado Exploring Expedition that manifests itself as the inhuman lust for ivory, the crippling intrigues and petty jealousies among the European wanderers over privileged positions and promotion, the hollowness of Kurtz's insatiable appetite for lying fame, sham distinction, fouled success, untrammelled but corrupt power and vainglory, and indeed the total loss of vision that reduces the whole colonial affair to a grand delusion. Conrad saw nothing that was really beneficial to the "savages" in the coming of Europeans to Africa. If anything, he saw their presence in Africa as the beginning of the dehumanization of Africans and the underdevelopment of their land, as Walter Rodney was later to make known in his seminal work: *How Europe Underdeveloped Africa*. In none of the passages of indictment mentioned above does Conrad celebrate the civilizing power of Europe. Had things been in their place, perhaps South Africa would not have been mangled by the monster of apartheid.

Achebe argues that *Heart of Darkness* is not a great work of art because it "eliminates the African as human factor" (Achebe 1988, 8) in an African setting. Surely, Africans are represented in the novella as rowers of boats, crewmen, carriers, prisoners, messengers, woodcutters, and helpers in the road construction work. Conrad presents such African characters as would enhance his indictment of the philanthropic pretence of the colonialists. Besides, Marlow's contacts with the natives are momentary and fragmentary, if not distant. The only exception is the relatively prolonged contact with the thirty crew members on the steamer bound for the Inner Station. Even then, Conrad had another major problem, the problem of incommunicability, which had to do with understanding the language(s) of the Africans, and which his four-month sojourn in the Congo made practically impossible. The problem bears direct relation on Achebe's criticism that Africans are portrayed as not capable of making coherent, intelligible speeches. "They exchanged short grunting phrases even among themselves." Achebe cites the two instances in which Africans use the English language in the novella. The first is the headman's request for human flesh to eat, while the second is the announcement by the manager's boy of Kurtz's death. (Achebe 1988, 6)

Had Conrad attempted to represent socio-cultural details and verities, it would certainly have produced the kind of distortion of which he is charged by Achebe; for the culture appears profoundly mysterious and incomprehensible to the novelist, who is expected to represent verbally what he does not understand, what is yet to be absorbed, what appears to him like a dream. The glow of fires as Kurtz's worshippers keep vigil, the throb of their drums, and the drone of their incantations all impinge on Marlow's mind as bewildering impressions. In such a situation, silence is golden. The resort to the nonverbal modes of communication in the novella is not accidental. Two examples will suffice. The first is Marlow's "speech in English with gestures" (Conrad 1973, 29) to the porters. Conrad recorded in his diary on Wednesday, 30 July, 1880: "Expect lots of bother with carriers tomorrow. Had them all called and made a speech which they did not understand. They promise good behaviour." (Conrad 1955, 169–170) The second is the look that the helmsman gives Marlow when the former receives his mortal wound. Achebe sees in the simile "like a claim of distant kinship" (Conrad 1973, 73)—that is, between a white employer and an African employee dying in the service of Western imperialism—the white man's pride of race. Conrad, on the contrary, hints at the bond that binds the two men in toil and mysterious origin. It is the profundity of the look that establishes for the reader the great partnership between the two men, Marlow's great sense of loss, the quality of the helmsman's hurt, and, above all, the oneness of human biological nature, for flesh is neither clay nor wood!

We begin to appreciate the enormity of the problem that confronts Conrad when we realize that Kurtz's mind disintegrates partly out of sheer loneliness. To exemplify the problem posed by the absence of verbal communication, we quote Marlow's remark on Kurtz: "This initiated wraith from the back of Nowhere honoured me with its amazing confidence before it vanished altogether. This was because it could speak English to me." (Conrad 1973, 71) (If Conrad calls Africans savages, he does not go as far as using "it" for them.) The fact that the African characters do not use language profusely in *Heart of Darkness* is not intended by Conrad as evidence of the people's lack of the natural capacity for language. Even the vision of Kurtz, who is said to be a talented orator, is given in broken phrases and fragmented sentences. Yet the meaning is not lost on the reader. No amount of words can express vividly what Marlow feels in his body and mind when he flings his shoe into the serpentine Congo because of the fear that he might not meet Kurtz alive. Besides, a profuse use of the English language by the African characters, who had not mastered the language, would have violated the law of verisimilitude and diminished the truthfulness of Conrad's art. Conrad, intuitively, through unalloyed fidelity to his own immediate sensations, translated language into action and magic in the scenes depicting Africans in *Heart of Darkness,* a feat that might not have been possible if he had found linguistic access to the mind of Africa.

"Certainly," Achebe wrote, "Conrad had a problem with niggers." (Achebe 1988, 9) As proof, he cited the following sentence: "A black figure stood up, strode on long black legs, waving long black arms." (Conrad 1973, 94) Conrad's expression hints at the idea of cultural and psychic integrity. With the hyperbolic repetitions, descriptive epithets, and grandiloquent, sesquipedalian images and nouns in the novel, Conrad is groping for a new mythopoeic prose style. He is struggling vaguely and unwittingly to wrest language from staleness and perversion and to restore words to their poetic origin.

The simple reason that cases of cannibalism are still reported on the pages of Nigerian newspapers absolves Conrad of the charge of portraying the crew as cannibals. (*The Punch*, 1, 8) His main interest, though, is not cannibalism per se but the basic biological need that drives man to it: the extreme and prolonged hunger that assails the crew. It is the kind of unrelenting hunger that would force survivors of a plane crash to feed on the corpses of their dead fellow-travellers. The externalization of primal emotions, especially at crucial moments of extreme agony and excruciating pain, when the trappings of "civilized" behavior are totally scraped off, bears testimony to the animal residue in man.

Achebe argues that the description of the African woman as "savage and superb, wild-eyed and magnificent" and of Kurtz's white fiancée as having "a mature capacity for fidelity, for belief, for suffering" exposes Conrad's racial bias. (Achebe 1988, 5–6) It is clear that Achebe misses the elaborate irony in Conrad's portraiture of Kurtz's "Intended": a dance of illusion and reality that is beautifully orchestrated during the long conversation between Marlow and Kurtz's fiancée, with which the novel ends. Like the other blind "civilized" folk, Kurtz's intended lives in a delicate but false dream-world of belief, illusion, hope, and love. Her knowledge of Kurtz, as a great, generous, good and noble man, is completely false. Marlow keeps her in the dark in order not to shatter her dream-world or shake her strong belief that Kurtz is good natured. He says: "I could not tell her. It would have been too dark—too dark altogether. . . ." (Conrad 1973, 111) The African woman may be wild, but she has integrity. The European woman's refinement is artificial, deceptive, and hollow.

Having seen the devilish side of human nature, the darkness in the human heart as manifested in its utter nakedness by Kurtz, Marlow knows better than the hypocritical and materialistic white people he meets in the streets to think that one race is biologically and morally superior to another, or that one race is destined to lead and salvage another. Conrad's brief sojourn in the Congo opened his mind to the sad facts of life. His remark to his friend Edward Garnett that "before the Congo, I was just a mere animal" (cited by Jean-Aubry, 175) testifies to that and reveals the degree of European blindness to the hidden truth of life. Hence, Europe is portrayed in the novella as a vast cemetery and its civilization as sham sophistication. She is rotten at the core, but glows outside. If Conrad depicts Africans as barbaric and uncivilized, but full of life, vigor and vitality, he represents Europeans as the living dead. African "culture" is portrayed as a crude and low form of existence, while European "culture" is depicted as embodying the germs of corruption and decay. Conrad exposes the weaknesses that inhere in the two cultures.

Conrad's vision in *Heart of Darkness* transcends the dubious division of the world into black and white. Achebe's reading of the novella is no doubt colored by his concern for African "culture" and by the anger bred by the burden placed on black people because of skin pigmentation. His interpretation of the text is totally uncharitable. It is writers like Conrad, who have the courage to tell us the bitter truth about our deplorable socioeconomic condition, who, ultimately, are our best friends. Had Ayi Kwei Armah, the author of *The Beautyful Ones Are Not Yet Born*, been white, Achebe would have been tempted to label him a racist, simply because Armah confronted us with our ugly image in his novel and revealed the truth about the degree of damage done by moral corruption in our society. (Achebe 1975, 13–14)

Works Cited

Achebe, Chinua. "Africa and Her Writers." Pp. 1–59 in *In Person: Achebe, Awoonor, and Soyinka,* edited by Karen L. Morell. Seattle: Institute For Comparative and Foreign Area Studies, University of Washington Press, 1975.

———. "An Image of Africa: Racism in Conrad's *Heart of Darkness.*" In *Hopes and Impediments: Selected Essays (1965–1987).* London: Heinemann, 1988: 1–20.

———. "An Image of Africa." *Research in African Literatures* 9 (Spring 1978): 1–15.

"Body of Slain Soldier Used for Soup." *The Punch* (Lagos), 6 November 1989: 1 and 8.

Conrad, Joseph. "Author's Note." Pp. vii–viii in *Almayer's Folly,* London: J.M. Dent and Sons, 1895.

———. "The Congo Diary." Pp. 169–170 in *Tales of Hearsay and Last Essays.* London : J.M. Dent, 1955.

———. *Heart of Darkness.* Middlesex, England: Penguin Books, 1973.

Emerson, Ralph Waldo. "The Method of Nature," p. 40 in *Nature, The Conduct of Life, and Other Essays.* London: J. M. Dent, 1963.

Fanon, Frantz. *Black Skin, White Masks: The Experience of a Black Man in a White World.* New York: Grove, 1967.

Harris, Wilson. "The Frontier on which *Heart of Darkness* Stands." *Research in African Literatures* 12 (Spring 1981): 86–93.

Jean-Aubry, Gerald. *The Sea Dreamer: A Definitive Biography of Joseph Conrad.* Trans. Helen Sebba. London: George Allen and Unwin, 1957.

Lee, Dennis. *Savage Fields: An Essay in Literature and Cosmology.* Toronto: House of Anansi, 1977.

Rodney, Walter. *How Europe Underdeveloped Africa.* London: Bogle-L'Ouverture, 1972.

Wright, Elizabeth. "Modern Psychoanalytic Criticism" Pp. 113–133 in *Modern Literary Theory: A Comparative Introduction,* edited by Ann Jefferson and David Robey. London: Batsford, 1982.

Chapter 11

Narrative Distancing and the (De)Construction of Imperialist Consciousness in "The Man Who Would Be King" and *Heart of Darkness*

Leonard A. Podis

Although a number of critics have, over the years, identified similarities in the works of Rudyard Kipling and Joseph Conrad (Sandison; McClure), their kinship as authors of empire has generally been deemphasized in the light of their markedly different attitudes towards imperialism and their dissimilar stature as artists. Kipling has been seen as a jingoistic apologist for empire, a second-rate writer with a knack for the short story (Fussell, 216–217), while Conrad has been accorded more respect as both a critic of imperialism and a consummate artist. Despite some rehabilitation of Kipling, the consensus remains that Conrad occupies higher ground both morally and aesthetically than does Kipling.[1]

Yet for all their differences, Kipling and Conrad did share important qualities as narrative artists, particularly in their fictional representations of the colonial situation. In this essay I will examine similarities of narrative construction in "The Man Who Would Be King" and *Heart of Darkness*, two tales of "vaulting imperial ambition" (Wurgaft, 131) that might be considered quintessential narratives of British colonial literature. In examining Kipling's and Conrad's use of narrative distancing I will argue that both stories undermine the visions of Eurocentric superiority that suffuse and inform them, albeit in different ways.

Conrad, of course, openly disavowed imperialism in *Heart of Darkness*, and yet the location of his story within the standard Eurocentric tradition of representing colonial lands and people has worked at odds with his nobler goals. Conrad's unenlightened depiction of Africans (Achebe 1977) betrays an inability to transcend the dominant colonial discourse of the era, thus perpetuating the colonial mindset in a work that is dedicated to challenging that mindset. Kipling unambiguously embraced imperialism (if not always the way in which the British were conducting it) and so would seem to be more in step with the discourse of imperialist superiority. Yet the "The Man Who Would Be King" contains strong and troubling undercurrents that challenge and destabilize the work's pro-imperial foundations.

At the level of plot, characterization, and theme, there are striking parallels between these two works that examine the attempt of European men to dominate "the dark places of the earth" (Kipling, 44; Conrad, 9). Both stories involve the unsavory exploits of imperialists who journey to a remote land to set themselves up as godlike rulers, initially succeeding, but ultimately failing, first losing their sanity and then their lives. In each case, firearms, superior technology, and the superstitious nature of the people allow the Europeans to establish dominance. The protagonists are similarly arrogant in their sense of superiority to the indigenous populations, both subscribing to the brutal mentality characteristic of empire-builders. Accordingly, in both stories, these supposedly superior rulers ruthlessly eliminate "rebels" and resisters, exhibiting a complete lack of regard for them as human beings. In both works, a major goal of the imperialist figures is to reap the spoils of the undeveloped world. Ultimately, in both cases, the would-be king brings ruin upon himself through overconfidence in his powers.[2]

Rather than conduct a detailed comparison of such features, however, I intend to examine a larger issue raised by the similarity of the two pieces: the function of narrative distancing in the authorial construction of the consciousness or subjectivity of the colonial adventurer. Understanding Conrad's and Kipling's use of narrative distancing from their colonial subject matter is of central importance in coming to terms with the type of imperial discourse represented by these works. It is useful to note, for example, that one reason for Kipling's and Conrad's inability to render colonized people and their cultures with much accuracy or sensitivity is that the type of imperial discourse in which "The Man Who Would Be King" and *Heart of Darkness* are situated, indeed help to define, can observe colonized people only across a vast ethnocentric distance related in part to what Hunt Hawkins calls "the solipsistic arrogance of the colonialists." (87)

This distancing of the colonized other through an ethnocentric lens that makes the colonizer the true focal point while relegating the colonized to a poorly defined background is part of a complex and subtle scheme of narrative distancing that operates in both these stories, a scheme that reveals Conrad's and Kipling's feelings of approach/avoidance towards the imperial enterprise and that finally undermines the stories' own ethnocentrism. Specifically, both stories employ five techniques that contribute to narrative distancing and mediation: (1) construction of an elusive identity for the conquering imperialists; (2) creation of an ambivalent relationship between the narrators and the conquering imperialists; (3) framing, or narration within narration; (4) instability of the participant-narrators (Peachey/Marlow); and (5) ethnocentric bias.

The first type of distancing common to both stories arises from Conrad's and Kipling's efforts to construct elusive identities for their conquering imperialists. As Fussell has noted, "The Man Who Would Be King" is concerned with the "layers of real and apparent identities" (220) of Dravot and Carnehan, who at one point literally disguise themselves as "native" priest and servant and who variously appear or represent themselves as loafers, laborers, adventurers, journalists, common soldiers, commanding officers, "heathens," royalty, and deities. Similarly, in *Heart of Darkness* one of Marlow's greatest challenges is the attempt to discover the "real" Kurtz, a mysterious figure whose identities cover the range from saint to maniac, "universal genius" to murderer, entrepreneur to plunderer, pious "intended" to licentious libertine, deity to devil.

In Kipling's story, the confusion over identity is evident not only in Danny's and Peachey's having toiled at many jobs and in their assumption of disguises, but also in their apparently ludicrous aspirations to royalty (which, ironically, they do realize, after a fashion). Early in the narrative it is significant that Peachey confides in the journalist that he has been "pretend[ing] to be correspondent of the 'Backwoodsman.'" (Kipling, 42) Likewise, Dravot, despite his stature as a "loafer" and "vagabond" is to be found "sleeping like a gentleman" on the train at the Marwar Junction. (42) Later they both appear in "native" disguises so well done that both the narrator and the "native" crowd are fooled. Fundamentally, the central action of the story involves Danny's and Peachey's attempt to represent themselves to the Kafiristanis as something they are not.

The issue of identity emerges similarly in *Heart of Darkness*. Kurtz's identity appears as a series of stark contradictions. On the one hand, he is a "remarkable" figure, one who represents the apex of western culture: "All Europe contributed to the making of Kurtz" (Conrad, 50), with his skills in the arts of music, poetry, rhetoric, and painting, and his lofty ideals. Apparently the most genuinely philanthropic of the company agents, he disgusts his supposedly more philistinistic colleagues with the high-mindedness of his goals. His prim, refined, nearly ethereal "Intended" back home can vouch for the rarity of his gifts and the righteousness of his behavior. The Congolese apparently regard him as a deity. Yet there are the other Kurtzes: the ruthless collector of ivory, the bloodthirsty ruler of his region, the conductor of "unspeakable rites," the lover of a "savage" woman, the chief devil of the land, the author of such phrases as "Exterminate all the brutes!"

On the one hand, the mysterious and contradictory aspects of the conquering imperialists' elusive identities pique the interest of each story's narrator in the central imperialist figure, emphasizing authorial feelings of approach towards the subject. The protean, shifting nature of the protagonists creates a challenge for narrator, author, and audience alike, a mystery to be contemplated, if not solved. On the other hand, the theme of elusive identity contributes to the distancing techniques at work in the pieces, as well, placing the conquering imperialists at a considerable remove from author, narrator, and reader by precluding any clear or definitive understanding of who they are.

The sense of authorial approach/avoidance towards imperial conquest is further enhanced in both stories by the creation of an ambivalent relationship between the primary narrators and the conquering imperialists. In both pieces, the result is a tension between attraction and repulsion. In "The Man Who Would Be King," both the epigraph and the opening paragraph suggest the journalist's attraction to Danny and Peachey. Despite their humble socioeconomic status, the narrator has befriended them: "fellow to a beggar if he be found worthy." (Kipling, 39) He similarly notes that he "came near to kinship" with Danny. Initially put off by Peachey's request that he deliver a message to Dravot, the journalist is drawn to Peachey and Danny once he realizes that they are fellow masons. He also states that Peachey is "a wanderer and a vagabond like myself." (40) His respect for them later increases dramatically when he witnesses firsthand the competence with which they carry out their impersonation of a priest and his servant. Of course the magnitude of their seemingly impossible quest, the fact that they achieved their goal, and the knowledge that they paid a high price for their boldness all contribute to his fascination with them. At the same time, the narrator's comments resonate with pity, contempt, and condescension as he considers the hapless fate of these obvious ne'er-do-wells. He is suspicious of them from start to finish, only reluctantly relays Peachey's message to Dravot, reports them to the authorities as potential blackmailers of the Degumber Rajah, and doubts their sanity and their competence, admonishing them that "even if you reached [the Kafiristanis] you couldn't do anything." (54)

Marlow has similarly ambivalent ties to Kurtz. Both he and Kurtz are employed by the same company, and, questions of their respective moral integrity aside, the fact remains that they work for a common purpose, to carry on the ivory trade for profit. Like the journalist in Kipling's story, Marlow is also awe-stricken by the magnitude of Kurtz's involvement in his colonial venture. As the journey progresses, he notes that his ultimate goal is to meet Kurtz. Despite the monstrous nature of Kurtz's crimes, Marlow is drawn to him and the mystique surrounding him. Like Kipling's journalist, too, Marlow is hardly hesitant to criticize, judge, or deplore the behavior of the conquering imperialist, as the circumstances warrant. Observing that "his soul was mad" (Conrad, 65), Marlow decries Kurtz's murderous "lack of restraint," pronouncing him "the nightmare of my choice" (64) and lamenting the invasion of the territory by "these mean and greedy phantoms." (67) Thus both "The Man Who Would Be King" and *Heart of Darkness* emerge not only as qualified celebrations of the charismatic hardihood, competence, and audacity of the central imperialist figures, but as didactic and admonitory works, as well.

Perhaps the most obvious likeness in the narrative techniques of the two pieces is the employment in both of a framing technique, so that the colonial experiences of Danny and Peachey and of Kurtz are not presented directly by an authorial narrative voice but are reported at second-, third-, or fourth-hand. In *Heart of Darkness,* which is somewhat more elaborately constructed, Kurtz's exploits are recounted by Marlow, whose tale in turn is reported to us by an anonymous figure, whose narration in turn is inscribed by Conrad. In "The Man Who Would Be King," the adventures of Danny and Peachey are told by Peachey to the journalist, whose narration in turn is recorded by Kipling.

Interestingly, the distancing effect is further enhanced in Kipling's story by the fact that Peachey as tale-teller specifically separates himself from Peachey as imperialist conqueror by flatly asserting that the Peachey who took part in the subjugation of Kafiristan died as a result of the adventure. Very near the beginning of his long tale, he tells the journalist, "There was a party called Peachey Taliaferro Carnehan that was with Dravot. Shall I tell you about him? He died out there in the cold. Slap from the bridge fell old Peachey. . . ." (Kipling, 66) Shortly thereafter, he refers to himself as "that other party, Carnehan." (67) Depicting Peachey in this fashion, as someone who returns to narrate a story about a version of himself that has "died," Kipling is able to add another layer to the scheme of mediations.

In the case of these imperial tales, one obvious function of this technique of multiple framing is that it serves to underscore the tortuous and indirect means by which narratives of empire must work themselves back to the metropolitan country. Both works essentially present the reader with reports from the front lines of the battle for empire, as told by firsthand witnesses to narrators who see fit to pass along what they have heard. In this sense the narrative of imperial conquest takes on a strong flavor of a folk tale about the exploits of men who have confronted the challenges of the unknown. In effect the technique reinforces the message to the stay-at-home audience that they are permitted to venture only so close to such figures and their deeds.

In both Kipling's and Conrad's use of such narrative framing there is also a suggestion of authorial approach/avoidance towards the imperial subject matter. On the one hand, the use of these particular chains of narrators conveys an optimistic attitude. Despite the difficult passage which such tales had to undergo, they have nevertheless been successfully relayed, and the tale-tellers/authors constitute an unbroken chain of imperialist adventurers. In the case of Kipling's story, Danny and Peachey are enterprising colonialists whose tale is narrated by another enterprising colonialist, the unnamed Anglo-Indian journalist, whose story is rendered by yet another enterprising colonialist, Rudyard Kipling, a pro-Empire Anglo-Indian acknowledged to be the first English writer "to travel widely throughout the British Dominions." (Carrington, 383) Likewise, in Conrad's novella, Kurtz's imperialist exploits are reported by a fellow imperialist, Marlow, whose tale is offered by the anonymous narrator (who holds forth enthusiastically about the glories of empire), whose tale is inscribed by Joseph Conrad, who is known to have written *Heart of Darkness* after serving as captain of a steamer owned by a company connected with King Leopold's private Congo state. (Mahood, 4) Conrad, in fact, noted that he forced himself to "get out" *Heart of Darkness* "for the sake of the shekels." (Baines, 223) That these authors of empire succeeded in being the last link in the narrative chains created in their stories, then, suggests that such a framing device constitutes, at least in this respect, a gesture of authorial approach to the subject of imperial conquest.

On the other hand, there is an element of despair, even terror, and possibly shame or guilt in the use of narrative framing in these stories, a definite gesture of authorial avoidance that manifests itself in Kipling's and Conrad's attempts to distance and dissociate themselves and their readership from the heart of the action. At some level, through their construction of multiple layers of narration, the authors seem to be saying, "These horrible occurrences can only be reported across great physical, temporal, and psychological distances, and it is just as well, for such deeds are best contemplated from a safe distance." In Conrad's piece, Marlow is left gloomily to report on the unhappy events of Kurtz's career and his own ill health, and the initially enthusiastic anonymous narrator, who began his tale with a paean to the greatness of the Thames, bearer of "the dreams of men, the seed of commonwealths, the germs of empires" (Conrad, 8) is, by the end, quite deflated, grimly observing in the last line of the story that the Thames "seemed to lead into the heart of an immense darkness." (76) Conrad, for his part, is obviously as pessimistic as the rest, if not more so. In Kipling's story, the mad Peachey must tell of his dead friend Danny as well as his own dead alter ego. The journalist, left to recount the facts of Peachey's madness and actual death, manages to maintain, like Kipling himself, an air of energy and indefatigability, but he is obviously shaken by the experience. There is, in other words, in the use of the narrative frames, the expression of a powerful desire to retreat from what has been reported at the center, a wish for layers of mediation to create a barrier between author/audience and the central action.

Further accentuating the sense of narrative distance in both works is a fourth type of mediation: the creation of a barrier or filter of psychological instability. In the case of Kipling's tale, the events are screened by a participant-narrator who has at best a tenuous grip on his sanity. Peachey, who announces his return to the journalist "with a dry cackle" (Kipling, 63) declares "I ain't mad—yet, but I shall be that way soon." (64) In fact, he is almost certainly mad from the moment he reappears. He exhibits mannerisms of madness or at least severe psychological disorientation throughout. Easily distracted, he occasionally loses his place in the story or goes off on a tangent. At one point, when the journalist decides to interrupt with a question, he does so "[a]t the risk of throwing the creature out of train." (72) His reference to himself as already "dead" also shows a deep confusion, since it was actually Danny who fell "[s]lap from the bridge" and died, not Peachey. Near the end of his tale, it is clear that he has been suffering from hallucinations, as he explains that his safe return to India was aided by Dravot's guidance: "'[F]or Daniel Dravot he walked before and said: "Come along, Peachey. It's a big thing we're doing." The mountains they danced at night, and the mountains they tried to fall on Peachey's head, but Dan he held up his hand, and Peachey came along. . . .'" (95) Subsequently, the journalist prepares him "for eventual transfer to the Asylum" (97), where he dies almost upon arrival.

Although Marlow is not in such poor shape mentally or physically as is Peachey, his experience has taxed him to the point that he did suffer some serious disorientation, creating in *Heart of Darkness* a similar filter of instability through which the central events are made to pass. We learn near the end of his tale that, following Kurtz's death, he experienced a serious illness that affected his perceptions. Consequently, when he returned to Europe and "tottered about the streets" (Conrad, 70), he was, by his own admission, not completely in his right mind. And while he does not appear to have suffered hallucinations in the manner of Peachey, he does speak, even as he sits on the *Nellie* with his acquaintances, of the near-hallucinatory nature of the whole adventure: "It seems to me I am trying to tell you a dream—making a vain attempt, because no relation of a dream can convey the dream-sensation, that commingling of absurdity, surprise and bewilderment. . . ." (30)

The fifth and final type of narrative distancing I will examine is that created by the ethnocentric point of view that governs both "The Man Who Would Be King" and *Heart of Darkness*. At an obvious level, the stories are ethnocentric in that they deny or simply ignore the possibility that the colonized people can have cultural or personal significance the equal of their own. Thus the Kafiristanis and the Congolese are not truly people but objects to be shuffled about. The stories offer the point of view of European men who, to use Hawkins' terms (72–73), borrowed from O. Mannoni (108), regard the colonial realm as "a world without men"—a world inhabited by inferior, even sub-human beings. Both works, of course, abound with what today constitutes offensive references to the indigenous people: "savages," "niggers," "heathens," and so forth.

As Martin Seymour-Smith notes in his biography of Kipling, "Not one of Kipling's audience could publicly question his or her ethnocentricity, or regard it as anything but absolutely right. They could not imagine that their [colonized] servants themselves had any such ethnocentric feeling." (Seymour-Smith, 54)

Such a statement clearly applies to Marlow, obviously the most morally sensitive figure in either story, just as fully as it does to Kurtz, Danny, and Peachey. Although Marlow doesn't dehumanize the Congolese to the extent that the others do, in that he doesn't believe they should be indiscriminately murdered if some practical reason for doing so arises, he is like the others in viewing them as second-class human beings. True, he reluctantly acknowledges their humanity when he shudders at his possible kinship to the mindless beings who "howled and leaped and spun" on shore, but it is clear that he regards them as savages, capable only of limited accomplishments: "No," he concedes in what he appears to think is a generous interpretation, "they were not inhuman." (Conrad, 37) One African for whom he expresses some appreciation is his fireman, whom he calls "an improved specimen" of savage because "he could fire up a vertical boiler." (38) Revealingly, Marlow further observes that, with the fireman's mimicry of genuinely human behavior, he reminded him of "a dog in a parody of breeches and a feather hat walking on his hind-legs." (38)

This presentation of a colonized servant as a junior or assistant human being, a pretender to real or full human stature, echoes a similar practice in "The Man Who Would Be King."[3] Like Marlow, Danny and Peachey make use of the services of "an improved specimen" of Kafiristani, the chief of Bashkai, whom they call Billy Fish. As Peachey notes, they named him Billy Fish "because he was so like Billy Fish that drove the big tank-engine at Mach on the Bolan in the old days." (Kipling, 74) It is especially significant that Billy and a select few others are given the names of British soldiers that Danny and Peachy have known. Like Marlow's "savage," who has achieved the stature of quasi-human being by becoming a fireman, Billy Fish shows sufficient merit to be named after a *full-ranking* human being, an Englishman. Like the improved specimen of savage in *Heart of Darkness* as well, Billy can mimic fully human behavior by giving the Masonic handshake and otherwise behaving like the members of the "master race," even if that behavior is little understood and partially motivated by superstitious fears, such as those exhibited by Marlow's fireman, who checks the steam gauge, lest "the evil spirit inside the boiler would get angry through the greatness of his thirst and take a terrible vengeance." (Conrad, 39) Ultimately, in what perhaps amounts to a Eurocentric gesture towards poetic justice, Billy dies at the hands of his own people, the price he had to pay for rising above his "natural" station by presuming to become a quasi-European. His fate resembles that of another "improved specimen of savage" in *Heart of Darkness*, Marlow's helmsman, who bleeds to death all over Marlow's shoes after being speared by one of his own kind. Just as Peachey laments the loss of Billy, whom he calls "a good friend of us all" (Kipling, 94), Marlow admits that he "missed [his] late helmsman awfully," acknowledging that although the "savage . . . was no more account than a grain of sand in a black Sahara . . . a subtle bond had been created" nonetheless. (Conrad, 51)

Ethnocentric distancing in these imperial narratives is evident not only in their stereotypically racist renderings of the colonial inhabitants as primitive, uncivilized, and dangerous, but also in their nearly total lack of genuine interest in the colonial territories and their cultures. While both stories do depict the remote regions of empire to which their protagonists have journeyed, the real concern of "The Man Who Would Be King" and *Heart of Darkness* is obviously with the effects of the imperial adventure on the imperialist. A prime example of this ethnocentric distancing of Kipling's and Conrad's narratives can be seen in the way both stories similarly treat the journey through colonial territory in order to emphasize the hardships faced by the western traveler.

Marlow's account of his journey to find Kurtz contains frequent references to the intolerable conditions. Even before the ship reaches the mouth of the Congo, "all along the formless coast bordered by dangerous surf, . . . Nature herself . . . tried to ward off intruders." (Conrad, 17) The French warship which is futilely firing rounds into the jungle is losing its crew to "fever at the rate of three a day." (17) Marlow himself shrinks at the prospect of enduring "the blinding sunshine of that land." (20) At his first stop he stays in a stifling hut where "big flies buzzed fiendishly and did not sting but stabbed." (22) On the way to the central station he broods about the "paths spreading over the empty land, through the long grass, through burnt grass . . . up and down stony hills ablaze with heat." (23) At the central station, disease is rampant. The manager laments that the agents "die so quick, too, that I haven't the time to send them out of the country—it's incredible!" (35) Once the steamer has been repaired and Marlow heads upriver, he confronts the "impenetrable forest," with the air "warm, thick, heavy, sluggish" and "no joy in the brilliance of sunshine." (35)

In both stories, the journeys are marked not only by heat and discomfort but also by various other sorts of dangers, fears, and loathing. For Marlow and his "pilgrims" there is the constant threat of shipwreck posed by the nightmarish conditions on the river. Marlow must be ever vigilant lest the unusually treacherous African river tear out the bottom of the riverboat, a mishap that had already befallen a previous captain prior to Marlow's arrival at the central station. There is also the hardship of poor rations, a nutritional problem that perhaps pales by comparison to the fears of the Europeans that their crew of "cannibals" might at any moment turn on them and "have a good tuck-in for once . . ."(Conrad, 42), especially in light of the fact that their "rotten hippo-meat" had been imprudently thrown overboard. Then there is the fear of attack from the shore. Marlow, for example, describes his steamer as struggling "slowly on the edge of a black and incomprehensible frenzy" (37); he and his boatload of faithless travelers are uncertain of the intentions of the "savages" on the shore, but are in any case "appalled, as sane men would be before an enthusiastic outbreak in a madhouse." (37) Indeed, the "natives" do attack the boat by shooting showers of arrows. (45–46)

In "The Man Who Would Be King," Danny's and Peachey's actual journey is similarly fraught with hardship and danger. The weather poses a threat, the way itself is treacherous, the rations are poor or non-existent, and they encounter considerable hostility from the "heathens." Adopting various disguises to avoid being killed outright, they soon encounter mountainous terrain. "And then [their] camels were no use, and . . . they killed the camels all among the mountains, not having anything in particular to eat. . . ." (Kipling, 66) After killing a man intent on robbing and possibly murdering them, Danny and Peachy take his mules and strike out "into those bitter cold mountaineous [sic] parts, and never a road broader than the back of your hand." (66) Of the country through which they travel, Peachey recalls that the mountains are "always fighting . . . and don't let you sleep at night." (65) Besides contending with fierce mountainmen, they have to handle mules that "were most contrary" and to be wary of "bringing down the tremenjus avalanches." (67) Eventually, they are forced to kill the mules, "not having anything in special for them or us to eat." (67) Like Marlow and his pilgrims, as they near their destination, they are exposed to a hostile action featuring "men with bows and arrows." (67)

In both stories, then, the colonial world is portrayed largely in terms of the hardships it poses for the conquering imperialist, not as a place worthy of contemplation in its own right. It is the antithesis of the "normal" (i.e., British) environment with which Marlow periodically contrasts it for the benefit of his auditors aboard the *Nellie*. With its inhospitable climate, its resistant and unyielding geophysical character, and its primitive and hostile inhabitants, it presents a monumental challenge to the would-be builder of empire. Clearly, such an approach to the colonial subject is ethnocentric in the truest sense; it creates a narrative viewpoint that actually has its focus on the western imperialist, even as it purportedly attempts to render the colonial world that serves as the location of the action.

Perhaps the greatest significance of this final type of narrative distancing, ethnocentric vision, is that all the western figures—the conquering imperialists who have the adventures, the narrators who recount them and the authors who shape the resultant narratives—appear boxed in from the beginning, unable to approach, explore, or fathom the colonized "other" in a less ethnocentric way. In the words of Ross Murfin, they have constructed a colonial landscape "violently emptied by pejorative interpretations of native peoples and biased decodings of their cultures." (111) The phenomenon of approach/avoidance is again evident here in that the authors signal their approach to the colonial subject in their putative attempts to depict it in their stories, even as they simultaneously avoid it by denying its more genuine essence in their portrayals.

Certainly the notion that *Heart of Darkness* questions the whole ethnocentrically determined imperial enterprise is nothing new. The many readers who see Conrad's novella as a forcefully anti-imperialist, antiracist work will readily agree that the novella does undermine the ethnocentric world view of the imperialist. Even those who hold the story to be virulently racist and embarrassingly Eurocentric must concede that certain aspects of the work call into question the *validity* of the racist views purportedly advanced: that is, the European characters depicted in the novella are patently *not* superior human beings. The pilgrims and the company officials are poor examples of a supposedly vaunted western civilization. Whatever positive attributes Kurtz and Marlow have, we must likewise question the validity of their credentials, especially those of Kurtz, to serve as model human beings for those "savages" who are given the role of assistant human beings within the Eurocentric vision.

Yet despite Conrad's obvious desire to undercut imperialist assumptions, *Heart of Darkness* works against itself by simultaneously promoting an imperialist epistemology and worldview. It is clear that Conrad did not perceive the serious contradiction inherent in using imperialist discourse, replete with its racist terms and reductive conceptions of the "dark continent," as the vehicle through which to express anticolonialist views. Conrad's inability to create a wholeheartedly anti-imperialist text calls into question the integrity of the novella. From our current vantage point, somewhat distant from the colonialist discourse, it is easy to see how situating an anti-imperialist story within such a linguistic framework worked at cross-purposes with the work's themes. Doubtless a Victorian readership, heavily steeped in that discourse and seeing it as "natural," would have questioned not the use of the discourse but rather the articulation of an anticolonial message. Such an imperialist worldview, after all, inevitably pointed toward the logic and desirability of European domination of supposedly inferior subject peoples. In any case, whether seen from our present viewpoint or a contemporary one, the discourse and the themes of *Heart of Darkness* tend to undermine each other.

In light of Kipling's jingoistic reputation, we might be surprised to note that "The Man Who Would Be King" also problematizes its ethnocentric vision of European superiority. Indeed, the element of European hypocrisy stands out more clearly in some respects in "The Man Who Would Be King" than in Conrad's story. As the protagonists in what must be acknowledged as an important narrative of European conquest, Danny and Peachey show themselves to be anything but the representatives of an intrinsically superior race. Like the journalist-narrator, they are "vagabonds." Greedy, shiftless, deceitful, and disputatious, they blunder into an alien land and oppress its people for their own gain. Their more admirable qualities of determination and resourcefulness notwithstanding, they are curious choices to play the role of emissaries of an advanced breed, for in many respects they do not make particularly impressive representatives of their supposedly enlightened civilization. It is probably naive to say that Kipling was unaware of the irony he was establishing by creating imperial rulers of supposedly "superior clay" who have so many glaring weaknesses. According to Mark Paffard in *Kipling's Indian Fiction*, "Such men were an anomaly and sometimes an embarrassment in India's tightly organized white enclaves" (76), a social fact of which Kipling would have been keenly aware. By creating such blemished idols to fill the role of conqueror, Kipling appears to be *distancing* himself from the pro-imperialist vision that his tale simultaneously advances. In this regard, "The Man Who Would Be King" stridently calls into question the ethnocentric premise of the need to civilize the savages upon which much of the rhetoric of imperial domination, including its own, was based.

Even as Kipling's and Conrad's narratives give strong expression to their ethnocentric vision, then, each in its own way deconstructs that vision. Both works, in this sense, finally express signs of authorial avoidance towards the invidious discourse they help to define. That a writer reputed to be as pro-imperialist as Kipling could express doubts about colonial domination might initially seem surprising. However, "The Man Who Would Be King" was written two years before Kipling "began his imperialism in earnest" (Seymour-Smith, 164), during a period when he was apparently more sensitive to the problems associated with imperial domination. Moreover, Kipling was clearly ambivalent in his feelings toward the colonized subjects; as Seymour-Smith notes, Kipling's "attitudes were not worked out. . . . His belief that Indians were inferior was undermined by his belief that they were not, and his belief that they were not was undermined by his belief that they were." (63) Conrad, of course, had generally been seen as an anti-imperialist author, a writer of consummate moral sensitivity, until the appearance of Achebe's critique of *Heart of Darkness,* which stressed Conrad's benighted acceptance of myths about the bestiality of Africans. As the debate has evolved, Conrad's novella has been defended by critics who "predictably stress Conrad's critical stance towards imperialism and also the wide acceptance of racist language and categories in the late Victorian period." (Brantlinger 1985, 363) In any case, an examination of "The Man Who Would Be King" and *Heart of Darkness* strongly suggests that both Kipling and Conrad had conflicting feelings about the imperialist endeavor.

Both "The Man Who Would Be King" and *Heart of Darkness* clearly have important implications for the study of the more recently established tradition of postcolonial literature. Indeed, Achebe's announced intention to write his early novels in order to gainsay the impression created by imperial literature that the history of his people was "one long night of savagery" (Achebe 1965, 162) supports the idea that one important purpose of postcolonial literature has been to counter, or problematize, the ethnocentric assumptions of imperial literature. Intent on forging their own literary traditions, recent third world writers have also been conscious of the need to work off of and against the earlier imperial writings. In recognizing Kipling's and Conrad's stories of conquest as kindred narratives that express complex, ambivalent feelings towards empire, students of postcolonial literature can appreciate the degree to which "The Man Who Would Be King" and *Heart of Darkness,* taken together, can be read as works that problematize Eurocentric hegemony, a process which postcolonial literature, in its attempts to establish and define itself, later takes to its conclusion.

Notes

1 Recent years have also seen some challenges to Conrad's status as an anti-imperialistic writer, however. Most notable is Chinua Achebe's claim that Conrad, in *Heart of Darkness*, reveals himself to be "a bloody racist." See "An Image of Africa."

2 Kipling's story in particular would seem to have predicted the actual path that decolonization was eventually to take, wherein the subject peoples learn European systems and appropriate European technology in order to drive out their imperial masters. See, for example, Rupert Emerson, *From Empire to Nation* (Cambridge: Harvard University Press, 1960). Conrad's novella, with its linkage of the spiritual deterioration of a supposedly superior group to atrocities perpetrated on supposedly "sub-human" people, seems eerily to have foretold the coming of the sort of ultimate imperial savagery that would manifest itself in Hitler's "final solution." In this sense it appears as a critique of imperial villainy whose textual antecedents are perhaps visible as early as 1729 in Swift's "A Modest Proposal."

3 Patrick Brantlinger discusses the figure of the "savage as sidekick" in British imperial fiction, noting that in such discourse, "No matter how astonishing their apings of white ways . . . they can never become the genuine article." See *Rule of Darkness*, pp. 58–60.

Works Cited

Achebe, Chinua. "An Image of Africa." *Massachusetts Review* 18 (1977): 782–794.

———. "The Novelist as Teacher." *New Statesman* 29 January 1965: 161–162.

Baines, Jocelyn. *Joseph Conrad: A Critical Biography*. New York: McGraw-Hill, 1960.

Brantlinger, Patrick. "*Heart of Darkness*: Anti-Imperialism, Racism, or Impressionism?" *Criticism* 27 (1985): 363–385.

———. *Rule of Darkness: British Literature and Imperialism, 1830–1914*. Ithaca, NY: Cornell University Press, 1988.

Carrington, C. E. *The Life of Rudyard Kipling*. Garden City, NY: Doubleday, 1955.

Conrad, Joseph. *Heart of Darkness*. Edited by Robert Kimbrough. 3rd ed. New York: W. W. Norton, 1988.

Emerson, Rupert. *From Empire to Nation*. Cambridge, MA: Harvard University Press, 1960.

Fussell, Jr., Paul. "Irony, Freemasonry, and Humane Ethics in Kipling's 'The Man Who Would Be King.'" *ELH* 25 (1958): 216–233.

Hawkins, Hunt. "Conrad and the Psychology of Colonialism." In *Conrad Revisited: Essays for the Eighties*. Edited by Ross C. Murfin. University, AL: University of Alabama Press, 1985: 71–87.

Kipling, Rudyard. "The Man Who Would Be King." In *The Phantom 'Rickshaw and Other Stories: The Writings in Prose and Verse of Rudyard Kipling*, vol 5. New York: Scribner's, 1911: 39–97.

Mahood, M. M. *The Colonial Encounter*. London: Rex Collings, 1977.

Mannoni, O. *Prospero and Caliban: The Psychology of Colonialization*. Trans. Pamela Powesland. New York: Frederick Praeger, 1956.

McClure, John A. *Kipling and Conrad: The Colonial Fiction*. Cambridge, MA: Harvard University Press, 1981.

Murfin, Ross C. "Introduction: The Critical Background." In *Joseph Conrad, "Heart of Darkness": A Case Study in Contemporary Criticism*. Edited by Ross C. Murfin. New York: St. Martin's, 1989.

Paffard, Mark. *Kipling's Indian Fiction*. New York: St. Martin's, 1989.

Sandison, A. G. "Rudyard Kipling." In *British Writers*, vol. 6. Edited by Ian Scott-Kilvert. New York: Scribner's, 1983: 165–206.

Seymour-Smith, Martin. *Rudyard Kipling*. New York: St. Martin's, 1989.

Wurgaft, Lewis D. *The Imperial Imagination: Magic and Myth in Kipling's India*. Middletown, CT: Wesleyan University Press, 1983.

AFROCENTRIC CHALLENGES TO COLONIAL AND POSTCOLONIAL HEGEMONY

As the inclusion of the term "colonial" in the heading of this section indicates, African literary challenges to imperial hierarchy began well before the current postcolonial era. Indeed, as Chris Kwame Awuyah writes in "Nationalism and Pan-Africanism in Ghanaian Writing: The Examples of Ottobah Cugoano, Joseph E. Casely-Hayford, and Ayi Kwei Armah," African writers were actively contesting European constructions of the "other" as early as the period of slavery. Awuyah supports this contention through his careful analysis of the work of the eighteenth-century Ghanaian writer, Ottobah Cugoano, which he follows up with a discussion of the writing of the early-twentieth-century novelist, Joseph E. Casely-Hayford. Awuyah convincingly argues that the themes and philosophies of both of these earlier authors have a strong affinity with the work of the postcolonial writer Ayi Kwei Armah, especially in his *Two Thousand Seasons*. Awuyah's analysis of these three writers establishes not only a tradition of resistance, but demonstrates a movement toward an Afrocentric philosophy.

In the Introduction to this book, we noted that one reason we have included Kofi Anyidoho's "IntroBlues: A Poetic Voyage into SoulTime" is that it challenges the conventional hierarchy in which the traditional scholarly essay is seen as superior to alternative modes of expression. The title alone should suggest ways in which Anyidoho mounts this challenge. Beyond considering the article's rhetorical challenge, however, we should note that Anyidoho conducts a highly personalized enactment of the Pan-African worldview. Anyidoho's piece is presented as a journey of the African psyche struggling to redefine itself within the oppressive confines of the western world. In his article, "my-story" becomes the saga of the contemporary African seeking to create a viable space amid hostile conditions.

Those hostile conditions also figure prominently in the next piece in this section, Vincent Odamtten's "Sojourners in the Lands of Former Colonizers." In this essay, Odamtten reminds the reader that an appropriate, indeed essential, prelude to the formation of an Afrocentric challenge is an examination of the damage done to the African psyche by the brutalizing colonial encounter, an encounter he traces in literature to Prospero's relationship with Caliban and Sycorax in Shakespeare's *The Tempest*. In attempting to comprehend "the preoccupation with colonialism and what it did to Africa and its peoples," Odamtten looks at the genesis of African literature and also several African works that involve the "journey from the periphery to the former centers of discredited empire." His exploration of this subject includes the analysis of Mustafa's doomed reversal of imperial conquest in Tayeb Salih's *Season of Migration to the North*, as well as the less violent efforts at remaking the image of the colonial encounter that are exhibited in some of the sojourner narratives of Ama Ata Aidoo. Such a process he calls "healing," seeing it as the sign of "a significant historical junction" from the "point, in our recent histories, when we were paralyzed by 'images' . . ." to the point at which we can "determine where we are going."

Saaka and Podis's "Representations of Cultural Ambivalence: The Portrayal of Sons and Daughters in Postcolonial African Literature" concludes this section by considering journeys as well, specifically the journeys taken by sons and daughters depicted in African literature. These journeys are sometimes literal, as in the case of Olunde, who has traveled to England and back to Nigeria in order to play a role in the maintenance of the Yoruba tradition referred to in the title of Soyinka's

Death and the King's Horseman. In other cases, the journeys are spiritual or metaphorical, as in the case of Njoroge's journey from a naive faith in the power of a westernized education to a realistic awareness of the debilitating impact of colonial oppression in Kenya, or of Jeffia's journey from a world of fear and soullessness to a community of security and love in Ben Okri's *Flowers and Shadows*. In essence, Saaka and Podis are concerned to show the range of issues and problems that contemporary African writers see as surrounding the effort to mount an Afrocentric challenge to the colonial legacy. In their reading of six works (three sons, three daughters), Saaka and Podis convey the idea that contemporary African writers are keenly aware of complex currents that swirl around African youth in their attempts to live productively in societies that are often deeply conflicted between traditional values and modern, often westernized ways.

Chapter 12

Nationalism and Pan-Africanism in Ghanaian Writing: The Examples of Ottobah Cugoano, Joseph E. Casely-Hayford, and Ayi Kwei Armah

Chris Kwame Awuyah

Two hundred years of Ghanaian writing, from Ottobah Cugoano to Joseph E. Casely-Hayford to Ayi Kwei Armah, has been marked by a commitment to nationalism and Pan-Africanism. These writers and many others have upheld the African mode of living as the primary, perhaps only, basis from which black people can march forward, collectively and positively. Cugoano's *Thoughts and Sentiments on the Evil . . . of . . . Slavery . . .* (1787), a personal testimony of an ex-slave, inaugurates a tradition of protest writing by refuting aspersions about black people in very clear terms and by questioning Europe's imperial quest in Africa. Casely-Hayford (*Ethiopia Unbound*, 1911) continues the tradition of affirming positive African values and passionately censuring Western institutions for failing to treat black people according to common standards of morality and decency. He is keenly aware of the struggles of black people everywhere, and he seeks to use his writing to provide an intellectual justification for these struggles. Like his precursors, Armah is a militant Pan-Africanist. In *Two Thousand Seasons* (1973), his artistic statement on the cause of black people, Armah sets forth a vision of the future based on a new philosophy which he describes as "the way."

In emphasizing the strong affinities among Cugoano, Casely-Hayford, and Armah, I am not simply acknowledging the obvious: their links to a common native soil. More significantly, I am affirming a bonding forged within the same historical, philosophical, and rhetorical space. Taken together, the three texts are narratives of major phases of African history: slavery, colonialism, and neocolonialism in the postindependence era. *Thoughts* is Cugoano's reflections on the evils of slavery, while *Ethiopia Unbound* is Casely-Hayford's insight into the struggle against colonialism. In *Two Thousand Seasons*, Armah undertakes a broad sweep of Africa's history, noting the struggle against slavery and colonialism, and going beyond to uphold some values of the precolonial past which are relevant to the present.

Such comprehensive accounts are necessary if Africans are to understand who they are, how they relate to the rest of the world, and how they can formulate action for the future. More specifically, by developing a historical consciousness we are able to define a frame of reference that encompasses the larger configurations of Ghanaian writing, its continuities and variations, and thus we can grasp the place of individual texts in relation to the Ghanaian literary system, thereby offering alternative readings to the pervasive approach of appropriating Ghanaian literary works within arbitrarily conceived points of reference, as was evidenced in Paul Edwards's reluctance to acknowledge the African cultural and political connections in the writings of Cugoano and other eighteenth-century African expatriate writers in Britain. (Edwards, 1968a, b) Charles Larson's interesting reading of Armah's novels (Larson, 117–119) is a similar example.

Thoughts and Sentiments on the Evil of Slavery

Thoughts is a narrative of Cugoano's experience of childhood, dislocation from family, humiliation at being auctioned off at a slave market, suffering on plantations, and eventual freedom. Writing from Britain as an ex-slave, he was conscious of the impact of his work on a society that was profiting from the labor of millions of black people held in bondage. In *Thoughts* Cugoano assumes a moral and intellectual position as he offers his individual experience as a "mirror" for white people to see the evil of slavery.

Thoughts is the bold effort of a writer whose confidence comes from his inner strength. Writing was for Cugoano what it became for Frederick Douglass, Mary Prince, and Harriet Jacobs: an act of empowerment, a counter-voice in condemnation of a system that dehumanized millions of black people. In *Thoughts*, Cugoano records his personal experience, defines his identity, and stakes a place of belonging, geographically, existentially, and philosophically.

Cugoano has fond memories of his childhood, which was idyllic, simple and innocent. He recalls his birthplace, his playmates, and the incidents that led to his kidnapping and enslavement from Fanteland:

> I was born in the city of Agimaque, on the coast of Fantyn; my father was a companion to the chief in the part of the country of Fantee, and when the old king died . . . I was sent for by his nephew, Amro Accasa, who succeeded the old king in the chiefdom of that part of Fantee known by the name of Agimaque and Assinee. I lived with his children enjoying peace and tranquility, about 20 moons, which, according to their way of reckoning, is two years. (Cugoano 1787, 6)

But *Thoughts* must not be construed simply as an exercise in nostalgia, a hallmark of most twentieth-century African negritudinists. For Cugoano's childhood, the only experience he ever had of Ghana, becomes his sustenance as he is subjected to slavery and as he witnesses the dehumanization of black people.

Cugoano gives specific details about how he was "brought from a state of innocence and freedom, and, in a barbarous and cruel manner, conveyed to a state of horror. . . ." (10) After being captured from their villages, the slaves are held in European fortresses at "Commenda, Cape Coast Castle, Fort Royal, Queen Anne's Point, Charles Fort, Annamabo, Winebah, Shidoe, Acra . . ." (94), locations in present-day Ghana, and subjected to the most extreme form of cruelty. According to Cugoano, the experience is benumbing:

> [N]o description can give an adequate idea of the horror of [the African slaves] feelings and the dreadful calamities they undergo. The

treacherous, perfidious and cruel methods made use of in procuring them, are horrible and shocking. (94–95)

During the sea voyage, the slaves are locked up in holds where they are exposed to hunger, misery, and death. From the ships the slaves are sent to the auctioneer's pen where often relatives and members of the same clan are sold separately. The agony is "heart-piercing" as husbands, wives, sons, and daughters cling to each other. But they are torn apart, nevertheless, or, if the hugging continues, "the flogger [is] called on, and they [are] soon driven away with the bloody commiseration of cutting fangs of the whip lashing their naked body" (96). There is virtually no remonstration about subjecting Africans to the most brutal treatment. Employing language similar to that used by Yambo Ouologuem (*Bound to Violence*) and Armah (*Two Thousand Seasons*), Cugoano states:

> Being in this dreadful captivity and horrible slavery, without any hope of deliverance, for about eight or nine months, beholding the most dreadful scenes of misery and cruelty, and seeing my companions often cruelly lashed . . . for the most trifling faults; this made me often tremble and weep, but I escaped better than many of them. For eating a piece of sugarcane, some were cruelly lashed, or struck over the face to knock their teeth out. (11)

Thoughts is written in the autobiographical mode, but Cugoano assumes a public speaking voice to make the individual experience a narrative of the collective experience of all black people. By this rhetorical mode, a common feature to slave narratives, writing is posited as a social act, thereby expanding the ambiance of the narrative. In his prefatory remarks in the 1791 edition of *Thoughts*, Cugoano states his determination to use his writing "to convey instructions to his oppressed countrymen" (Cugoano 1791, 6), that is, black people throughout the world.

Cugoano confronts the issues of slavery and racism in the public arena by condemning the European slave traders, their African collaborators, and the church, government, and monarchies of Europe. These institutions and organizations are the "authors of African graves." (Cugoano 1787, xii) Africans, Cugoano notes, must bear their share of responsibility for slavery. He is blunt in condemning the practice in Africa of subjecting prisoners of war and debtors to domestic slavery. He observes with deep regret the action of some Africans who kidnap and sell fellow Africans to European traders. Cugoano himself was kidnapped by one of these traitors.

> I must own, to the shame of my own countrymen, that I was first kidnapped and betrayed by some of my own complexion, who were the first cause of my exile and slavery. (12)

Although Cugoano holds that Europeans are ultimately responsible for the transatlantic human trafficking, he also—as Armah does two hundred years later in *Two Thousand Seasons*—condemns African slave hunters and portrays them as despicable creatures who have been corrupted by Europeans. (26)

Cugoano maintains a distinction between a form of Christianity which, in his opinion, is based on universal love, and one that is exploitative and used for enslavement and colonization. He is passionate and direct in censuring Christian and Western institutions for failing to live by their true principles and for encouraging the activities of the merchants, planters, buccaneers, and slave traders. Cugoano examines the role of Christians in relation to slavery, racism, and imperialism, issues that are at the heart of much of modern African writing. The tendency in *Thoughts* to condemn the negative activities of the missionaries and evangelists while affirming the positive values of true Christianity has been taken up with urgency in such later black writing as Richard Wright's *Black Boy* and Ngugi wa Thiong'o's *A Grain of Wheat*.

Cugoano challenges stereotypical views of black inferiority and invalidates the preposterous arguments of proslavery advocates that Africans are descendants of Ham. Cugoano refers to that argument as malicious and specious. He asks, since the supposed descendants of Ham include Europeans and Asians, why it is only Africans who must suffer from Noah's curse? Cugoano also dismisses as racist propaganda the myth that Africans are subhumans and therefore can be enslaved:

> The external blackness of the Ethiopians, is as innocent and natural, as the spots in the leopards; and . . . the difference of color and complexion, which in [it] hath pleased God to appoint among men, are no more unbecoming unto either of them, than the different shades of the rainbow are unseemingly to the whole, or unbecoming to any

> part of the apparent arch. It does not alter the nature and quality of a man, whether he wears a black or white coat, whether he puts it on or strips it off, he is still the same man. (47)

Neither skin color nor texture of hair could determine a person's character and morality. The same sentiments and convictions have been expressed, nearly two hundred years later, by Rev. Martin Luther King, Jr., from the pulpit and at public rallies as he sought to enlighten the consciences of Americans about the ungodliness and ignominy of racism and unjust treatment of black people in America.

Cugoano believes in the liberating power of education. As writing gives Cugoano an effective voice that enables him to demonstrate the capabilities of a liberated mind, he feels that with education Africans could be in control of their own society. Cugoano calls for the general education of Africans and for instruction in the true teachings of Christ. Ex-slaves should be sent back to Africa to teach "useful learning and the knowledge of Christian religion." (132) Slaves on plantations in the West Indies should be freed immediately and ex-slaves should become wage earners. Cugoano makes a general appeal to abolish slavery:

> While ever such a horrible business as the slavery and oppression of the Africans is carried on, there is not one man in all Great Britain and her colonies that knoweth anything of it, can be innocent and safe, unless he speedily riseth up with abhorrence of it in his own judgement, and to avert evil, declare himself against it, and all such notorious wickedness. (103)

Cugoano's commitment to racial equality is an early expression of the international struggle of black people for liberation, justice, and equality. He anticipates the writings and teachings of W. E. B. DuBois, Kwame Nkrumah, and Rev. Martin Luther King, Jr. He indicates the global dimensions of the anti-imperialist struggle by noting the unparalleled brutality perpetrated by the Spaniards upon the aborigines of South America. (77, 82)

As a typical slave narrative, *Thoughts* served well to rally support for the antislavery movement. However, Cugoano went much further than Olaudah Equiano and the other slave narrative writers of the nineteenth century in addressing the issue of black liberation throughout the world. Considering that he was writing in late-eighteenth-century Britain, where the humanity of blacks was held in doubt, Cugoano's personal courage, his positive image of himself, and his claim of his identity as an African are amazing.

It is unarguable that the writings of Cugoano (and of Wilhelm Anton Amo and Ignatius Sanchos as well) represent some of the early chapters missing from the literary history of Ghana. It is clear that Cugoano's declarations of anger and cynicism toward Western values, his projections of the moral and intellectual qualities of black people, and his advocacy of indigenous African culture are early expressions of themes and concerns that have figured prominently in later black writing. Keith Sandiford rightly notes the significance of *Letters of the Late Ignatius Sancho* (1782), *Thoughts*, and *The Interesting Narrative of the Life of Olaudah Equiano* (1789):

> Their importance as precursors in the literary tradition that has addressed itself to ontological and existential issues definitive of subsequent Black Writing is this: They set the agenda of values for such authorship that has shaped permanently the meaning of literacy and the profession of letters in post-colonial and still-colonized Black societies. (Sandiford, 151)

The thrust of *Thoughts* is positive and affirmative toward authentic African values, confrontational toward those who threaten the African tradition, and offensive against those who undermine or harm African people.

Ethiopia Unbound

Like his compatriot Cugoano, Joseph Casely-Hayford's life and writing were committed to teaching the world about black civilization. Writing in Ghana in 1911, nearly a century after the abolition of slavery in Great Britain, Casely-Hayford was spared many of the indignities suffered by Cugoano and other Africans. He also benefited from an early formal education at Cape Coast, studies in journalism at Fourah Bay College, and law at Cambridge University. He joined movements against colonial rule and soon distinguished himself as an activist and prolific author. In his non-literary writings, *Gold Coast Native Institu-*

tions (1903) and *The Truth About the West Africa Land* (1913), and at public forums, Casely-Hayford challenged Britain's acquisition of territories in Ghana and other parts of Africa. A master of the art of persuasion, Casely-Hayford was effective whether addressing the League of Nations or a political rally in Accra. He spoke against exploitation and cruelty, and he campaigned for unity among black people.

Casely-Hayford's nationalist commitment is strongly expressed in his fictional work, *Ethiopia Unbound*, a title that highlights his call for black liberation. Ethiopia, the only black African country where there was no extended European occupation, becomes for Casely-Hayford a symbol of black freedom and aspiration. The fictional hero of this book, Kwamankra, Casely-Hayford's alter ego, becomes the voice of this early Ghanaian nationalist as he attempts to rebut racist arguments about Africans. Kwamankra is a Pan-Africanist who has studied in Britain and has returned to the Gold Coast to campaign for change in his society and to fight for dignity and self-respect. He is contrasted with his schoolmate, the ironically named Whitely, a missionary in the Gold Coast.

Casely-Hayford advocates cultural nationalism as a means of attaining self-reliance. He implores Africans to go back to the precolonial past, and he favorably compares African to Western institutions. In *Ethiopia Unbound*, Kwamankra calls for the establishment of a national university in each African country and for the teaching of indigenous African languages such as Fanti and Hausa. Kwamankra is aware of the importance of external symbols, recommending, for example, the use of national attire instead of Western academic gowns in the national universities:

> The distinctive garb of students, male and female, was national with an adaptability suggestive of the advanced state of society. It was recognized that the best part of the teaching must be done in the people's own language, and soon several text-books of known authority had, with the kind permission of authors and publishers, been translated into Fanti [and other African languages], thereby making the progress of the student rapid and sound. (Casely-Hayford, 167)

His call for the establishment of endowed chairs in African Studies in national universities across Africa shows Casely-Hayford's foresight and determination to develop the cultural and human resources of Africa. Is it not surprising that more than eight decades after Casely-Hayford made his landmark statements about the promotion of African studies, only a handful of universities in Africa have taken concrete steps toward establishing institutes of African Studies?

To claim that Casely-Hayford was an African nationalist should not be misconstrued to mean that he opposed all Western values. As a matter of fact, he supported the use of values and technology that were relevant in the African context. Specifically, Casely-Hayford recognized the contribution of Western education reformers like A. G. Fraser, the first principal of Achimota College, who, during his service in the Gold Coast, promoted the use of local languages for instruction in the colonies. However, Casely-Hayford was against indiscriminate introduction of Western values and technology into Africa. In *Ethiopia Unbound*, Kwamankra questions how an educated African could maintain his individuality and identity if he is not familiar with his own history and customs. How can the black person be taken seriously when all he does is ape white manners and assimilate white values?

As well, Casely-Hayford condemns Western institutions that exploit black people. In *Ethiopia Unbound*, he censures the colonial administration and the missionaries and portrays the colonial adminstrators as corrupt and callous:

> With the gin bottle in one hand and the Bible in the other, [the colonial administrator] urges moral excellence, which, in his heart of hearts, he knows to be impossible of attainment by the African under the circumstances; and when the latter fails, his benevolent protector makes such a failure a cause for dismembering his tribe, alienating his lands, appropriating his goods, and sapping the foundations of his authority and institutions. (69)

Casely-Hayford shows that the behavior of the colonial administrator is pathetic and absurd. For instance, one of the fictional characters, Mr. Bilcox, condemns some of his colleagues who altruistically work for the progress of Ghanaians. In the words of Mr. Bilcox, such people are "a mere handful of white fools who are blind enough not to see where the bread is buttered and who advocate equal rights for the natives and all that sort of tommy rot." (78)

In another interesting episode, Whitely refers to black people as "nothing but a pack of dishonest people." (81) This colonial chaplain believes that a "natural gulf" (83) separates him and his likes from the local Ghanaian people. He institutes apartheid in all spheres of social and church life and even rules that "on no account would [Europeans] commingle their dead with the dead of 'niggers.'" (83) Whitely demands that "European and native cemeteries" be separated by a "path, thirty-six feet wide." (84)

Like Cugoano, Casely-Hayford questions "how far the conduct of Christian nations in relation to aboriginal races, conformed to the Christian standard of morality." (95) Several of the missionaries the church sends to Africa serve effectively as "soldiers" in the interest of colonialism. In a parallel case (*A Grain of Wheat*), Ngugi dramatizes the colonization of Kenya through the Bible and the gun.

Ethiopia Unbound is the work of an eclectic mind, one that is well aware of the contribution of black people to world culture. Casely-Hayford refers to the Pan-African struggle for justice, liberty, and equality in various parts of the world. In the chapter "Race Emancipation—Particular Considerations: African Nationality," Kwamankra notes:

> Whether in the east, south, or west of the African continent, or yet among the teeming millions of Ethiopia's sons in America, the cry of the African, in its last analysis, is for the scope and freedom in the struggle for existence. (Casely-Hayford, 167)

Casely-Hayford discusses the works of Booker T. Washington, W. E. B. DuBois, and Edward Blyden. In *Ethiopia Unbound,* Kwamankra speaks at Hampton, Virginia, about these contemporary black scholars. However, he wrongly criticizes Washington and DuBois (especially the latter) for being provincial and therefore limited, since they are only concerned with the problems of black people in America, and then endorses the position of Edward Blyden, whom he considers to be an internationalist. Blyden calls on Africans in the diaspora to go back to their true roots.

Also, Kwamankra rejects DuBois's idea (*The Souls of Black Folks*) that black people manifest a double consciousness:

an American, a negro, two thoughts, two unreconciled strivings, two warring ideals in one dark body, whose dogged strength alone keeps it from being torn asunder. (Casely-Hayford, 180)

African Americans, unlike the Hebrews in Egypt, were unable to preserve their language, manners, customs, religions, and household gods. (164) However, Kwamankra appears to have contradicted himself when he urges Africans in America to assert their African identity and to see their presence in America as temporary, "sojourning in a strange land." (165) It seems that in calling on African Americans to imbibe "all that is best in western culture in the land of their oppressors, yet [remain] true to racial instincts and inspiration, customs and institutions" (173), Kwamankra is advocating DuBois's well-known double consciousness.

Casely-Hayford's subject in *Ethiopia Unbound* is the state of the black person, and the vitality of black culture in spite of centuries of slavery, colonization, and racism. He advocates Pan-Africanism and the development of African personality which he believes would lead to liberation and development. Casely-Hayford continues the tradition of affirming positive African values in furtherance of nationalism. The Pan-Africanist George Padmore, who became Kwame Nkrumah's confidant, described Casely-Hayford as the "John the Baptist" who prepared the way for Nkrumah. F. Nnabuenyi Ugonna, in an introduction to the 1969 edition of *Ethiopia Unbound*, praised the book for promoting positive African values:

> *Ethiopia Unbound* is undoubtedly one of the most important contributions to the literature of African nationalism. Although it is primarily a work of fiction and so properly belongs to the field of African literature, it contains ideas that are indispensable to all those interested in African studies. (xix)

Ethiopia Unbound is one of the earliest works to give literary treatment to the philosophy of African personality, and the concepts of nationalism and Pan-Africanism.

Two Thousand Seasons

The issues of slavery, colonialism, and the African tradition are central in *Two Thousand Seasons*. Like Cugoano and Casely-

Hayford, Armah attempts to dispel wrong assumptions about Africa's history, advocates adjustment of the way we apprehend the past, and calls for an assertion of traditional African values. He uses details from the indigenous tradition to demonstrate its vitality, to make a statement about the African way of life, and to define his artistic vision.

In taking a stand in favor of African value systems, Armah posits his writing as a counter-force against prevailing Western assumptions about Africa. For Armah, as it was for Cugoano (though under different circumstances), writing becomes a subversive act in opposition to the forces that have controlled the destiny of Africa. In *Why Are We So Blest?*, Armah states:

> [I]n the world of my people that most important first act of creation, that rearrangement without which all attempts at creation are doomed to falseness remains to be done. Europe hurled itself against us—not for creation, but to destroy us, to use us for creating itself. America, a growth out of Europe, now deepens that destruction. In this wreckage there is no creative art outside the destruction of the destroyers. In my people's world, revolution would be the only art, revolutionaries the only creators. All else is part of Africa's destruction. (Armah 1974, 231)

Armah takes writing seriously and with urgency. He sees art as a means of coming to terms with the past and redefining the course of action for the future. Art becomes for Armah a social dynamic to bring about change in Africa.

Armah is motivated by a passion to write his version of African history. He is aware that what has been offered as Africa's history has been constructed from Western materials. The history of Africa, he observes, has been skewed in reflection of the biases of the dominating European powers who have enslaved and colonized it. Africans cannot continue to see their past through the tainted lenses of Europeans. Armah notes with concern:

> The air everywhere around is poisoned with truncated tales of our origin. That is also part of the wreckage of our people. What has been cast abroad is not a thousandth of our history even if its quality were truth. The people called our people are not the hundredth of our people. But the haze of this fouled world exists to wipe out knowledge of our way, the way. These mists are here to keep us lost, the destroyers' easy prey. (Armah 1974, 1–2)

Armah is referring to Western writers such as Joseph Conrad, Rider Haggard, and Joyce Cary, who have depicted Africa as the context for elemental struggles, both physical and psychological; a place where "civilized" Europeans must battle with the characteristic darkness of Africa. This myth has been promoted by the forces that have exploited Africa for centuries. The challenge for African writers (Achebe, Armah, and Awoonor, for example) is to expose this propaganda, and to present African experience from an African perspective.

In *Two Thousand Seasons* Armah describes the epic struggles of black people during their odyssey of two millennia. Black people have strayed from "the way"; they have spent long and tiring seasons groping for their true path. Their tribulation has been predicted by Anoa, a female principle and a principal seer of black people, who has a prescience of seasons of suffering, death, and destruction in stock for black people. She predicts "two thousand seasons of destruction" consisting of "a thousand dry, a thousand moist [years]." (Armah 1973, 25)

Africans have spent hundreds of years "wandering amazed along alien roads." (Armah 1973, xv) The great wandering of black people involves a treacherous journey across the desert, which threatens the creative principle or "the way." The desert, as Armah reveals in his prologue, only "takes" and "knows no giving. . . . There the devotees of death take life, consume it, exhaust everything." (ix) The desert represents destruction: "It is a carrier of death." (xi) Spring water "runs dry" (xi) and all species are threatened.

In their migration across the desert black people face the onslaught of fierce Arabs. Ironically these Arabs, as Armah points out, are welcomed by the people of Anoa, but they betray and murder their hosts. In the chapter "The Ostentatious Cripple," Armah notes that the Arabs engage in unrelenting massacre and turn the "women [of Anoa] into playthings for their decayed pleasure." (Armah 1973, 31) He calls the Arabs hedonists who satiate themselves with sex, sodomy, and rape. (13)

These are the activities of the people who "know nothing of reciprocity. The road to death . . . that is their road." (Armah 1973, 11) In contrast to other African writers (Senghor and

Laye), Armah makes it clear that the Arab factor in African history is no less disastrous than is the Western involvement that came after it. The Ghanaian writer attacks both Christianity and Islam for their destructive impact on Africa.

The next thousand seasons witness the succession of the death-dealing Arabs by visitors from across the sea, white people who, in collusion with some Africans, unleash another millennium of "the destruction of souls, the killing of bodies, the infusion of violence into every breath, every drop, every morsel of your sustaining air, your water, your food." (Armah 1973, 26–27) Immediately following their arrival in Africa, the destroyers from the sea "killed half the people of the town and built a stone house for themselves on the hill closest to the sea." (120) Then they waged war on all living things and even inanimate objects: they seized and transported black people to America (129); they razed mountains in search of precious metals; they slaughtered elephants for their tusks, appropriated the most fertile lands, and forced the indigenous people to do manual labor. For several hundreds of years, the people of Anoa fought battles to defend their homesteads from the white invaders and their local allies.

Armah's depiction of whites in *Two Thousand Seasons* has provoked an interesting debate. He has been accused of reverse racism, racial chauvinism, and historical inaccuracy. Among others, Bernth Lindfors and Derek Wright are troubled by what they perceive as Armah's simplistic equation of whiteness with death and destruction, and blackness with life and creativity. Wright labels *Two Thousand Seasons* "a therapeutic exorcism" (Wright, 234), while Lindfors denounces the Ghanaian writer for his "cartoon . . . history" and for his advocacy of "black ethnocentricism." (Lindfors, 90)

While not holding brief for Armah—*Two Thousand Seasons* speaks for itself—I wish to state that it is puzzling why these critics are troubled by Armah's attack on Arab and white predators, but are silent about his negative depiction of African collaborators (the Askaris and Zombis) of the slave traders. Unlike his critics, who are selective with whom they empathize, Armah attacks *all* who violate the rules of "the way." Anyidoho shows insight when he states:

> There are indeed no good or beautiful Whites in this novel, but we
> are not offered a simplistic choice between Whites and Blacks. Armah's

fierce rhetoric is even more relentless in depicting Blacks who have become part of destruction's forces. (Anyidoho, 109)

There is no doubt about the abrasiveness of Armah's art. Nor does he discriminate in his attack on betrayers and destroyers. Armah condemns the death-dealing Arabs and whites, and the likes of Koranche, Kamuzu, and Bradford George, the African traitors. None is spared. Again Anyidoho notes:

> In Armah's visionary world, we are not offered the chance of seeking refuge in any neutral zones. There are no such zones in the world of *Two Thousand Seasons*. We must participate in a clear-cut opposition between the devotees of death and a people devoted to survival and to life. (Anyidoho, 109)

There might be a feeling of discomfort with Armah's attack because of its forthrightness and intensity, but he is against all exploiters, whether they be foreigners or indigenous people.

The Ghanaian novelist seems to have anticipated the concerns of some of his critics when he announces through his fictional character, Isanusi, that the anger of the people of Anoa is measured and their cause is just:

> This has been no useless explosion of rage animating us, hurling us singly into the brief, senseless acts of momentary, particular revenge. In us has been the need to spend life, against the present killing arrangements, . . . to spend life cutting through deceiving superficialities, to reach again the essential truth the destroyers must hide from the spirit if their white road is to prevail; to spend life acting on the truth against destruction's whiteness; to spend life working with our people, searching for paths to our way. (Armah, 246)

Armah strips bare the truth about the African past that has been concealed beneath layers of Western myths. His language is blunt and direct. He does not conceal his message beneath pointless ambiguities nor worry about propriety. He must "cut through deceiving superficialities" that are routinely offered as accounts of African history. Armah's abrasiveness is necessary.

Lindfors also criticizes Armah for inaccuracy and for lacking verisimilitude. However, he has only made use of his poetic license, the privileges that artists from all traditions and locations exercise. There is no such thing as pure and objective truth, certainly not in art. Art is shaped by various factors,

including writers' sensibilities and prevailing cultural and ideological formations. In any case Armah has no illusions about
the reaches of art. Verity is only a possibility in creative art.
The collective narrative voice in Armah's novel declares:

> What we do not know we do not claim to know. . . . We have no need
> to claim to know. . . . We have thought it better to start from sure
> knowledge, call fables fables, and wait till clarity. (Armah 1973, 5)

In his essay "Beyond Self-Depreciation and Racism: Versions
of African History in *Bound to Violence* and *Two Thousand Seasons*," Abioseh Porter offers an eloquent defense of Armah's
novel:

> It is remarkable that though critics have generally and correctly pointed
> out the presence of exaggeration and distortion in [*Two Thousand
> Seasons* and *Bound to Violence*], a good number of the critics seem to
> forget that hyperbole and distortion have been essential ingredients
> in various forms of literature (oral and written) from the earliest times.
> From passages such as those depicting the exploits of peoples as dif-
> ferent as the Israelites in the *Bible*, the Romans in Virgil's *Aeneid,* and
> Africans in works such as *Soundjiata* and *Chaka* (to name just a few
> examples), it can be seen that an effective use of exaggeration and
> the grotesque has been a major factor for the success of certain liter-
> ary classics dealing with the history of a people. (Porter, 5–6)

According to Porter, Armah uses techniques that are basic to
creative writing. He advises critics of Armah (and Ouologuem)
to use "a less racially defensive and a more literary approach."
(13)

To censure, for example, Alexander Pope's "The Dunciad"
merely because of the use of exaggeration is to demand a different poem or poet. To eliminate the fantastic and gross in
The Beautyful Ones Are Not Yet Born is to sanitize this novel.
Similarly, the vitality of *Two Thousand Seasons* is in Armah's
departure from strict verisimilitude.

It is needless to mention that *Two Thousand Seasons* is not a
documentation of African history. It is a re-creation, an interpretation of the African past. Even real historical accounts give
only a partial view of an event. History involves a process of
selection. Each historical account bears the imprint of such
factors as the historian's perspective, skills, ideology, and available data:

There is no such thing as a complete history, a history which represents the past as it truly was. The past as total experience of a people remains an unretrievable whole of which various accounts of history can only provide more or less accurate fragments. Nor is there any such thing as "the" history of a people. There is only a plurality of histories, each offering its special permutation of selected details, each serving the ideological needs of one group or another. History, whether recorded or remembered, is always a process of selection and omission. (Anyidoho, 109–110)

The nineteenth-century French novelist and essayist Stendhal (Marie Henri Beyle) declared that the novelist is a historian on horseback. The novelist is more prone than the historian to grasp but a fragment of a phenomenon. However, it does not mean the novelist's interpretation of a historical event is any less significant than that of the historian. As a matter of fact, if one goes by what classical scholars claim, one might rate the novelist as being more capable of apprehending a substantive meaning of events than the historian. In the *Poetics*, Aristotle declares that poets are capable of attaining higher truths than historians.

The novelist presents events without any special obligation to maintain strict verisimilitude. Instead, he molds them to correspond with his artistic vision. In *Two Thousand Seasons*, Armah's subject is African history, but he diminishes the importance of empiricism. As Hayden White reminds us in *Tropics of Discourse*, history is not determined by a collection of facts, but by *representations* of events, a series of interpretations.

Armah's knowledge of the past comes from collective memory, remembered knowledge shared by the African communities, knowledge by intuition and knowledge interpreted by the prophets. In *Two Thousand Seasons* the story about the origin of the people of Anoa is told in a series of prophetic utterances:

We speak of the central prophecy that heard the curse of our present coming before its violence burst upon heads, we speak of the vision that saw our scattering before the first shattering stroke exploded from the desert's white light . . . of destruction's two thousand seasons against us. (Armah 1973, 19)

The prophets and seers keep alive knowledge of the collective identity of black people. Armah's novel is based on black experience as lived according to prophecy. Thus informed, with remembered knowledge, he attempts to subvert the Western version of African history.

Armah also offers a corrective vision of the way some Africans interpret their history. He looks at Africa from within. Armah makes distinctions between the legitimate prophets of the people, like Anoa, who fight with the people, and those court singers and griots, lackeys, who bestow undeserved praises on leaders who in most instances work against the people. Armah dispenses with the practice of many African historians and writers (such as Senghor) who beatify the past.

In *Two Thousand Seasons*, Armah is scornful of Kamuzu, a buffoon who "found an old singer with a high, racing voice to sing for him and a hireling drummer [to] beat out the words on mercenary skin for his flattery." (Armah 1973, 97) He lashes out at the ancient Malian, Mansa Kanka Musa, ironically referred to as "the Golden One," who, in A.D. 1324, went on a pilgrimage to Mecca:

> Have we forgotten the stupid pilgrimage of the one surnamed—O, ridiculous pomp—The Golden One: he who went across the desert from his swollen capital twenty days journey from where we lived; he who went with slaves and servants hauling gold to astonish eyes in the desert. (97)

According to Armah, Mansa Musa's journey to the Middle East opened a gateway into Africa, bringing adventurers with "flaming greed that brought us pillage clothed in the idiocy of religion." Such rulers are no celebrants; they betrayed their people. Armah chastises African historians and griots who glorify these "ostentatious cripples" (97) and who perpetuate myths of the great kingdoms of the past.

History is a continuing experience, and if Africans are to stop repeating their past errors, they must confront the past. Armah believes that certain vices of the present have roots in the past. He denounces the négritudists' holistic residual yearning for Africanness in reaction to Western brainwashing. Such nostalgic affirmation of an ideal African tradition has no place in *Two Thousand Seasons*. For Armah, going back to the past must not mean "blind groping backward along a nostalgic road." (Armah 1973, 233) Going back to the past must involve selecting only ideals and values to which the contemporary society might aspire.

In *Myth, Literature and the African World*, Soyinka observes that Armah's relation with the African tradition is "essentially one of combination of respect and irreverence." (Soyinka, 215) According to him, Armah's objective is to redefine the values and perspectives of the present society:

> Armah's vision is a secular and humane vision despising alike the flatulence of religious piety and its proselytising aggressiveness, insisting on a strict selectivity from the past in designing the African future. (114)

Soyinka praises *Two Thousand Seasons* as a major effort to retrieve the values of the African tradition in order to define new directions for contemporary African society: "the visionary reconstruction of the past for the purposes of a social direction." (106) Armah strongly believes that African writers must, in the words of Chinua Achebe and Kofi Awoonor, respectively, "heal the wound in the soul" (Achebe 44), and "search through the debris of [Africa's] history for pieces with which to build the true self in his own image." (Awoonor, 30)

The healing process involves, among other things, offering a corrective vision, one that is based on authentic African traditions. Armah posits the philosophy of "the way," "the living way," "our way" as the source of authentic African values. As a positive affirmation, "the way" is community, reciprocity, connectedness, and fruition. The negation of its principles leads to fragmentation, destruction, and death:

> Our way is reciprocity. The way is wholeness. Our way knows no oppression. Our way is hospitable to guests. The way repels destroyers; the way destroys oppression. Our way produces before it consumes. The way produces far more than it consumes. Our way creates. The way destroys our destruction. (Armah 1973, 27)

"The way" encapsulates Armah's artistic vision; it is a philosophical construct and a metaphor for his artistic endeavour in *Two Thousand Seasons*:

> Our vocation goes against all unconnectedness. It is a call to create the way again, and where even the foundations have been assaulted

and destroyed, where restoration has been made impossible. Simply
to create the way. (Armah 1973, 13)

"The way" serves as a conceptual framework for the entire
novel, embodying Armah's view of history and commitment.
He does not define "the way" directly or in precise terms. Instead, its attributes are manifested throughout the novel and
experienced by black people, the people of Anoa. The meaning of "the way" emerges from the narrative process. In a sense,
increase in knowledge of "the way" deepens our understanding of the novel and, indeed, Armah's philosophy. Thus the
search for the meaning of "the way" becomes the process of
interpretation of *Two Thousand Seasons*.

In consonance with his use of history, Armah constructs a
counter-myth to interpret Africa's experience. He subverts and
at the same time elevates history to the level of myth. Armah's
recall of African history is linked with his remembrance of the
myth of the origin of black people. In place of the distorted
accounts and half-truths about African history, Armah reconstructs an epic of the long and tiring seasons of migration. He
warns: "[A] people losing sight of origin are dead. A people
deaf to purposes are lost." (Armah 1973, xiii) Like Ngugi and
Soyinka, Armah molds his novel in the form of a myth. But at
the same time he moves away, much further than the Kenyan
and Nigerian writers, from the actual rituals of the myth of
creation. Armah extends the spatial and temporal constraints
within which Ngugi and Soyinka, respectively, realize their
Gikuyu and Yoruba myths. He creates a modern myth to reflect the African experience, one that embraces the entire Pan-
African world.

In *Two Thousand Seasons*, myth supplies the effective symbolic structure for Armah's interpretation of history. It is a
force of the creative process that results in the novel, obviously, and that enables him to establish the philosophy of "the
way." He re-creates the story of the origin and experience of
black people. Armah reconstructs myth to fit his vision and
the result is a merging of myth and creativity to become
mythopoiesis: the making of myth.

Mythopoiesis, Okpewho points out, is an act of creativity:
"[T]he ultimate resource and the object of mythopoiesis is
imaginative or intellectual play." (Okpewho, 264) He argues

that *Two Thousand Seasons* is a mythical novel which departs from the old theory (as in Fraser's *The Golden Bough*) that sees myth as sacred tales. Armah, Okpewho explains, engages in mythmaking in order to transcend the constraints of "time-bound reality." According to Okpewho:

> By his attachment to history, therefore, Armah may be seen to have given up any need or desire for symbolic reading. This would have been true but for the amazing scope that he has given experience—and scope is one of the real mainstays of myth-making. (14)

Thomas Knipp reaches a similar conclusion about the use of myth for creativity:

> Myth, the larger construction that fuses concept and emotion, is usually narrative: a story or a gathering of stories. When these stories are, or purport to be, a chronological and interpretative arrangement of actual events causally explained or connected, they are called history. (Knipp, 40–41)

Knipp adds: "History is myth; it is the reorganization of the past according to the needs of the present." (41) And so in *Two Thousand Seasons*, Armah transcends empirical reality and factual account to attain another form, the creative order.

Following the examples of Cugoano and Casely-Hayford, Armah articulates the consciousness of his society in the process of change. Along with his commitment to promote positive values for contemporary African society, Armah reverts to the ways of Anoa. Okpewho explains:

> What Armah has done in his book is to identify one transcending concept—"the way"—and stretch it over a massive landscape of time, within which the various events of black historical experience can be seen only as symbolic illustrations of the eminence of "the way." (14)

Armah searches through the "debris" of the African past and selects the philosophy of "the way," an embodiment of the collective destiny, which eschews individualism.

The symbolic structure of Armah's novel reinforces the process of mythmaking. In furtherance of this, many of his characters (Okai, Soyinka, Irele, Isanusi, and Nandi) are recognizable personages. Similarly, the hazardous desert crossing and the journey toward the treacherous coastline have symbolic importance. Drought, treachery, and hardship are rites for the physical and spiritual initiation of the entire race. Also, the regular recourse to prophetic language is indicative of the attempt to rise beyond historical time-constrained reality. Thus, through mythopoeisis Armah defines his vision of Africa.

Characterization is in relation to group experience; individual strength is dedicated to group interest. Armah's personages are multiethnic, drawn from different parts of Africa. He praises positive figures of the African liberation struggle: past (Moliwe, Sekela, and Nandi) and present (Soyinka, Okai, and Irele). Armah emphasizes the difference between these people and another group, the so-called heroes, whom he describes as single peacocks strutting against each other's glory.

Armah dramatizes the futility of individual action in his earlier novels, *The Beautyful Ones Are Not Yet Born* and *Fragments*. Individual action is ineffective and doomed to failure in these two novels. Positive resolution is deferred in *The Beautyful Ones* and Armah warns against excessive individualism in *Fragments*. By contrast, Armah promotes collective action as a force for the liberation of black people everywhere in *Two Thousand Seasons*. Indeed, the artistic disposition throughout the novel is in furtherance of this principle. In characterization and in narrative style, as well as general philosophy, the commitment is to the promotion of a collective destiny.

The quest for group identity is expressed through the adoption of a communal narrative voice. Anyidoho makes the following observation of *Two Thousand Seasons*:

> It is indeed remarkable that the word *I* occurs only in a rare situation, a situation in which it is directly rejected. The search for *I* which is so basic to most novels is not part of the universe of this work. (Anyidoho, 125)

The narrative "I," that most personal of pronouns, is rejected because it cannot adequately express the values of "the way." In effect "the way" is a leitmotif, serving as an anchor by which the narrative is secured. The collective voice is strengthened through the unity of single voices.

The rejection of marked individualism is dramatized in a striking scene when Abena, one of the initiates who was betrayed by her King and sold into slavery, was asked why she did not try to save herself even though she knew of the plot:

> "Saved myself apart from all of us?" Abena asked.
> Silence. "There is no self to save apart from all of us.
> What would I have done with my life, alone, like a
> beast of prey?" (Armah 1973, 174)

In this episode, individual action is integrated with the collective will as the people of Anoa struggle to discover "the way."

Throughout *Two Thousand Seasons* the proclivity to individual action and philosophy is condemned: "Pieces cut off from their whole are nothing but dead fragments." (2) Armah warns, the individual is an easy prey to aggressors:

> Beware of the destroyers. It is their habit to cut off fingers from the hand itself uprooted from its parent body, calling each fallen piece a creature in itself, different from ears, eyes, noses . . . and entrails, other individual creatures of their making. Is it a wonder we have been flung so far from the way? That our people are scattered even into the desert, across the sea, over and away from this land, and we have forgotten how to recognise ourselves? (Armah 1973, 2)

As Armah states, the lack of continuity of knowledge can obliterate the sense of identity of the people and thus threaten their existence.

Individualism can lead to internecine fighting. There is self-destruction in fragmentation. There is chaos where there is no common purpose.

> A people are already trapped in spirit when they agree to the use of things to hurl against each other. The root of the disease is not in the things themselves but in the use of things; the disease is not in the abundance of things but relationships growing between users. (Armah 1973, 315)

The common adage that when two brothers fight they abandon their inheritance to strangers holds true in this novel as it has in Africa's past and present history.

While in *The Beautyful Ones* and *Fragments* Armah presents his diagnosis of the cause of the atrophy in his society, in *Two Thousand Seasons* he goes beyond the analyses in his earlier novels to provide a cure to eliminate the malady. He makes a rousing call for collective action for common interest. Armah advocates an affirmation of common African roots and a Pan-African identity of black people. He calls on black people everywhere to tell their story. Armah himself feels obligated to construct his people's experience:

> The destroyed who retain the desire to remake themselves and act upon that desire remake themselves. The remade are pointers to the way, the way of remembrance, the way of knowing purpose. (Armah 1973, xv)

He believes that the survival of the denigrated depends upon how they interpret their experiences.

We are reminded of Achebe's maxim that unless Africans know where the rain started beating them they will not be able to dry themselves. Armah supports this philosophy: "Our way begins from coherent understanding. It is a way that aims at preserving knowledge. . . ." (61) Throughout the years of fragmentation and wide dispersal, black people have kept alive the memory of their common African origin that has led to a continuity in awareness about a collective destiny. This collective action is the dynamic force behind Pan-Africanism. The successful revolt of the youths of Anoa is indicative of the possibilities for black people when they act in common:

> There is indeed a great force in the world, a force spiritual and able to shape the physical universe, but that force is not something cut off, not something separate from ourselves. It is an energy in us, strongest in our working, breathing, thinking together as one people; weakest when we are scattered, confused, broken into individual, unconnected fragments. (Armah 1973, 151)

With each person working together for the common goal, black people can hopefully overcome their present adversities. According to Anyidoho,

> Armah is not merely recounting history but interpreting it into an ideal which can guarantee survival and purposeful life for his people as a community, not as individuals each seeking to carve a piece of the earth for his personal glory. (Anyidoho, 127)

There is only "one cause, all else are branches" (Armah 1973, 26)—the cause of Pan-Africanism. There is only one course, "the living way" (26)—the way of Anoa. Through "the way" black people become a part of a force so powerful that it transcends, enlightens, and even heals. *Two Thousand Seasons,* like *Thoughts* and *Ethiopia Unbound,* is an expression of active Pan-Africanism.

Conclusion

Thoughts, Ethiopia Unbound, and *Two Thousand Seasons* mirror the development of African literature and the history of Africa. These texts intersect at several points in their reflections on major historical events in Africa. Cugoano, Casely-Hayford and Armah deal with the common themes of the struggle against slavery, colonialism, and neocolonialism, and with black liberation from an African nationalist and a Pan-Africanist perspective. These writers are committed to using Africa as a basis for appraising African experience, that is, seeing Africa through Africa's eyes, or what a contemporary African-American scholar, Molefi Asante, calls "Afrocentricity." Such a commitment will help Africans not only to understand themselves, but also determine how they view themselves in relation to the rest of the world.

Another subject common to the three texts and no less important is the concept of change, which runs through all the phases of African history that these works represent: change from slavery to liberation; change from colonialism to independence; change from neocolonialism in the postindependence era to social revolution and affirmation of traditional African values. Cugoano does not present enslaved Africans as victims awaiting a change of heart by their white captors. He records the various ways he himself and several others resist slavery, question the morality and basic beliefs of European institutions that condone and profit from that heinous trade, and offer concrete proposals for the development of Africa using African resources. Casely-Hayford's program for Pan-Africanism is still currently and urgently required. He understood the importance of using symbols for revitalizing African culture. Casely-Hayford advocates the use of African languages as media for instruction in African universities, and the establishment of chairs in African studies in African national universities. As a measure of how far Casely-Hayford was ahead of his time, it is interesting to note that at the dawn of the twenty-first century, almost all universities across Africa still use Western languages as their primary media of instruction. What is more, only very few of these institutions have given any serious consideration to the call for setting up endowed chairs in African languages and literatures. For his part, Armah calls for a social revolution, one that is based on traditional African values or "our way." In *Two Thousand Seasons*, as in *The Healers*, Armah offers a solution to the social, economic, and political malaise in Africa.

In a point related to their preoccupation with change, the three writers see their art as subversive of the existing social order. Art is used to galvanize support for a new social and political order. Art is used as a counter-force against prevailing assumptions and actions against black people. In place of distortions about Africa, prejudice against black people, and self-destructive acts by black people, Cugoano, Casely-Hayford, and Armah advocate Pan-Africanism to foster a sense of pride, solidarity, and community, and to promote social change.

Works Cited

Achebe, Chinua. *Morning Yet, On Creation Day*. London: Heinemann, 1975.

Anyidoho, Kofi. "Historical Realism and the Visionary Ideal: Ayi Kwei Armah's *Two Thousand Seasons*." *Ufahamu* 11.2 (1981/82): 108–130.

Armah, Ayi Kwei. *Two Thousand Seasons*. Nairobi: East Africa Publishing, 1973.

———. *Why Are We So Blest?* London: Heinemann, 1974.

Awoonor, Kofi. *The Breast of the Earth*. New York: Doubleday, 1976.

Casely-Hayford, Joseph. *Ethiopia Unbound* [1911]. Introduction by F. Nnabuenyi Ugonna, London: Frank Cass, 1969.

Cugoano, Ottobah. *Thoughts and Sentiments on the Evil and Wicked Traffic of the Slavery and Commerce of the Human Species*. London, 1787. Unless otherwise specifed, references in the text are from this edition.

———. *Thoughts and Sentiments on the Evil and Wicked Traffick of the Slavery and Commerce of the Human Species*. London, 1791. The 1787 edition, which is a longer and more complete version, is preferred by most recent scholars.

Edwards, Paul. "Introduction." *Thoughts and Sentiments on the Evil and Wicked Traffic of the Slavery and Commerce of the Human Species* (1787). London: Dawsons of Pall Mall, 1968a. Edwards argues that Sancho and Cugoano are very much part of the British literary tradition. "[O]nly occasionally do we hear the voice of the African and former slave in these works." (i) See also Edwards's introduction to *Letters of the Late Ignatius Sancho* (1782). London: Dawsons of Pall Mall, 1968b.

Knipp, Thomas. "Myth, History and The Poetry of Kofi Awoonor." *African Literature Today* 11 (1980): 39–61.

Larson, Charles. "Ayi Kwei Armah's Vision of African Reciprocity." *Africa Today* 21.2 (1974): 117–119; See also Ayi Kwei Armah. "Larsony: Fiction as Criticism of Fiction." *First World* 1.2 (March–April 1977): 50–56.

Lindfors, Bernth. "Armah's Histories." *African Literature Today* 11 (1980): 85–96.

Okpewho, Isidore. *Myth in Africa*. Cambridge: Cambridge University Press, 1983.

Porter, Abioseh. "Beyond Self-Depreciation and Racism: Versions of African History in *Bound to Violence* and *Two Thousand Seasons*." *Journal of Black Studies* 20.1 (1989): 3–14.

Sandiford, Keith A. *Measuring the Moment*. London and Toronto: Associated University Press, 1988.

Soyinka, Wole. *Myth, Literature and the African World*. Cambridge: Cambridge University Press, 1976.

Wright, Derek. *Ayi Kwei Armah's Africa: The Sources of His Fiction*. London: Hans Zell, 1988.

Chapter 13

IntroBlues: A Poetic Voyage into SoulTime

Kofi Anyidoho

There is a journey we all must make into our past in order to come to terms with our future. In the last decade or so I have journeyed into various spaces of the world. And everywhere I go I must confront dimensions of myself I did not know were there. I discover new purposes I did not know I could have made my own. There is something of my-story, something of my mystery, carved into every tombstone in all the graveyards of the world, something of my history enshrined in every monument and in every anthem ever erected in honor of the spirit of endurance. Back home in Africa, we perform our resurrection dance in the company of hyenas pretending to be royal ancestors. Some tell us our salvation lies in a repudiation of our history of pain and of endless fragmentation. But once upon a time, I journeyed from Africa to Giessen in the heartland of AryanEarth, and there, in the company of Mervyn Morris and Carolyn Cooper, of Caryl Phillips and Joan Riley and Marlene Nourbese Philip, of Chenjerai Hove and Anthony Nazombe, together, we sorted out our differences and recovered an ancestral unison in the midst of provocative distractions.

The official program defined our being brought together in terms of the common alien tongue grafted into our creative souls by civilizing fires of an extinguished colonial empire; we were representative contributors to *The New Literatures in En-*

glish, an alternate term to what used to be *Commonwealth Literature* until the CommonWealth Ideal could no longer be reconciled to the arrogant opulence of the few in full view of the despair and the misery of the rest of us.

As a people whose life is eternally defined/refined by the paradoxes of Africa's historical consciousness, we gathered in Giessen on the premise of our shared inheritance of English as an uncommon language of creativity, but we soon discovered that there were shared concerns and shared ways of articulating those concerns in a manner our common linguistic legacy could neither explain nor contain. Sometimes even the "owners" of this proud legacy would stand puzzled as we wandered through history into myth and memory, seeking lost landmarks, often proceeding with a ruthless primal logic marked by a geography of scars and by the tormented remembrance of that inescapable "living wound under a patchwork of scars."[1] We would shock ourselves with unsuspected ecstasy as we stumbled upon hidden paths, paths that pointed in directions of a future unmarked by scars, a future relieved of the eternal burdens of an enslaved people, a future deprived of the recurring nightmares of a generation without elders and often without heirs:

> *In the half-life, half-light of alien tongues,*
> *In the uncanny fluency of the other's language*
> *We relive the past in rituals of revival,*
> *Unravelling memories in slow time; gathering the present.*[2]

Ours is the **IntroBlues**, the forever journey into **SoulTime**. It is the quest for a future alive with the energy of recovered vision, a future released from the trauma of a cyclonic past and from the myopia of a stampeded present. It cannot, must not be that the rest of the world came upon us, and—often with our own connivance—picked us up, used us to clean up her mess, then dropped us off into trash, and moved on into a new era of celebrative arrogance, somehow hopeful that we would forever remain lost among shadows of our own doubts. With so much waiting to be done, with so much left so long undone, to keep calling our situation a dilemma is just a bad excuse for inaction.

Somehow we must recall that we are a people who once rode the dawn with civilization's light still glowing through our mind. And if today we seem lost among shadows, we must probe the deep night of our blood and seek out our birth cord from the garbage heap of history's crowded lies. A people once enslaved, they say, are too often too willing to be a people self-enslaved. That is why Brother Obiba defines slavery as "the living wound under a patchwork of scars." The wounds must be sought out and washed clean with the iodine of pain. The trauma of death must be transformed into the drama of life, the destabilized soul purged of the heavy burden of permanent sorrow and of recurring seizures of rage.

The quest for recovered vision begins as a confrontation with the gray mythology of little minds forever lost in the blinding flash of the electrocuted dream. Always we must recall the fate of those who fought to the death of the last warrior, fought to the death of the final hope.

They say Christoph Colomb rode the waves and landed in a dream. They say he discovered a people as organized as the beehive. They say he claimed the honey for the unquenchable thirst of His/Her Imperial Majesty the King/Queen of Spain. They say he set the hive ablaze to quench his own greed for fame. Four Hundred and Ninety-Eight Years later, I journey from Africa into Santo Domingo and find an island still kneeling in a sea of blood, lying deep in the path of hurricanes. In 1992, in this Year of Their Lord, an uncaring world celebrates Christoph Colomb in full knowledge of the anguish of those who still pay the price of other people's ecstasy.

The Taino-Arawaks, the Amerindian people who discovered Christoph Colomb and died upon their inalienable love for their Earth, they are now but mere mementos casually packaged into flimsy toys for tourist collectors of little treasures. A people who once built a civilization of rare glory are now but doubtful memories on the faded pages of world history. And we must speak in low whispers about the inexplicable Five Hundred Years of the Latin American Solitude, and of the elusive Magical Realism of García Márquez and of Alejo Carpentier. And yet the troubled presence of the Amerindian absence casts long shadows upon the marbled whorehouses along the sandy beaches of Santo Domingo, this stolen legacy.

The Taino in 1992[3]
for Manuel Vargas
for Wilson Harris

Ao! Amigo   Los Amigos
Adios   Domingo
Adios   Santo Domingo
Hispaniola   Hispaniola   Hispaniola
Lost Land of the Taino

Christoph Colomb   Christoph Colomb
Duarte   Sanchez   Mella
Imperial Statues in a Sea of Blood.

The turbulent memory of the Taino
And a hurricane of Arawak Sounds.

So they wiped them out?
Drowned their screams
Burned their nerves and bones
And scattered their ashes
Across the intimidating splendor
Of this young history of lies.

StormTime in these CaribSeas.
Soon the Hurricanes   the Hurricanes
Shall spring loose
From places of ancient ambush.

They will gather once more
The ancestral anger
Of this land of hostile winds.

In the dying howl
Of Hurricane Columbus
We yet may hear once more
The rising growl
Of the Taino Chieftain
Who opted out of Christ's Kingdom
Where they insist the old Sea Dog
May come to sup with ArchAngel and God.

Through the infinity of centuries
Forever lost to trauma and to amnesia

We ford ancient oceans of blood
In that final backward glance

Into old chambers
Jammed with precious stones

And firstfruits gathered in savage
Haste from fields nurtured with love
By those careful Guardians of the Earth:

> *"We do not inherit the Earth*
>   *from our ancestors;*
> *We borrow it from our Children."*

Christoph Colomb   Christoph Colomb
Hispaniola   Hispaniola   Hispaniola

Adios   Domingo
Adios   Santo Domingo.

Adios Domingo. And yet must I take with me memories of those who put some meaning to my nightmare. Pedro Muamba Tujibikile, the brother Catholic padre from Zaire, now doing missionary work among the peasants of Republica Dominicana. He it was who wrote and spoke of *La Resistencia cultural del negro en America Latina: Lógica ancestral y celebración de la vida.* Perhaps one day we may learn of just how this ancestral logic works. How do these lost African people, trapped as they are in this twentieth-century sugar plantation colony, how do they celebrate life in a land where all people of African descent are mislabeled *Indios,* and you could not call yourself a Negro no matter how far you insist on journeying into **SoulTime**? We must decode their fiestas of painful joy, perhaps? *Adios Domingo.*

My journey from Santo Domingo into Havana was like making a connection between two lifetimes separated by a final death of the soul. Many telexes back and forth, and against the best judgment of travel agents who could not find Havana listed in their most comprehensive travel guides, I finally sit on Cubana Air and hop the brief distance into another life, across the Bay of Pigs. And Havana was alive and well, but quiet and thoughtful of the sudden death of old comrades, as the Eastern Block collapsed from weight of communal dreams pressed too hard against the push of risky freedomways. And Havana's solitude is also Havana's fortitude. *Socialismo o Muerte!*

And this indeed is Cuba of the fabled Bay of Pigs?

The Royal Palm
Standing still among her Island Solitude:

Tall.   Proud.   Erect
against the storm.
Full of erotic energy.
And yet overwhelmed
by ecstasy of old victories
won in a sea of hurricanes.
Lying low & lying deep
in the armpit of the Buffalo Bull.

Now that you've lost all friends
to freedom cyclones of our time
For how long may you survive
the inspiring hate of enemies?
For how long must all your goals
be measured between angles set by devoted opponents?
Suppose the inevitable logic of history
rolls in upon the next hurricane
and deprives you of your dearest enemy,
would you still be firm and steady and royal like the palm?
or would you loosen your hold on the prime purpose for which
José Martí and Antonio Maceo and Che Guevara
and all the endless line of valiant ancestors
fought against their doubts and died their own deaths
so that life may be deprived of its eternal hesitations?
                                        ("Havana Soul")

And so I come to the U.S. of A., and in the year of **Crisis in the Gulf**. You could feel the gentle stirrings of the winds, then the rising burst of self-righteous anger, the sudden rumbling of the airwaves. And then of course the DesertStorm. And Americana was livid with the ecstasy of the game of war. And ABC and CBS and NBC and CNN carried it all for every living moment of death, every sudden boom of hopes exploding into glorious fragments against a weary sky. And then of course the total blankout on our Liberian Civil War.

So Akofa came back home from school with a Social Studies prep: telephone numbers of Congressmen and Senators; she could call and give them her opinion on whether the world should go to war against Saddam Hussein. But somewhere in her twelve-year-old mind, she figured it couldn't be right. "I don't want to talk about their war," she protests. "After all, they don't care about Liberia?" But that is the point, my young woman. People should fight their own wars, count their own losses, and celebrate their own victories, if indeed we still can talk of the victory of war, any war. And yet, how am I to explain that the Gulf Crisis is *Our* Crisis? Back home in structurally adjusted Ghana, the price of fuel jumps from four hundred cedis to one thousand cedis per gallon. Overnight. All because somebody on Wall Street *speculated* that the war could last for years, or maybe the Gulf would dry up from excessive nuclear heat. And then of course the Dow Jones Industrial Average could take a suicidal plunge. Fairly simple arithmetic of life. The Quantum Physics of Existential Inequality, according to Brother Atukwei Oshamraku Okai, Organ-Grinder to Man and God.

And about Liberia, Akofa: It would of course be nice, really nice, if the U.S. of A. could care. Especially since as you remember from the history book, after the Americana Dream had used up so many of our people and didn't need them anymore, she gathered a whole lot of them and re-exported them all to Liberia. But you see, we have a real problem here, and we must sympathize with the Americana position. The Liberian War is an Africana problem and then of course it is a *civil war*. This means that for no reason at all, people of the same family decide that they must destroy themselves by killing one another. And they would do it with or without help from anyone. And then of course the United Nations would not permit anyone, not even the United States, to interfere in a family quarrel. The Gulf War was clearly different: The United Nations said anyone who wanted to give exercise to his soldiers could send them to fight Saddam Hussein, because Saddam's War was the Mother of All Wars.

Somehow we survived that screaming hysteria of war fever. Now it's time for the victory parade. And as the yellow ribbons of War Joys float along the avenues must I still remind myself of how somewhere there may be many fellow humans who even now must wear the blood red banderas of mass slaughter?

And as I pack up my dreams and head back home to Africa, I must keep a firm hold on the memories that bring meaning and substance to my brief sojourn here at Cornell, where the Africana Studies & Research Center is separated from the main campus with its centers of knowledge and power, separated by a waterfall and a deep gorge linked by a narrow bridge closed to traffic for half my stay. I remember Mama Daisy Rowe and her daily hopes for a son called into the DesertStorm. I remember Sister Carolyn Wells and her sorrow poem for Winnie Mandela on her way to those caves of hate that kept her Nelson in for a generation of nameless pain. I remember quiet Sheila Towner and her silent hope for a more friendly environment for work and play and rest. I remember Anne Adams and how she made time to care for everything and for everyone but herself. And Abdul Nanji, the eternally youthful Mwalimu who makes Kiswahili an alternative official language for the business we must conduct for Africana Studies. *Nenda salama, rafiki yangu.*[4]

I must recall the many other scholars who came as visitors and moved on before we could find the time to compare notes. Among them, Pathe Diagne, the Senegalese/Wolof warrior whose whisper is the lion's roar; he who set the house aflame with the broken energy of Bakari II, the mystery Mansa of Ancient Mali who with his 10,000 men and 2,000 boats sailed the secret air corridors of our turbulent Atlantic and disappeared into South America in A.D. 1312, generations before the birth of Christoph Colomb. In Elmina in Ghana, we still can see footprints of Christoph Colomb. But somebody forgot to tell us why poor Colomb just had to come first to West Africa before sailing off into his dream.

I go back home to Africa with one regret: With each one of us caught so deep in our private resistance, there was hardly time for a sustained intellectual fellowship, the deep probing and frank sharing of dreams and doubts beyond our eternal good intentions. Next time for sure, we would say, but then Time runs into Eternity even as we get stuck at deadends, even as we pause and hope and fling our anger at the hostile winds. The gorge that separates Africana Studies from the Mainland Cornell campus, that gorge like all the many other gorges of our history, cannot be bridged with corpses of our rage, but with an expanded vision of our mission. When our students—inheritors of our dream—speak with pride about sunrise glories of Ancient Egypt, we must confront them with the fragmented reality of the Modern African Global Community. We cannot celebrate vanished civilizations as though beyond the birth and the death of light those who now people our dream could never count for much.

Yesterday I took Akofa to the Corning Museum of Glass. The exhibits, of course, begin with Ancient Egypt. But the official museum history claims the first glass vessels were made in Mesopotamia. The archaeological evidence of Mesopotamia's pride of place may only be excavated from the mythic imagination of the official historian of this magnificent museum of false images and translucent distortions of reality forever fractured in the sharp angle of creative truth.

We cannot assume that Truth speaks for itself. Despite Cheikh Anta Diop. Despite George G. James. Despite John Henrik Clarke. Despite Yosef ben-Jochannan. Despite Ivan van Sertima. Despite Theophile Obenga. And despite all the countless other despites, we have had to wait for *Black Athena* for the issue to appear on the official agenda of the academy. And even now, Martin Bernal is still debating footnotes with his very learned colleagues.

In spite of the concrete archaeological evidence of our claim to the world's premier civilizations, we still must sort out for ourselves, how and why and where we lost our own truth and must live and die by the alien lies we now believe with the reckless passion of teenage love. That is why the Brodah-Sistah Communion is hardly enough, unless it means holding hands and together digging deep even into the mess we swim through on our way to everywhere but our desired destination.

Mallam Femi Taiwo, my companion for this season of soulsearch, says he is still looking for someone who could relieve him of his brains. For a philosophy teacher in a world that would not associate thought with Africa, Femi certainly has a problem. But Mallam Femi, I'm afraid you are stuck with your own brains. And you will need it all to survive the onslaught of the new mythology of infantmen laying ambush in a jungle of war machines zooming down the brink of imagined galaxies.

Some have tried to negotiate their way around the sadness we call our Blues. Others have tried believing it wasn't there at all. Still others will swear this ain't the way it is supposed to be and so they couldn't care a tiny bit. But still the Blues remains.

And it grows so deep it sometimes tastes like indigo and infrared, burning paths of solitude into all our carnivals of hope. And once every so often we must start revolutions that never move beyond the talking stage.

Yesterday, after two decades, we finally saw through the clouds and gave Osagyefo Dr. Kwame Nkrumah a doubtful hero's reburial. Some people we know are in the habit of making heroes out of even infamous criminals. We have mastered the art of converting our most likely heroes into infamous criminals. Is it any wonder then that we shop around the world craving for other people's ancestors so we can worship them with the turbulent passion of the newly converted devotee? But yesterday, after two decades and a generation of stray bullets and stray hopes and lost memories, we actually saw a slender light rising through the clouds, and we woke up with the dawn, and gave Nkrumah the Osagyefo a doubtful hero's funeral, with the cemetery gates firmly locked against the crowd of dispossessed kinsmen and kinswomen whose case he once took up with the gods of greed. But now, after the last post and twenty-one cannon salute, we must settle back into the stale silence of lost fortune seekers.

At his death in 1972, there were the professional cynics among us who insisted we abandon his corpse to his so-called alien and socialist waywardness. Today we wake up to find that those who abandon their dead to the savage mercy of the crows may not in their turn have even the owls to hoot over their corpse. We can still recall the great debate that took the place of the hero's funeral. And we must recall the final word of the African-American Lolita Jones, the mythical voice from our turbulent past-future:

Lolita Jones[5]
for Dzifa   for Maya

And so they says ma Name is Lolita Jones?

But that aint ma real Name.
I never has known ma Name   our Name

I cud'a been Naita   Norwetu
Or may be Maimouna   Mkabayi
Asantewaa   may be Aminata   Malaika.

Ma Name cud'a been sculptured
Into colors of the Rainbow
Across the bosom of our Earth.

But you see:
Long ago   your People sold ma People.
Ma People sold to Atlantic's Storms.

The Storms   first it took away our Voice
Then it took away our Name
And it stripped us of our Soul.

Since then   we've been pulled   pushed
kicked   tossed   squeezed   pinched
knocked over   stepped upon   and spat upon.

We've been all over the place
And yet
We aint got nowhere at all.

That's why when the Black Star rose
I flew over to find ma Space

And aint nobody like this Brother
Who gave me back ma Soul.

But you   you kicked him out
you pushed him off
you segregated him from his SoilSoul.

And yet since that fucking day
You all aint done nothing worth a dime!

Now his Soul is gone on home
You sit out here   you mess your head
You drink palm wine   you talk some shit
Just shuckin'   n jivin'   n soundin'
All signifyin' Nothin'!
You all just arguin' funerals.

Aint nothing gone down here at all
And you all is nothing worth ma pain.
I'll gather ma tears around ma wounds
I'll fly me off to ma QueenDom Come.

I've got me a date with our SoulBrother
And this aint no place for our Carnival.

Just hang out here
And grind your teeth
And cry some mess
And talk some bull
And drive some corpse to his KingDom   Gone.

Why dont you talk of Life for a change?
You all is so hang up with the Dead
And I aint got no time to die just now.

I cudnt care to wait for judgment of your Gods.
There never was no case against our SoulBrother.

It's you all is trial here
But I cudnt care to wait
And hang you even by the Toe.

You didnt even invite me here at all
But I came   &   I spoke ma Soul.

So we must go back across the Middle Passage, go over to consult with Ma Rainey for a redefinition of the Blues:

> I never could stand no silence. I always got to have some music in my
> head somewhere. It keeps things balanced. Music will do that. It fills
> things up. The more music you got in the world, the fuller it is. . . .
>   White folks don't understand about the blues. They hear it come
> out, but they don't know how it got there. They don't understand
> that's life's way of talking. You don't sing to feel better. You sing 'cause
> that's a way of understanding life. . . .
>   The blues help you get out of bed in the morning. You get up know-
> ing you ain't alone. There's something else in the world. Something's
> been added by that song. This is an empty world without the blues. I
> take that emptiness and try to fill it up with something.[6]

And we cannot talk about the Blues without coming to terms
with Jazz. For, as you may remember from way back before the
clouds, Jazz is the flip-side of the Blues. Some may talk of the
African American Jazz as a study in dissonance, as a reflection of the spiritual and cultural travail of a people uprooted
and flung up into the bosom of the storm. There is much historical and psychological truth in this view of our people's art.
But the jazzy hoarseness of history's ArmStrongs is more than
the lyrical agony of the vanquished. Above all else, beyond all
doubt, Jazz is a reaffirmation of hopes once denied, a celebra-

tion of that piece of life which survived the storm. Jazz&Blues is an aesthetic definition of an experience that took away our laughter only to find that nature abhors vacuums, and so it fills our being with stirring vibrations of the soul.

> And so still we stand so tall among the cannonades
> We smell of mists and of powdered memories.
>
> And those who took away our Voice
>   They are now surprised
> They couldnt take away our Song.
>   ("EarthChild," 1985)

But then, quite clearly, it is not enough for us to sing the Blues and play all that Jazz, especially when we look around and find that those who cause the pain in the first place, still get so much Joy and so much High from all our Sorrow Songs. Especially when we look around and find that these days at the annual Jazz Festival at Carnegie Hall, we are often not invited at all. Clearly, quite clearly, it is not enough for us to sing the Blues and blow the Jazz. But like I said a little while ago, some have tried to negotiate their way around the sadness we call our Blues. Others have tried believing it wasn't there at all. Still others will swear this ain't the way it is supposed to be and so they couldn't care a tiny bit. But still the Blues remains. And it grows so deep it sometimes tastes like indigo and infrared, burning paths of solitude into all our carnivals of hope.

That is why in the end, no matter how far away we try to hide away from ourselves, we will have to come back home and figure out where and how and why we lost the light in our eyes, how and why we have become the eternal orphans living on crumbs and leftovers. For we are the dog who caught the game, but later sat under the table, cracking our hopes over bones over droppings from the master's hands.

So let's just say that I've tried to take you into the physical and mental geography of our history of pain and of endless fragmentation. Let's say that I've dwelt too much too long on the living wound we call the **IntroBlues**, the forever journey into **SoulTime**. Let's say just for the sake of reconfirmation that too much focus on pain, however delirious, may bring death home to the soul. So now, I want to remind you that in spite of it all, we can say without a doubt that as a people, we do hold the world record for survival against the most unreasonable odds. Yes, we hold the most spectacular survival record. But we must hasten to remind ourselves that just to survive is not and can never be enough.

Notes

1   Obiba Opoku-Agyemang, "Cape Coast Castle: The Edifice and the Metaphor," in *Dubois Centre Selected Papers,* vol. 1 (Accra: W. E. B. DuBois Memorial Centre for Pan African Culture), forthcoming.

2   Abena P. A. Busia, "Migrations," in *Testimonies of Exile* (Trenton, NJ: Africa World Press, 1990), p. 9.

3   This poem and others quoted here, unless otherwise indicated, are part of my collection, *AncestralLogic & CaribbeanBlues* (Trenton, NJ: Africa World Press, 1993).

4   Kiswahili, meaning "Stay well, my friend."

5   The occasion is that of the death in exile of Kwame Nkrumah, the deposed first president of Ghana. There is an imaginary trial going on in Ghana to decide whether he deserves to be brought back home for a hero's burial. Lolita Jones is the final and uninvited witness, testifying to Nkrumah's Pan-African legacy. See "In the High Court of Cosmic Justice," in my earlier collection, *Earthchild* (Accra: Woeli, 1985).

6   August Wilson, *Ma Rainey's Black Bottom* (New York: New American Library, 1985).

Chapter 14

Sojourners in the Lands of Former Colonizers

Vincent O. Odamtten

Some time ago, I came across a copy of Thomas Stevens and
A. H. Collins's *Babes of the Empire: An Alphabet for Young England*. At first, the images of the various people who were colonized by Europeans, specifically the British, seemed so crude
in their deprecation and objectification of these human beings. But, on further consideration, the combination of form
and content would be especially seductive for the intended
audience of "Young England":

> D is a Dervish from sunny Soudan;
> He dances no more his eccentric can-can,
> But, trained to our manners, is eagerly fain,
> When Britain once calls him, to dance in her train. (Stevens and
> Collins, 8)

In many ways, this verse marks the start of an intensification
of the process of image-making and its refinement in the literatures of the European Empire builders begun in
Shakespeare's *The Tempest*. As much as these texts were for
consumption by the children of colonizers, they also signified
a self-centered "dialogue" with the colonized.

At a significantly more sophisticated level than *Babes of the
Empire*, is Robert Browning's poem, "Caliban upon Setebos."[1]
The coincidence of reading Browning's poem and *Babes of the
Empire* prompted this essay examining the perspective of Afri-
can writers on the darker issues intimated by those *dramatic
dialogues*—issues which had so haunted the European imagina-

tion from the time of the *encounter*, when the prospective colonial subject, *the Other*, had invaded the consciousness of the European. Shakespeare's record of that encounter has come, in many ways, to symbolize the totality of that momentous meeting and the subsequent ambiguous relationship.

Although Shakespeare's work is obviously Eurocentric, it raises the central issues that were to become the hallmark of the colonial encounter: the expropriation of land by the colonialist; the subjugation of the Other by violence, technological advantage (*the* **magic** *of the English bard's version*), and language; the dehumanizing of Caliban and the imprisonment of Sycorax; the paranoid fear of the colonized subject's possible revolt; and, almost as an afterthought, the probable rape of the colonizer's *vestal possession—his woman.* Caliban's well-known response to such a violation of **his humanity**, by Prospero—

> You taught me language, and my profit on't
> Is, I know how to curse. The red plague rid you
> For learning me your language!
>   (*The Tempest,* Act I, ii)

—becomes the rallying cry to all colonized people to resist oppression and regain their autonomy and agency. To create and work for **their own** benefit.

Browning's revision of Shakespeare raises other issues which, despite the placing of the words in Caliban's mouth, reveal the English poet's concern with the hierarchical stratification of society, the displacement of spirituality by science, and the valorization of progress as exemplified by increasing materialism and industrialization. Of particular significance in Browning's poem is the reinvention of Setebos as the Christian God we find in Milton's *Paradise Lost*, not as Caliban's mother's "god." Browning's re-creation of Caliban, as a romantic noble savage, serves as the sounding board for *Browning's* metaphysical speculations about the ways of God, thus enabling him to justify the ways of the colonizer to the colonized. The final meditation of Caliban suggests as much: "Fool to gibe at Him! / Lo! 'Lieth flat and loveth Setebos!" (Browning, 147) One is reminded of Ngugi's observations about the effect of what he describes as imperialism's "cultural bomb," [which] annihilate[s] a people's belief in their names, in their languages, in their environment, *in their heritage of struggle*, in their unity, in their capacities and ultimately in themselves. It makes them see their past as one wasteland of non-achievement and it makes them want to distance themselves from that wasteland. (Ngugi 1986a, 3 [emphasis added])

Unlike Robert Browning's revision of the existential quandary of Shakespeare's Caliban, African writers have been engaged in a *creative and critical dialogue*, with each other and their former masters' myth-makers—Western writers. Over this period, the nature of that palaver or dialogue has shifted marginally; however, its overall objective has remained consistent.

Ngugi wa Thiong'o, in *Writing Against Neocolonialism*, states that the African writer, since the late 1940s, has gone through three stages or phases which, more or less, correspond to "the age of the anticolonial struggle; the age of independence; and the age of neocolonialism." (Ngugi 1986b, 1) Such a characterization is, because of its simple clarity of conception, still valid as we approach the twenty-first century. We may quibble about this or that detail; however, it must be understood that *Writing Against Neocolonialism* is a general guide to the aesthetic-ideological nature of African writing in the last half-century. As such, it not only charts the various histories of selected African writers, but it also outlines the political tendencies which have marked the histories of contemporary Africa.

As responsible and responsive social beings, we should be and are challenged by Ngugi's closing remarks:

> . . . the African writer of the eighties, the one who opts for becoming an integral part of the African revolution, has no choice but that of aligning himself with the people: their economic, political and cultural struggle for survival. . . . Such a writer will have to rediscover the real languages of struggle in the actions and speeches of his people, learn from their great heritage of orature, and above all, learn from their great optimism and faith in the capacity of human beings to remake their world and renew themselves. (Ngugi 1986b, 19–20)

Such compelling words urge us, as readers, to discover a means by which we can more critically read those works which not only trace the footprints Africa's histories have left us; but, as readers, to confidently find those works in which there is a recognition "that the eighties and nineties will see a heightening of the war against neocolonialism."(19) If there are writers who are writing against neocolonialism, there should be reader-critics who complement the work of such writers. Given that those to whom Ngugi refers are, to a greater or lesser extent, subject to similar overdeterminations within our historical memory, then it would seem necessary that we also learn, like the committed writer in the application of her craft, *to read against neocolonialism*—to read as active and critical subjects attempting to understand our histories, our languages, and symbols. To critically read, in this way, is to read in opposition to Africa's inherited colonial and neocolonial arrangements—to begin to develop a polylectic understanding of our economic, political, and cultural actualities.

A *polylectic* critical method, or understanding, demands that we approach a work of art in a self-interpellative manner, bringing to our reading and critique the knowledge which allows an evaluation that accounts for as many of the complexities of the specific (con)text(s) of the literary/cultural product(s) as possible. Thus we begin to see the text(s) and its surround as part of the personal, local, and global dynamic. Simply put, a polylectic criticism calls for the acknowledgment of the *interdependencies*, even as it recognizes the *overdeterminate autonomies of writer, text, audience, and the social whole*. The use of the word "polylectic" serves, in part, as a verbal reminder that we need to conceptualize this dynamic relationship in terms that prevent the more vulgar reductionist and mechanical conceptions of the traditional "dialectic." However, this phrasing does not displace the materialist or historical basis of a Marxist analysis. Such an analysis must recognize that the "other" and her practices are knowable. Further, a meaningful dialogue with the "other's" practices and her products (which are produced in purposeful, meditated activity) is possible. This dialogue, for example with Aidoo's literary texts, becomes more productive, since a polylectic criticism admits that these *not-wholly-Western* art-works, as products of a human agency, constitute what S. P. Mohanty calls "complex historical phenomen[a], available to us only through the process of hermeneutical comparison and specification." (Mohanty, 23)

Our critical reviewing will trace the trajectory of African literature as it engages in the struggle to re-create and protect *itself*; firstly on its own ground, in its own terms, then, more notably, in the lands of the former colonizers and their neocolonial inheritors. This struggle has entailed the disestablishment of colonizing myths like those propagated in Browning's "Caliban on Setebos" and *Babes of the Empire*. The struggle has also tangentially revealed that the colonizer's project of continued domination—even after the end of formal colonialism—needs to be resisted with even more determination. To this end, we will focus on a sampling of works by Chinua Achebe, Tayeb Salih, and Ama Ata Aidoo.

The anticolonial period of modern African writing may be said to have begun with the cultural assault of Négritude. As a movement born in Paris during the late thirties and forties, Négritude was a "revolutionary" artistic and cultural force, the main objectives of which were the formulation of ideological weapons for reclaiming a sense of pride in things African, of preparing the ground for the political and psychological struggle for independence, and an end to racial discrimination. Although somewhat limited in its untheorized acceptance of "race" as a fundamental category, it pushed African intellectuals in a more progressive direction, stressing a Pan-African underpinning of the struggles for political independence which was to accelerate after the Second Imperialist War. In part, the physical relocation of the Négritude writers, in the *foreign* city, enhanced their visions of *home*. By the 1950s, the Anglophone writers and intellectuals had made their appearance on the literary scene with the publication of Amos Tutuola's *The Palmwine Drinkard* (1952) in London.

The emerging writers, whether they were of the Négritude school or not, adhered to three basic assumptions, as listed in an editorial in *Présence Africaine* 11 (1967) "1. No nation without a culture. 2. No culture without a past. 3. No authentic cultural liberation without political liberation first." Generally speaking, these early works sought to create an authentically *African* literature, through the use of proverbs, legends, folktales, literal translations from indigenous languages etc., even as the writers expressed themselves in the languages of the European colonizers. These writers were aware of the problems inherent in using non-African genres and languages to convey the African spirit; nevertheless, to a greater or lesser extent, their works successfully conveyed that spirit of resistance.

Chinua Achebe's *Things Fall Apart* has been described as "a response to and a record of the traumatic consequences of the impact of western capitalist colonialism on the traditional values and institutions of the African peoples." (Palmer, 63) As far as this brief characterization of that impressive work goes, it only begins to suggest the re-viewing of the colonial encounter. More than anything, Achebe's work is a reply to Prospero's arrogance and paternalism. It reinscribes Africa in the record of history, even as it challenges the sin of excess, by both the colonizer and the African, represented by Okonkwo. This reply and reinscription negates Conrad's image of Africa as the *Heart of Darkness*. As Achebe notes:

> Africa . . . [is] a metaphysical battlefield devoid of all recognizable humanity, into which the wandering European enters at his peril. . . . The real question is the dehumanization of Africa and Africans which this age-long attitude has fostered and continues to foster in the world. (Achebe 1989, 12)

Things Fall Apart rehumanizes the African landscape of Conrad's "battlefield." Rather than the views and solutions proffered by Prospero, Mr. Kurtz, or the pompous District Commissioner, Achebe's novel shows the African as more completely human in his and her strengths and weaknesses. The view of colonialism is not flattering. It does not suggest some noble mission to civilize the "natives," or "when Britain once calls him, to dance in her train." Rather, Achebe's work, which belongs to that period Ngugi describes as "the age of the anticolonial struggle," focuses our gaze on the complex and internally regulated African society. For society it is, with its own values and practices, its checks and balances, albeit a society in the midst of change.

Yet, despite the evidence of things seen, many failed to see the true nature of colonialism. The extent of its corrupting legacy was often underestimated, in practice. Frantz Fanon's radical psychosocial examination of colonialism revealed its manichean organization, its valorization of the dichotomies of good and evil, white and black, civilization and savagery, emotion and intellect. Abdul JanMohamed rightly noted that

> [t]he colonial society, then, embodies a rejection of the colonizer by the colonized and vice versa. This opposition, however, is accompanied by an equally profound dependency, particularly on the part of the colonialist. (JanMohamed, 4)

This co-dependency, as it is manifest in the colonized[2] during the age of independence, is explored by such writers as Tayeb Salih in *Season of Migration to the North* (1970), which focuses on Mustafa Said's journey into the belly of the beast, the seat of the British colonial empire and his return to a village in the Sudan. The novel's structure, the use of two narrators, and its major thematic concern, the consequences of colonialism, reverses the European model of conquest and subverts the primacy of the written form. Mustafa, a self-conscious, highly intelligent "native," goes to London to continue his University education; however, even as he acquires that education, he embarks on a conquest of his own. Pandering to the colonizer's dependency, her desire to *orientalize* the colonial subject, to weave an erotic fantasy around the body of the Other, he proceeds to seduce a number of English women. The result of this reversal, the fulfillment of the colonizer's worst nightmare, is the suicide of the women, the murder of one, and Mustafa's imprisonment. He eventually returns to Africa where he meets the narrator, who was also educated in England; however, they belong to different generations.

After telling his story to our young narrator, Mustafa drowns in the Nile. It is never clear if he committed suicide or died accidentally. Although Mustafa had obligated the narrator to be guardian of his widow, Hosna Bint Mahmoud, the narrator fails to prevent the "seventy-year-old Wad Rayyes" (Salih, 87) from marrying the thirty-year-old widow. Hosna, in a replay of her dead husband's activities in London, castrates and kills Wad Rayyes on their wedding night. Unlike the case of her husband, her suicide is unambiguous, and it leaves our narrator to care for her children. Salih's complex rewriting of the *encounter* suggests that the new generation of intellectuals— the narrator has pretensions of becoming a poet—have learnt nothing about the truth or consequences of the colonial legacy.

For Salih, Mustafa Said's return to the belly of the imperialist beast exposes the "profound dependency" of the colonizer and the colonized, especially in sexual terms. The violence of the various sexual encounters symbolizes the manner in which the imperialist project perverts and contaminates all human relationships, even the most private. In addition, the work unveils the insidious nature of hegemonic practices, such as patriarchy, which provide what is ultimately only a short-lived privilege; since those who claim that privilege are ironically dehumanized in the very practice of it.

Ama Ata Aidoo has likewise sought, in her various works, to reveal the oppressive consequences of not only patriarchy, but also colonialism and other exploitative practices. For Aidoo, as with Tayeb Salih, the belly of the imperialist beast may become the site for the incubation of a clearer vision; however, Aidoo's works depart from Salih's violent politico-sexual phantasmagorias, opting instead for more polyvalent nightmares. Sissie, the protagonist of "Everything Counts," the opening story in her collection, *No Sweetness Here*, returns from England where she has been studying. Her sojourn allows her to not only see her fellow expatriates in a new light, but to know "them as intimately as the hems of her dresses." (Aidoo 1970, 1) Such knowledge comes from *being out of Africa*, from being exposed to an alien culture and history that is at once familiar and strange. This experience intensifies Sissie's need to return to her old familiar land, the nostalgia of an exile. There is the felt desire to give something back to Africa from which so much has been taken, but the return is an unexpected shock. (Aidoo 1970, 3–4) All that she and her "brothers" in England had discussed, argued about returned with a clarity that was truly disturbing:

> she could not stop the voice of one of the boys as it came from across the sea, from the foreign land, where she had once been with them.
> "But Sissie, look here, we see what you mean. Except that it is not the real point we are getting at. Traditionally, women from your area might have worn their hair long. However, you've still got to admit that there is an element in this wig-wearing that is totally foreign. Unhealthy." (Aidoo 1970, 5–6)

Even though on some level "the boys" had been right, they were also wrong in a more fundamental way. "[N]early all of

them were still abroad . . . they found the thought of returning home frightening." (Aidoo 1970, 7) She had returned. And
in so doing, she had been able to confront the demon that had
sent her into temporary exile in the first place.

A late night on the New York City subway becomes the venue
for another epiphany. This time, the vision is in the shape of
an old black woman who sits across from another exile, Kofi,
the narrator of "Other Versions." (Aidoo 1970, 133–134) In
this final tale of Aidoo's collection, Kofi recounts the significant role of his mother in his life. He feels resentment and
anger, when his mother insists that he give four pounds of his
first and subsequent paychecks to a father who has sacrificed
nothing for his own son's upkeep and education. (Aidoo 1970,
131) Even as he advances up the educational ladder, Kofi is
gnawed by the inequity of a matrilineal society's ideology subsumed by a system of patriarchal privilege compounded by
the abuses of neocolonialism. The consequences of such a
confluence, internalized and accepted as "normal," inhibit his
mother's ability to accept the gift from her son, the fruits of
her labor. As Aidoo has noted, because

> of the colonial experience we still, unfortunately, are very much lack-
> ing in confidence in ourselves and what belongs to us. It is beautiful
> to have independence, but it's what has happened to our minds that
> is to me the most frightening thing about the colonial experience.
> (cited in Pieterse and Duerden, 26)

But the colonial experience, with its overt manipulation of
the colonized subject, has assumed other, more covert guises
in the contemporary world. The neocolonial subject is still at
the mercy of the subtle machinations of imperialist economic
and ideological interests; and even Kofi's presence in the
United States is not accidental. He is the recipient of a business syndicate's scholarship, a syndicate that had been "looking out for [an] especially bright. . . . African." (Aidoo 1970,
132)

Kofi only begins to understand the reasons for his mother's
refusal to accept his money when, after a dinner in which "the
main course for the evening was me" (Aidoo 1970, 132) at the
Merrows' "high and mighty hut" he meets the cook, Mrs. Hye.
It is in this racist situation that he makes the link between the
"invisible" cook and other African American mothers, who

toil without recognition, and his own Mother back home in Ghana. A few days after the fateful meeting with Mrs. Hye, Kofi meets another "Mother" on the subway. He feels compelled, "like one goaded with a fire-brand," to acknowledge what she symbolizes by giving her "twelve dollars." (Aidoo 1970, 134) Politely, she refuses his gift. Kofi realizes that the greatest gift that he can give to his mother is to be true to himself. By eschewing the irresponsible, exploitative, and opportunistic route, Kofi's dramatic narrative eloquently asserts the possibility of "Other Versions" of this reality which so strongly tries to insist that there is "No Sweetness Here."

Even as "Other Versions" metaphorically recalls Sycorax's important role and marginalization in our neocolonial, colonial, and precolonial histories, Ama Ata Aidoo's first novel, *Our Sister Killjoy: or Reflections from a Black-Eyed Squint* enables Sycorax's avatar, Sissie, to respond to the indignities of centuries of confinement and abuse. Aidoo, through a melange of prose and poetry, examines the four-part journey to maturity of Sissie, the young university-educated protagonist. She has been chosen to represent her country (Ghana), in Europe, as a member of an international youth organization: INVOLU. Sissie's experiences in Germany and England are narrated, for the most part, by an omniscient storyteller, "Sister Killjoy" or "the Bird of the Wayside," whose perceptiveness and sharply ironic "squint" stand in contradistinction to Sissie's early innocence. In this work, we have an extended treatment of the process of awakening, the incubation to consciousness of the neocolonial subject in the belly of the former colonizer. After the Bird of the Wayside's emphatic opening assertion that we are **"Into a Bad Dream,"** we are left with the rest of page one and the whole of page two as blank paper, and page two has no pagination. We are tricked, quite literally, into "the blank of whiteness"; or perhaps, we are invited to take a journey so familiar, yet so unlike Marlow's trip into *The Heart of Darkness*. The reversal of Conrad's central metaphor for the exploration of the imperial project marks Aidoo's overt departure from the aesthetic-ideological paradigm that supports that other journey. The Bird of the Wayside knows that despite the psychological damage wrought by that blank whiteness in our history, there are people whose resistance and work will take us

out of a "bad dream" towards those "dazzling conclusions. . . ." (Aidoo 1977, 3–5)–Sycorax will have her freedom.

Rather than one moment of illumination, "Our Sister Killjoy" recounts the accumulated series of insights that eventually save Sissie from premature death within the dead womb
of the former colonial empire. *Our Sister Killjoy* becomes the
record of the cutting of the umbilical cord that has almost
strangled one of the *Babes of the Empire*. After leaving Ghana
and its "academic-pseudo-intellectual" (Aidoo 1977, 6) representative, Sammy, Sissie flies to Germany. She stays in a castle
in Bavaria where, during her free time, she meets and befriends
Marija, a young lonely middle-class housewife (Part Two: "The
Plums"). As their friendship develops to the point of physical
intimacy, Sissie draws back when she realizes that the dynamics of the relationship are, in essence, as exploitative as conventional wisdom characterizes heterosexual ones. Sissie avoids
the manichean bind that results in the colonial subject acqui-
escing to that dictum that "your [the colonizer's] servant loves
you." Sissie's arrival in London, and her experiences with her
lover (Part Three: "From Our Sister Killjoy"), her "precious
something," and other African expatriates confirm the inequali-
ties of such relationships, and she decides to return *home*, since

> that felt like fresh honey on the tongue: a mixture of complete sweet-
> ness and smoky roughage. Below was home with its unavoidable
> warmth and even after these thousands of years, its uncertainties.
> (Aidoo 1977, 133)

In the closing section of the work, "A Love Letter," the narrator allows Sissie to tell her own story. This letter is intended
for her ex-lover, but it is never sent to him. Sissie, in this letter,
is finally able to fully articulate her fears and hopes, her experiences and desires. The letter becomes a poignant document
of her growing strength and maturity. It marks Sissie's commitment to find and utilize a language of her own, in order to
combat the ignorance and the wrongs—past and present,
political and personal—which she recognizes as the bane of
Africa.

In one respect, the preoccupation with colonialism and what
it did to Africa and its peoples is a process of healing. The
journey from the periphery to the former centers of discred-

ited empire is part of this process of renewal. It is a necessary *review* of where the rain started to beat us, as Achebe characterizes it, a recovery of what Prospero attempted to deny was our inheritance, our culture, and our birthright. As neocolonial subjects, interpellated by the ideological hailings of shared histories of oppression and exploitation, of resistance and struggle, we find ourselves at what seems to be a truly significant historical junction of forces and tendencies. We are more able to review and evaluate the consequences of colonialism and its effect on the independence phase of our history. In addition, as we grapple with the complexities of neocolonialism in order to move beyond the present undemocratic and exploitative arrangements on a new trajectory, we will be enabled to fully realize that,

> we
>   no
>   more
> fear
>   these images of
> hell.

In order to reach that point at which "these images of / hell" really hold "no / more / fear" for us, we need to start at that point, in our recent histories, when we were paralyzed by such "images" and more. This project, in the context of a so-called "new world order," means that despite the end of formal colonialism, Africa's writers will take us and their characters to the remains of former centers of past empires, not in a fit of nostalgia, but purposefully, to learn. If we do not know how we have arrived at this place, how are we to determine where we are going? The work of these few writers and, unfortunately, those which have been omitted, have given Caliban and his mother, Sycorax, their dignity as human beings. They no longer need "'[l]ieth flat and [love] Setebos"; because, like Prospero, the colonizer must return to the metropolis, "the blank of whiteness," and confess:

> Now my charms are all o'erthrown,
> And what strength I have's mine own,
> Which is most faint. . . .

  .   .   .   .   .

> . . . Now I want
> Spirits to enforce, art to enchant;
> And my ending is despair
> Unless I be relieved by prayer,
> Which pierces so that it assaults
> Mercy itself and frees all faults.
> As you from crimes would pardoned be,
> Let your indulgence set me free.
>   (*The Tempest*, V, i)

Yet, Prospero's plea will not be granted in the manner that he wishes. Sycorax's children, who have been sojourners in the lands of former colonizers will no longer *indulge* the usurper, despite his neocolonial bag of tricks, for they have learned more than his language, seen more than his charms and art.

Notes

1 Browning's poem, written in 1860 and published in 1864, coincides with the heightened debates about American slavery, abolition, and the U.S. Civil War.

2 The "colonized" here, as elsewhere, also involves the notion of a gendered subordination arising from patriarchy as well as an imperial domination.

Works Cited

Achebe, Chinua. *Hopes and Impediments*. New York: Anchor Books/ Doubleday, 1989.

———. *Things Fall Apart*. London: Heinemann, 1970.

Aidoo, Ama Ata. "Everything Counts" and "Other Versions." In *No Sweetness Here*. Harlow, UK: Longman, 1970.

———. *Our Sister Killjoy: or, Reflections from a Black-Eyed Squint*. Harlow, UK: Longman, 1977.

———. "Tomorrow's Song." In *Someone Talking to Sometime*. Harare, Zimbabwe: College Press, 1987.

Browning, Robert. "Caliban Upon Setebos; or, Natural Theology in the Island." In *Dramatis Personae*. Boston: Ticknor and Fields, 1864: 133–147.

JanMohamed, Abdul. *Manichean Aesthetics*. Amherst, MA: University of Massachusetts Press, 1983.

Mohanty, S. P. "Us and Them: On the Philosophical Bases of Political Criticism." *Yale Journal of Criticism* 2 (1989): 1–31.

Ngugi wa Thiong'o. *Decolonizing the Mind*. London: James Curry, 1986a.

———. *Writing Against Neocolonialism*. Wembley, Middlesex: Vita Books, 1986b.

Palmer, Eustace. *The Growth of the African Novel*. London: Heinemann, 1979.

Pieterse, Cosmo, and Dennis Duerden, eds. *African Writers Talking*. New York: Africana,, 1972.

Salih, Tayeb. *Season of Migration to the North*. London: Heinemann, 1970.

Stevens, Thomas, and A. H. Collins. *Babes of the Empire: An Alphabet for Young England*. London: Heinemann, 1902.

Chapter 15

Representations of Cultural Ambivalence: The Portrayal of Sons and Daughters in Postcolonial African Literature

Yakubu Saaka and Leonard A. Podis

As Kenneth Harrow observes in *Thresholds of Change in African Literature,* change is the "one overriding issue facing African literature now. . . . The issue of change appears in the preoccupations of [both] authors . . . and . . . characters." (Harrow, 3) Within the larger subject, a particularly challenging problem is that of cultural ambivalence regarding the dynamics of change, especially as it relates to either the violation or projection of tradition.[1] For example, while Buchi Emecheta's *The Bride Price* disparages "traditional superstition," it simultaneously affirms the lingering power of "the old taboos of the land." (Emecheta, 168) In Soyinka's *Death and the King's Horseman*, Olunde, the African character who most clearly embodies western values in his role as a medical student in the United Kingdom, gives his life to preserve the Yoruba tradition referred to in the play's title. In *The Bride Price*, the daughter, Aku-nna, yearns for a "modern" education, but is eventually undone by her flouting of tradition; in Soyinka's drama, the son pursues westernization but ultimately is himself fiercely determined to uphold tradition.[2] This essay argues that studying the depiction of sons and daughters in contemporary African literature yields key insights into African writers' representations of the conflicts between tradition and change that have tended to pull at the fabric of African society, conflicts that have in some cases left the continent "turning around and

around on itself like a thoroughbred horse caught in a fire."
(Kane, 12)[3]

A taxonomy of the various types of sons and daughters that
appear in the literature would reveal many categories: preserv-
ers of tradition, rebels against "outmoded" ways, those who
withdraw or try to escape, expatriate sons/daughters, return-
ees, religious zealots, freedom fighters, and both willing agents
and naive dupes of neocolonialism. However, creating such a
taxonomy is beyond the scope of the present paper. This essay
instead discusses the roles played by a half-dozen sons and
daughters, examining them as representative types whose characters and actions contextualize specific cultural values and
beliefs. In addition to Olunde and Aku-nna, this paper will
focus on Njoroge (Ngugi's *Weep Not, Child*); Sissie (Aidoo's *Our
Sister Killjoy*), Tambu (Dangarembga's *Nervous Conditions*); and
Jeffia (Okri's *Flowers and Shadows*).[4]

Any discussion involving the views of African authors with
regard to the issue of tradition versus change of course re-
quires some contextualization within the considerable amount
of scholarship devoted to this controversial topic. In *Muntu*,
an early, influential study on the subject, Janheinz Jahn observes that most commentators have felt that Africans must
"either . . . accept modern civilization and survive, or . . . per-
ish with their own traditions." Jahn's view is rather that "Africa can master modern technology yet retain a modified African culture. . . ." (Jahn, 12) "African intelligence," he notes,
"wants to integrate into modern life only what seems valuable
from the past." (16) In a work more directly concerned with
the relationship of African literature and African writers to
tradition and change, Emmanuel Obiechina observes that, even
as the emerging West African novelists were celebrating change
by adopting the western genre of the novel, they "were driven
in the direction of . . . affirming the past of the ex-colonial
people, validating their autochthonous values (especially so
far as these survive into the present), often at the expense of
the received new values." (Obiechina, 14)

While Jahn and Obiechina offer useful frameworks for understanding the challenges confronting African societies and
writers and for analyzing the potential sources of ambivalence
and conflict, Jahn's statement about the retention of the *most*

valuable elements of tradition is open to question. Much African literature suggests that it is not necessarily the most valuable elements, chosen purposefully by the intelligence, that will be retained; rather, it is the most potent and deeply-rooted elements, those that have the strongest psychological hold on people, that tend to prevail. Similarly, Obiechina's parenthetical observation that West African novelists attempted to validate especially those traditions that "survive into the present" (Obiechina, 14) is debatable, for the literature itself suggests that often there must be a conscious effort to reclaim traditions that have been obliterated by imperialism.

Indeed, recent postcolonial writers, such as Achebe in *Anthills of the Savannah* (1987), Rushdie in *Shame* (1983), and Ngugi in *Petals of Blood* (1978), have strongly suggested that many of the "most valuable" elements of traditional culture have not been able to survive what Rushdie calls the "palimpsest" (Rushdie, 92) of the colonial/neocolonial era, whereby hundreds, even thousands, of years of tradition were covered over with colonialism and its various legacies. Thus the notion that the most valuable traditions can simply be "retained" has been challenged by authors like Achebe and Ngugi, whose works insist that such traditions must actually be *recovered* through such fictional constructs as Idemili and the elder from Abazon in *Anthills of the Savannah* and Ndemi and Nyakinyua in *Petals of Blood*. (Podis and Saaka, 121)

In his article on tradition in the plays of Wole Soyinka, Oyin Ogunba also raises several important points about the conflict between tradition and change. In particular, in his discussion of *The Swamp Dwellers*, he asserts that Soyinka criticizes the use of tradition to promote the agenda of the "tradition monger": "self interest, disguised in traditional ritual and religious sanctions, encumbers the ground and keeps the people just above starvation level and so makes them perpetually subservient. . . ." (Ogunba, 5: 111) At the same time, Ogunba sees warnings in Soyinka's plays, particularly *The Lion and the Jewel*, against a hasty, ill-conceived modernism based on apings of western practices that are ill suited to the African situation. (5: 111–114)

One of the most memorable sons in postcolonial African literature is Olunde, son of Elesin, the doomed horseman of

Soyinka's *Death and the King's Horseman*. Soyinka's play is set in the 1940s, a time when comparatively few Nigerians traveled to England to attend university. Olunde has been singled out for westernization by Pilkings, the District Officer who later unknowingly serves as the catalyst in Olunde's death. Nevertheless, Olunde stands as an absolute pillar of tradition, sacrificing himself when his father defaults in his duty of committing suicide following the king's death. Although Soyinka denies in his preface that the play is primarily about anything so simple as "a clash of cultures" between East and West, it is clear that Olunde stands simultaneously for both tradition and change, and that considerable ambivalence surrounds the victory of tradition, which comes at the expense of a tragic conclusion.

Yet while it is true that Olunde's character *represents* both change (leaving home in order to study medicine in the United Kingdom) and tradition (committing suicide in his father's place), Olunde in fact does *not* feel himself divided but rather resolved and determined to appreciate and uphold his Yoruba heritage.[5] From the moment he enters the action in Scene 4, confronting Jane Pilkings with an unwavering determination to act on behalf of "the welfare of my people" (Soyinka, 57), Olunde is obviously the agent of Yoruba tradition. Dismissing Mrs. Pilkings' unenlightened observations with a reserved but nonetheless palpable contempt, he is determined to act out his part by burying his father. For Olunde, it is unthinkable that Elesin could still be alive: "I know he is dead" (63), he erroneously remarks. When he learns the truth, he quietly takes Elesin's place so that tradition may be upheld. As Olunde's body is borne along in the funeral procession, Iyaloja bitterly mocks Elesin: "There lies the honour of your household and of our race. . . . The son has proved the father Elesin, and there is nothing left in your mouth to gnash but infant gums." (75)

Ironically, the staunch preserver of tradition in this case is a son who, in light of his westernization, ought to reject such "a horrible custom." (Soyinka, 29) With his "modern" education, his "been-to" status, and his aspirations to be "a first-class doctor," Olunde should be expected to revile "ritual murder." (26) Elesin thus reproaches Pilkings: "You stole from me my first-born, sent him to your country so you could turn him into something in your own image." (62–63) Contrary to

Elesin's expectations, however, Olunde's exposure to western influences has actually strengthened his allegiance to traditionalism.[6]

Olunde's immersion in western culture has only served to strengthen his devotion to Yoruba tradition. As he tells Mrs. Pilkings, going to England helped him finally to appreciate his identity: "I am grateful to your country for that. And I will never give it up." (Soyinka, 54) Indeed, despite Soyinka's insistence that "The Colonial Factor is an incident, a catalytic incident merely" (Author's Note), western challenges to tradition are presented as naively insidious. The "modern" approach fails thoroughly, being redeemed only insofar as it has caused Olunde to harden his resolve as a defender of the faith. In the final analysis, the mixture of the western and the traditional proves to be a recipe for disaster. As Iyaloja admonishes a "tired" Pilkings, "The gods demanded only the old expired plantain but you cut down the sap-laden shoot to feed your pride." (76) In Soyinka's drama, the intrusion of change has resulted not in enlightenment or the "stamping out" (26) of "savage" customs, but in a monstrous inversion of the parent-child relationship. Olunde, the supposedly westernized child is forced to turn nature upside down, to become a "young shoot [that] has poured its sap into the parent stalk. . . ." (75) Olunde's experience ultimately affirms tradition within the context of change.

Like Olunde, Aku-nna, the protagonist in *The Bride Price*, gains exposure to modernizing influences, mainly through her upbringing in Lagos, where she lives an urban life and has a "western-style" education. Unlike Olunde, however, Aku-nna sees the traditions of her culture as constraining and repressive. In particular, her enforced relocation to rural Ibuza after the death of her father precipitates a crisis that threatens to end all her hopes of escaping the destiny for which her relatives feel she was born: to enter an arranged marriage in order to fetch a handsome bride price.[7]

Aku-nna vigorously rebels against tradition by violating her family's prohibition against marrying Chike, a descendant of slaves. Boldly rejecting what the narrative voice calls a "superstition" and running off with Chike in the absence of the payment of a bride price, Aku-nna ironically appears to fall prey to the very thing she had flouted, fulfilling the traditional prophecy by dying in childbirth. Although other possible reasons for her deterioration are mentioned in the narrative, great prominence is given to the power of the curse put upon her by her uncle/stepfather, Okonkwo. *The Bride Price* seems to suggest that some traditions are merely destructive superstitions to be cast aside, while also giving the impression that such traditions still have an inexplicable power and are rejected only at one's peril. Emecheta underscores the ironic complexity of this situation by stating in the novel's final paragraph that "Chike and Aku-nna substantiated the traditional superstition they had unknowingly set out to eradicate." (Emecheta, 168) According to the narrative voice, the details of Aku-nna's unfortunate story are told to all young girls born in Ibuza in order to teach them that "If a girl wished to live long and see her children's children, she must accept the husband chosen for her by her people, and the bride price must be paid." (168) Ironically, Aku-nna's desperate attempts to rebel have resulted in her being used as a warning against future rebellions.

Like *Death and the King's Horseman*, then, *The Bride Price* affirms the view that tradition and change are, at least potentially, a toxic combination. Even though Soyinka's play is fundamentally sympathetic to the Yoruba traditionalism embodied by Olunde and Emecheta's novel is largely sympathetic to the rebellious "modern" goals of Aku-nna, both works recognize that extremely powerful forces are unleashed by the interaction of old and new. Despite Emecheta's apparent support for challenges to Igbo ways that might be considered patriarchal or sexist, she ultimately affirms the immense "psychological hold" of tradition. Indeed, *The Bride Price* is constructed so as to accentuate Emecheta's own ambivalence: though she appears to be determined, like Aku-nna, to break free of "superstition," the novel itself gives considerable credence to the potency of a controversial aspect of traditional Igbo spirituality: Okonkwo's "juju." Despite the fact that Aku-nna is deliberately not told about the doll that Okonkwo has had created in her image because supposedly "these things do little harm if the intended victim is not aware of them" (Emecheta, 157), the magic apparently works. When Okonkwo commissions a second, more expensive doll whose "aim was to call Aku-nna back

from Ughelli through the wind" (162), we learn shortly thereafter that that is precisely what the doll does, as Aku-nna tells
her father-in-law that "[Okonkwo] calls me back in the wind,
when I am alone." (163) Of course other more "scientific" reasons for Aku-nna's swift decline are continually given, as well:
her delicate constitution, her "extremely anaemic condition"
(165), and "bad feeding in [her] youth." (162) But in leaving
open the very real possibility that the protagonist was undone
by Okonkwo's magic, *The Bride Price* itself effectively makes
the point that Aku-nna's creator, no less than Aku-nna, finds
that the traditional ways remain extremely potent and resistant to "modern" challenges.

Significantly, Aku-nna is a daughter and, as such, faces a
different array of problems than does Olunde. As the relatively empowered scion of Elesin's lineage, Olunde can act
decisively. Privileged with a medical school education, he can
choose to use his westernization in the service of tradition. At
stake in *Death and the King's Horseman* are overtly political
matters, such as the degree to which the British imperial government may be permitted to intervene in Yoruba traditions.
As a son, Olunde can exercise agency in this rather public
sphere, something he might not have been able to do as a
daughter.

Aku-nna's trials as a daughter, by contrast, are played out
within the private sphere of family relations. Indeed, one might
easily overlook the existence of any interest in such a political
issue as "westernization" in *The Bride Price* and simply dismiss
Aku-nna's rebellion as a poignant but highly particularized
instance of individualism quashed by a group-oriented society, the sort of issue that David Cook identifies when he notes
that "the problem for the leading character in an African novel
is . . . how to assert an individual viewpoint without becoming
a total outcast." (Cook, 16) However, it is important that Aku-
nna's rebellion does take place within the context of a modernizing, post-World War II Nigerian society. Although the
signs of westernization are subtle, they are none the less pervasive. Nna, Aku-nna's father, for instance, succumbs at the
start of the book to an old war wound received while fighting
for the British in Burma. Not only his death, but his livelihood
as well, as a railroad worker, has resulted from the British pres-

ence. Moreover, Aku-nna's urban upbringing and her persistent pursuit of a western-style education are indications of the presence of change.

Indeed it is education upon which Aku-nna pegs her hopes. However, while Olunde, as a son, was naturally singled out for advanced education, Aku-nna, as a daughter, is only grudgingly allowed to remain in school over the objections of family and friends. Her initial involvement in schooling is ascribed to an unwise and unfortunate idiosyncrasy on the part of Nna. After Nna's death, it is only the greed of Okonkwo that enables her to continue her studies, as he is convinced (albeit against his better judgment) that Aku-nna's education will translate into a much larger bride price for him.

Aku-nna's rebellion, in short, is feminist in nature, as *The Bride Price* pits change in the form of a western-style education for women against a somewhat jaundiced depiction of traditional Igbo patriarchy. In fact, in Emecheta's novel, the victimization of Aku-nna by an insensitive patriarchy presents change as a much-needed corrective for what Emecheta characterizes as paralyzing Igbo traditions. In this sense, Aku-nna, as a daughter, represents a radically different view of the tradition-versus-change conflict than does Olunde, as a son.

Much like Aku-nna, Njoroge, in Ngugi wa Thiong'o's *Weep Not, Child*, is completely dedicated to receiving a western-style education, and like Aku-nna, sees such learning as the solution to virtually all problems. Like *The Bride Price*, Ngugi's novel takes place in the late colonial period, immediately following World War II, when the memory of sacrifices made to help the British in the war is still fresh. Of course Kenya at the time is in a period of tremendous upheaval over settler domination, a form of colonialism that did not apply to Nigeria. Whereas Aku-nna, as a daughter, understandably turned to western-style education in an attempt to gain freedom from what Emecheta depicts as a repressive patriarchy, Njoroge actually has the wholehearted support of not only his immediate family, but the entire village.

In this regard, we can see a marked difference not only between the circumstances surrounding Njoroge's attempt to "modernize" through education and those of Aku-nna, but also between those of Njoroge and Olunde. Even though Olunde ultimately rededicated himself to Yoruba tradition, his immediate community was clearly suspicious of the western education for which Pilkings had singled him out. In the case of Njoroge, there are no such obstacles to face. So supportive is his family that when his father, Ngotho, is unable to pay for Njoroge's schooling, Njoroge's brother, Kamau, assumes the responsibility. Even the revolutionary brother, Boro, counsels Njoroge to continue the necessary and important task of being educated. Clearly, what stands in Njoroge's way is the viciously racist and repressive colonial system, which will allow him an education only as long as he is perceived as being no threat to the interests of the white settlers.

Central to Njoroge's worldview is the belief that education is the path through which he and his people can regain the ancestral lands. Partially, at least, he learned this from his father, who believes that "Education was good only because it would lead to the recovery of the lost lands." (Ngugi 1964, 39) Kamau, too, tells Njoroge, "'Education is the light of Kenya. That's what Jomo says.'" (38) Not surprisingly, Njoroge allows himself to become obsessed with the power and potential of education: "Before he went to sleep he prayed, 'Lord, let me get learning' . . . He fell asleep and dreamed of education in England." (44)

For a time it seems as though Njoroge's plan will work. He is an exemplary student and progresses rapidly along the path to success. During the periods of these small triumphs, he envisions himself as the savior of his people: "[H]e was lost in speculations about his vital role in the country. He remembered David rescuing a whole country from the curse of Goliath." (Ngugi 1964, 94) As conditions deteriorate around him with the escalating "emergency," he clings even more tenaciously to the hope of education and sees himself as the comforter of others: "Hope of a better day was the only comfort he could give to a weeping child." (111) As long as Njoroge is allowed to sustain his dream of being educated in order to help his people reclaim their sacred lands, his sense of any ambivalence between tradition and change is not strong. Indeed, he views change as the means whereby tradition will be reinvigorated. Ultimately, however, the harsh irony foreshadowed throughout the book strikes home as, at the apex of his education in Siriana, he is summarily removed by the authorities, detained in prison, and tortured before being released to survey the ruins of his family and community.

As the narrative voice observes, Njoroge "did not know that [his] faith in the future could be a form of escape from the reality of the present." (Ngugi 1964, 111) Humiliated and degraded, he is reduced to working for the Indian shopkeeper who is known for treating his African employees and customers poorly. As he listlessly tends the shop, the horrible recognition of his delusions comes home to him:

> Children came to the shop. They were coming from school. Njoroge saw their hopeful faces. He too had once been like this when he had seen the world as a place where a man with learning would rise to power and glory. (129)

Rather than leading himself and his people along the paths of glory, then, Njoroge, with his deluded faith in a "modern" education, must confront the folly and hopelessness of his youthful dreams. By itself, Njoroge's abiding faith in western-style education is useless. As long as all political power resides in the hands of the colonial government and the white settlers, the sons of Kenya will get nowhere, though they possess all the knowledge in the world.

While the message conveyed by the portrayal of Njoroge and his tribulations is rather bleak, the aura surrounding the depiction of Sissie, in Ama Ata Aidoo's *Our Sister Killjoy*, is just the opposite. Permeating this novel is a palpable sense of optimism, strength, hopefulness, and determination to blend the traditional and the modern in order to discover "which factors out of both the past and the present represent for us the most dynamic forces for the future." (Aidoo, 116) Njoroge and Sissie are alike in that both are essentially children of the community and both seek to synthesize the traditional and the modern. In this regard, they are different from Aku-nna, for example, who works as an individual against the community and who is enamored with westernization as a form of escape.

Despite the similarities between Sissie and Njoroge, there are significant differences beween them. For one thing, there is a tremendous dissimilarity in their situations and their fortunes. Instead of finding herself in the grim circumstances of the Kenyan liberation struggles of the early 1950s, Sissie emerges from the immediate postindependence period in Ghana, and she exudes the hope, even euphoria of that era. Indeed, not even her status as a woman can hold her back, for here we have a daughter of the community who acts in essence like a son—with all the agency and decisiveness that we saw in Soyinka's Olunde.

For another thing, whereas Njoroge has a naive faith in western education, Sissie is highly skeptical of western institutions. A dynamic daughter who does not suffer fools gladly, she is ready to challenge superficial assumptions about the supposed superiority of western ways, as when she mocks the attitude of her countryman, Sammy, who fatuously acted as though "going to Europe . . . was like a dress rehearsal for a journey to paradise." (Aidoo, 9) So willing is she to question European ways, in fact, that she is accused of having an "anti-western neurosis" (119), a designation she considers hyperbolic.

All in all, Sissie is probably the most remarkable daughter, perhaps the most remarkable character altogether, in contemporary African literature. Brimming with confidence and determination, she sets off for Europe as a new type of "been-to": one who is ready to engage in a form of *reverse imperialism*, as, in effect, she "conquers" and briefly "colonizes" Marija, the German woman who befriends her. In Sissie we also see a clear-cut instance of a daughter who attempts the *recovery* of positive traditions blotted out by the "palimpsest" of the colonial era. Indeed, through Sissie, Aidoo offers her own metaphor that predates Rushdie's palimpsest figure by several years, but which similarly suggests the damage done to cultural traditions by the incursion of imperialists: "An enemy has thrown a huge boulder across our path. We have been scattered. We wander too far. We are in danger of getting completely lost." (Aidoo, 118)

The clearest example of Sissie's attempts to recover lost indigenous traditions is seen in her representing her own strength (or, to the male expatriates she confronts, her *audacity*) as not something western and "modern," but as a resurrection of the assertive behavior of her precolonial foremothers. Although she is a feminist who embodies the strength and potential of modern African womanhood, she does not view the problems facing African women as something solely created by an oppressive African patriarchy. Rather, she focuses on reclaiming the precolonial tradition of strong African women, a positive element of the past that she believes was obscured by western influences:

> [I]t seems as if so much of the softness and meekness you and all the brothers expect of me and all the sisters is that which is really western. Some kind of hashed-up Victorian notions, hm? . . .
>
> See, at home the woman knew her position and all that. Of course, this has been true of the woman everywhere—most of the time. But wasn't her position among our people a little more complicated than that of the dolls the colonisers brought along with them who fainted at the sight of their own bleeding fingers and carried smelling salts around, all the time, to meet just such emergencies as bleeding fingers? (Aidoo, 117)

In this case, the "boulder" of imperialism disrupted the traditional path of the strong African woman and confused her path with that of the submissive western woman. *Our Sister Killjoy* is clearly feminist in a different sense from a work like *The Bride Price* in that Sissie's resistance to domination is presented as the latter-day manifestation of a tradition of strong African women. It is, in short, an Afrocentric feminism that values tradition. In depicting Sissie as a true descendant of those strong precolonial African foremothers, Aidoo aims to rediscover a usable past.

Further, Sissie, as narrator of part of *Our Sister Killjoy* ("A Love Letter"), criticizes the English language itself as another of those "boulders" that the colonizers threw "across our path." But in this case, she does not attempt to restore precolonial language, per se. Rather, she shapes English to her purposes. Here she achieves that much sought-after but elusive synthesis of the traditional and the modern: She is a precolonial-style assertive African woman using the linguistic tools of a western education masterfully in order to make her strength known to the world and in order to criticize not only the colonizers who left her with the "gift" of English, but also the language itself. At the start of her "Love Letter," all of these elements coalesce in a stunning moment of recognition:

My Precious Something,

    First of all there is this language. This language. Yes, I remember promising you that I was going to try and be positive about everything. Since you reminded me that the negative is so corrosive. But how can I help being serious? . . . Since so far, I have only been able to use a language that enslaved me, and therefore, the messengers of my mind always come shackled?

    . . . I [mean this] symbolically, referring to many areas of our lives where we are unable to operate meaningfully because of what we have gone through. (Aidoo, 112–113)

In this passage, Sissie is clearly identifying the English language itself as a part of the palimpsest that obscures pre-colonial African traditions. Yet at the same time that she criticizes this western import, she puts it to good use, making it serve tradition by revealing the positive attributes of traditional African women (embodied in her own narrative persona!) and reviling those fellow Africans who would misuse their modernization.

In many ways, then, Sissie is the embodiment of Jahn's view in *Muntu* that "Africa can master modern technology yet retain a modified African culture. . . ." (Jahn, 12) Her plea to the gathering of expatriates in London that they should take what they have learned and return to Ghana in order to improve conditions at home illustrates her commitment to this approach. Showing her characteristic traditional strength, she "got up to attack everybody, pleading that instead of forever gathering together virtuously spouting beautiful radical analyses of the situation at home, we should simply hurry back." (Aidoo, 121) Sissie indeed is the daughter of the whole community, serving as the conscience of that community, exhorting a group of men to use the benefits of their westernization to be true to their families, culture, and traditions.

Sissie narrates only a part of *Our Sister Killjoy*, but the voice of Tambudzai, the daughter-protagonist of Tsitsi Dangarembga's *Nervous Conditions*, dominates the entire novel. Whereas Sissie behaved much like a son, Tambu literally takes the place of one, assuming her brother's position at the mission school after his death. Tambu's role as narrator is especially significant because it points up a sharp distinction between the beliefs of Tambu as the young daughter experiencing the events and Tambu as the reflective woman, looking back upon her experiences and those of her family, particularly her cousin, Nyasha, and her brother, Nhamo. /

Nervous Conditions technically unfolds in the very late colonial period when Zimbabwe is still Rhodesia, but in design is contemporaneous with the action of *Our Sister Killjoy*. Both works show the *process of development* of a radical consciousness of the female protagonist. While *Our Sister Killjoy* presents Sissie as a full-blown, already shaped character, a strong African daughter ready to take on colonial and neocolonial hegemony in all its manifestations, *Nervous Conditions* illustrates how one daughter followed a path from blind ambition, in which she nearly lost her soul to the material temptations of westernization, to eventual recognition and an awakened consciousness of the violence done to her people and their traditions.

Nervous Conditions is perhaps unique in its bold attempts to play out the various possibilities for African sons and daughters with regard to different models of westernization. In Nhamo, for example, we see the sad tale of one who submits wholeheartedly to "modernization" and indeed does lose his soul and, shortly thereafter, his life. In Nyasha, who serves almost as an alter ego for Tambu, we see the ruin of a strong, capable African daughter who gets caught between tradition and change and is rendered a misfit. Near the end of the novel, as she sits pathetically in her mother's lap in the throes of her nervous breakdown, "looking no more than five years old," Nyasha is ironically able to pinpoint the truth: "'Look what they've done to us . . . I'm not one of them but I'm not one of you.'" (Dangarembga, 201)

Tambu, however, as protagonist and narrator, remains the focal point of the novel. An exceptionally intriguing daughter/son in terms of what she represents with regard to the conflict of tradition versus change, Tambu remains, for most of the novel, an ambitious seeker of a more westernized life style. In this sense, she is "feminist" in a way simiar to Aku-nna. Like Aku-nna and Njoroge, she exhibits a strong determination to go to school. Early on she faces many of the patriarchal obstacles that confronted Aku-nna, but she is a much stronger, more assertive character than Aku-nna, who is actually, despite her inner determination, rather meek. Later, after her brother's death, she enjoys some family support for her education, mainly through Babamukuru and his family, but she never experiences the unqualified communal support that Njoroge had, mainly because no one, herself included, sees her education as having much potential to ameliorate the "nervous conditions" under which the people live. Still, her desire to be accepted in a world of men and her growing taste for luxury (along with her revulsion for the "brutal squalor" of her old home life) drive her on.

Tambu's relentless quest for a western-style education is rather surprising, given that her own narrative casts such pursuits as hypocritical. Thus, she hates her brother for having rejected his roots, but is herself unable to recognize that the same thing is happening to her. Oblivious to the irony of her actions, she seeks for herself that which she deplores as abominable in others. As such, she appears at this point to represent the type of feminist daughter who fails to see that pursuit of western "emanicipation" for women inevitably results in the loss of a valuable Afrocentric balance between issues of gender and racial discrimination.

One of the most powerful illustrations of Tambu's misguided behavior is her callous disregard of her mother's distress. When her mother learns about Tambu's wishes to follow in the dead Nhamo's footsteps, she is inconsolable. Despite her mother's terrible anxiety and impassioned pleas that Tambu remain at home, she refuses to alter her course. Coldly and dispassionately, Tambu recounts:

> . . . I went to the mission all the same. My mother's anxiety was real. In the week before I left she ate hardly anything, not for lack of trying, and when she was able to swallow something, it lay heavy on her stomach. By the time I left she was so haggard and gaunt she could hardly walk to the fields, let alone work on them.
>
> "Is mother ill?" whispered Netsai [Tambu's sister], frightened. "Is she going to die too?"
>
> Netsai was frightened. I, I was triumphant. Babamukuru had approved my direction. I was vindicated! (Dangarembga, 56–57)

Here the juxtaposition of Tambu's mother's great suffering with Tambu's insensitive self-absorption underscores Dangarembga's disapproval of such behavior by a daughter. Yet Tambu-as-participant is shockingly unaware of the cruelty and hypocrisy of her actions.

Of course Tambu-as-narrator is aware of this hypocrisy. Early in the book, she notes that she "was like a vacuum . . . taking in everything, storing it all in its original state for future inspection." (Dangarembga, 63) Although this passage specifically refers to her listening to Nyasha's account of the history of the mission, it would also seem to speak to the general technique of Tambu-as-narrator, whose approach throughout is to show us how Tambu-as-participant experienced the events, with minimal commentary. Thus it is that the change in Tambu's attitudes toward the worth of a westernized life style appears only late in the novel, because it is only late in the story that Tambu-the-participant began to change her attitudes.

The two events that precipitate Tambu's awakening are Babamukuru's orchestration of a Christian wedding for Tambu's parents and the nervous breakdown of Nyasha. Initially, Tambu is rather favorably disposed towards Babamukuru's plan to have Tambu's parents married "in church before God" so that they would no longer be "living in sin." (Dangarembga, 147) She muses that "the more I saw of worlds beyond the homestead the more I was convinced that the further we left the old ways behind the closer we came to progress." (147) But Nyasha's lecture to Tambu appears to make an impact on her:

> Nyasha . . . became quite annoyed and delivered a lecture on the dangers of assuming that Christian ways were progressive ways. "It's bad enough," she said severely, "when a country gets colonised, but when the people do as well! That's the end, really, that's the end." (147)

Thereafter, Tambu begins to make known her uneasiness with the wedding plans, with "this plot which made such a joke of my parents, my home and myself." (Dangarembga, 149) Ultimately she turns on the procedings with a vengeance, declaring that "the whole performance was ridiculous. The whole business reduced my parents to the level of the stars of a comic show. . . . I did not want to see them brought down like that and I certainly did not want to be part of it. . . . A wedding that made a mockery of the people I belonged to and placed doubt on my legitimate existence in this world." (163) Tambu's mentioning the "doubt on my legitimate existence" of course has direct reference to the view of Christianity that a traditional marriage such as that of Jeremiah and Mainini, Tambu's parents, would be illegitimate and that any offspring would be illegitimate as well. At another level, this concern with the "illegitimacy" of a traditional marriage symbolizes the general view of the colonizers that the values and standards of the colonized people as a whole are worthless. The message is clear: to have legitimate children, one must have been married in a Christian ceremony; to have viable values altogether, one must subscribe to the "progressive" beliefs of the colonizer.

In a crucial moment of recognition, Tambu perceives that, to an extent, her history of enthusiasm for the "modernization" offered by Babamukuru "had stunted the growth of my faculty of criticism, sapped the energy that in childhood I had used to define my own position." (Dangarembga, 164) In an action that marks the beginning of her true rebelliousness as a daughter, Tambu avoids the wedding and receives "fifteen lashes" and is made to assume the housekeeper's chores. Tambu's "rebelliousness" contrasts sharply with the action of Aku-nna, who turns against tradition by pursuing a modern education. Tambu rebels against the "modern" ways of westernization in order to affirm tradition.

Tambu's radicalization intensifies at the end of the novel with Nyasha's breakdown, which is closely identified with the brutalizing impact of colonization. Ceasing to blame "tradition," Nyasha launches into a lengthy and caustic indictment of imperialism:

> "It's not [my parents'] fault. They did it to them too. . . especially to [Babamukuru]. . . . But it's not his fault, he's good." Her voice took on a Rhodesian accent. "He's a good boy, a good munt. A bloody good kaffir," she informed in sneering, sarcastic tones. Then she was whispering again. "Why do they do it, Tambu," she hissed bitterly, her face contorting with rage, "to me and to you and to him? . . . They've taken us away. . . . All of us. They've deprived you of you, him of him, ourselves of each other. We're grovelling. . . . I won't grovel."
>   . . . Nyasha was beside herself with fury. She rampaged, shredding her history book between her teeth ("Their history. Fucking liars. Their bloody lies."), breaking mirrors . . . jabbing the fragments viciously into her flesh. . . . "They've trapped us. . . . I don't hate you, Daddy. . . . They want me to, but I won't." (Dangarembga, 200–201)

In this incredibly poignant speech, *Nervous Conditions* allows the devastated and disconsolate Nyasha to speak for Tambu, as well. If Tambu remains the more emotionally stable of the two, it is none the less clear that she has come to appreciate the insights into the soul-destroying practices of colonialism that Nyasha offers. In the process, Tambu's feminism, like that of Nyasha (and of Sissie), has become more complete.

Thus it is that, by the novel's end, Tambu-as-participant and Tambu-as-narrator merge into one. They fuse into the persona of Tambu the enlightened daughter, who understands that she must be assertive, must "question things and refuse to be brainwashed." (Dangarembga, 204) This is the Tambu who recognizes that one way in which she can make a contribution to the restoration of the integrity of her people is to become Tambu-as-narrator, the one who will "set down this story." (204) As she notes in the final sentence of the novel, "It was a long and painful process for me" (204), and it is precisely the book's success in presenting this process by which Tambu develops from an unenlightened daughter into an enlightened woman that distinguishes *Nervous Conditions* as central to any discussion of the depiction of sons and daughters in contemporary African literature.

In *Flowers and Shadows*, Ben Okri presents an even more complex picture of the relationship of tradition and change through his protagonist, Jeffia, who illustrates the unhappy plight of the African middle class despite being the benefactor of the modernization brought about by western education. Jeffia faces the dilemma of modern success in a corrupt, neocolonial environment, with the focal point of that corruption being his own father, Jonan, a dishonest businessman who is aptly described by his mistress as one of those "people who press other people down . . . who sail on, crushing people." (Okri, 82) Ironically, Jeffia symbolizes the hope for a brighter future in that despite the welter of corruption that surrounds him, not only in the misdeeds of his father, but in the rampant misconduct of doctors, police, and government officials, he emerges as a beacon of stability and morality. At an even more profound level, this sensitive son of neocolonial Nigeria possesses a degree of understanding and awareness that characterize him as a feminist son. If Sissie was a feminist daughter who could act with the agency of a son, Jeffia is a feminist son who does not shrink from acting with all the compassion of a daughter.

Tradition plays a large part in the positive development of Jeffia's character, and his mother's influence upon him is strong and salutary. In contrast to his father, an abuser of women, Jeffia respects and supports the women in his life. As a matter of fact, the flowers that he associates with his mother (and which his father disparages) symbolize Jeffia's positive attributes, and the shadows (the dark side of human behavior) are his father's influence upon him. While embracing all that the flowers represent, Jeffia must acknowledge the shadows as a factor of which he must remain aware, and against whose effects he must guard. As his father tells him, "No one is ever free from a father's shadows. We all have intangible influence of those who have gone before . . . behind you are a thousand and one shadows you are heir to." (Okri, 124)

The influence of tradition notwithstanding, one of the strongest impressions created in *Flowers and Shadows* is of the moral bankruptcy of the modern world. In many ways, the book depicts modern Lagos life realistically. Jeffia, for example, lives in a huge house in an exclusive neighborhood. In distinctly un-African fashion, this palatial residence is occupied by only three people—Jeffia (an only child), his mother, and his father. Even Babamukuru, coopted though he is by "the man," invites relatives to help him occupy the mission house. The Okwes also own three cars (including a Mercedes for Jonan) and they have a chauffeur. They are, in short, westernized to a degree unknown in many other African novels. In creating a son who lives in such circumstances, Okri is clearly concerned to explore the challenges of tradition versus change that present themselves in postcolonial Africa.

It is, of course, highly ironic that such trappings of westernization do not result in anything very positive. Indeed, the novel is full of frightening depictions of a society that is running out of control:

> People trudged down the streets as though they had lost their souls. . . . At bus-stops people furiously struggled among themselves to get onto the buses, while the drivers laughed. Near a petrol station two men were fighting. One had been flung in the mud, had got up,

and picked up a bottle. Somewhere in front a dog had been run over
by a car. The animal's bloody innards spread out on the road like a
testament of man's cruelty. (Okri, 124)

Much to his credit, Jeffia is appalled at the excesses spawned
by the modern world upon his society. Unlike the nameless
protagonist in Ayi Kwei Armah's *The Beautyful Ones Are Not Yet
Born*, who is despondent at similar signs of social deterioration in Ghanaian society, Jeffia responds to the evidences of
injustice and decay not with a hopeless existential cynicism,
but with a more traditionally African sense of communal feeling. In particular, it is the influence of his mother to which his
attitudes and behavior can be traced, especially to her exhortations that "the real meaning of living was not to possess but
to express one's self in the noblest endeavors. . . ." (Okri, 49)
Given his own sensitivity, it is not surprising that Jeffia is drawn
to the nurse, Cynthia, who, like Jeffia's mother, serves as a foil
to the corrupt male figures in the novel.

In light of the patently empty nature of such "modernity," it
is easy to see why, in this novel, some of the more controversial aspects of African tradition burst to the surface, in particular the juju to which Jonan turns when he is in trouble.
However, it is important to note that it is not Jeffia, the son,
who calls "on the spirits of his ancestors and invok[es] his juju."
(75) Indeed, Jeffia is a son intent on rejecting the soulless aspects of change and preserving only the life-affirming
elements:

> To Jeffia's troubled mind the ritual seemed like a last resort; as if
> whatever evils were lurking about in realms of pre-manifestation had
> to be countered. (75)

It is fitting in *Flowers and Shadows* that the first twenty-one
chapters are narrated in third-person point of view, whereas
Jeffia serves as the first-person narrator of the final three chapters. The break comes, appropriately, after the death of Jonan,
and the shift to Jeffia as narrator appears to represent his
empowerment. The final sections bespeak a hopefulness toward the future, and the symbolism of the modern as corrupt
and the traditional as positive is rather clear. As Jeffia's mother
recovers from her injuries and Cynthia comes more fully into
Jeffia's life, the sense of a "happy ending" grows. Crucial to

the overall effect of increasing optimism is the move from the opulent house of Jonan to the two-room shack in what Jeffia calls a slum. Though the remaining Okwes would appear to have "come down in the world," in fact they have spiritually gone up in it, as they settle into circumstances that put them more in touch with "the people."

Although Jeffia doesn't entirely abandon his connection to the modern in that his father's house is being held "in care of some housing agents . . . for me when I was old enough to own it" (Okri, 200), he clearly renounces what it represents, or at least what it signified for his father. Jeffia appears to see hope in the fact that the once-gaudy edifice is itself returning to a more natural state:

> The last time I went there the grass had grown all round the house. The mango tree had borne fruit and birds had started coming there again. Some of the flowers had withered and died but others had survived . . . and the lawn had grown wild. And there was a big hole in one of the windows where somebody had thrown a stone. (200)

Jonan's splendid residence, which had represented the vanity and pretentiousness of one who had been seduced by the spoils available to corrupt agents of neocolonial capitalism, appears at last to be overwhelmed by an abiding nature.

At the same time, the "dirty compound" to which Jeffia and his mother move, although it represents "a big drop down," is the site where this son of postcolonial Nigeria will experience a resigned contentment, an opportunity to rebuild his life under the benign influence of "flowers" (which is, not surprisingly, the title of the last section of the book, the three chapters narrated by Jeffia), rather than the questionable influence of shadows.

There is much that could be said in examining the depiction of these half dozen sons and daughters. The circumstances in which they operate remain disorientingly complex. In all cases, tradition remains a given, a necessary force with which all of the sons and daughters must come to terms. The "psychological hold," of which Emecheta speaks in *The Bride Price*, may have its disadvantages, but what is most noteworthy is that it exists because it serves a purpose. Whether the sons and daughters fight that traditional hold or welcome it, it represents a definite point of orientation. It is an expression of culture that serves to define where one stands. In some cases, as in that of Jeffia, for example, even the controversial aspects of tradition, those troubling "superstitions" that burst through the "palimpsest," can be understood as rough counterparts of the controversial aspects of modern life, an interpretation suggested in Jeffia's resistance to *both* the traditional *and* the modern behaviors of his father. In other cases, as in that of Sissie or the more enlightened manifestation of Tambu (as narrator), tradition emerges as something palpably of value, as a crucial instrument in the struggle to ward off the lingering legacies of colonial incursion. These and other depictions of sons and daughters in modern African literature reveal significant aspects of the conflicts between tradition and change that continue to unfold.

Notes

1   We have consciously chosen "change" rather than "modernity" or "modernization" to emphasize that we do not here subscribe to the common binary opposition that pits African tradition against western notions of progress. The use of "change" implies that it is possible, indeed desirable, for African societies to alter in a positive direction—that is, to "modernize" themselves—without doing so along strictly or even primarily western lines. For discussion of this issue, see C. S. Whitaker, Jr., *The Politics of Tradition: Continuity and Change in Northern Nigeria, 1946–1966* (Princeton, NJ: Princeton University Press, 1970). By tradition, we mean historically African values and practices, uninfluenced by Western or Middle Eastern cultures. Some African literature is based on a different conception of tradition. See, for example, Cheikh Hamidou Kane's *Ambiguous Adventure* (London: Heinemann, 1972), which deals with the conflict between tradition and westernization, but in which the "tradition" of the Diallobé people is one already heavily altered by the influence of Islamic culture.

2   It is important to recognize that Soyinka's plays do not always uphold tradition. In "The Traditional Content of the Plays of Wole Soyinka" (*African Literature Today*, vols. 4–5), Oyin Ogunba examines several of the earlier works and concludes that "Wole Soyinka's attitude to tradition is unflattering. . . . [Soyinka] wants to do away with cant, to expose 'illustrious ancestors' and the stratagems of Messiahs. . . ." (5: 114–115)

3   In the political sphere, there has been less apparent conflict over the change from traditional paradigms. As Rupert Emerson observed more than three decades ago in *From Empire to Nation* (Cambridge, MA: Harvard University Press, 1960), African political attitudes and practices had changed sufficiently by mid-century to allow many former colonies to rise up and cast off their colonizers by adopting the ideas of nationalism that the westerners had themselves introduced. However, even in the area of politics, there have been some misgivings voiced about the loss of traditional forms. See, for example, Basil Davidson, *The Black Man's Burden: Africa and the Curse of the Nation-State* (New York: Random House, 1992).

4   For a brief discussion of the role of sons and daughters in earlier works by Mongo Beti and Ferdinand Oyono, see Harrow (84–85).

5   Olunde's insistence on committing suicide in his father's place clearly echoes the sort of "affirmation . . . of autochthonous values . . . often at the expense of . . . received new values" discussed by Obiechina. (14)

6   In this regard, Olunde's behavior is consistent with the historical record, which shows that while British authorities expected their westernized imperial subjects to become more committed to imperialist culture, the opposite, in fact, tended to occur. See, for example, Hugh Tinker's *Men Who Overturned Empires* (London: Macmillan, 1987) and Bernard Porter's *The Lion's Share: A Short History of British Imperialism, 1850–1983*, Second ed. (London: Longman, 1984).

7   Even though Obiechina (85) is referring primarily to the early works of Achebe in the following passage, it would seem appropriate to the plight in which Aku-nna finds herself as she tries to resist the forces arrayed against her: "The social and political institutions of the traditional society have perfected the art of exacting conformity from the individual and discouraging deviations and subversion of the common will." Moreover, Ogunba's (5: 11) observation about the exploitation of "traditional rituals" would seem to apply to the selfish and manipulative behavior of Aku-nna's uncle/stepfather, Okonkwo, who, in the process of insisting that the bride price be paid, initially seeks it solely in order to increase his own wealth and who eventually wishes to punish Aku-nna and Chike primarily to exact revenge.

Works Cited

Achebe, Chinua. *Anthills of the Savannah*. New York: Doubleday, 1987.

Aidoo, Ama Ata. *Our Sister Killjoy*. London: Longman, 1977.

Armah, Ayi Kwei. *The Beautyful Ones Are Not Yet Born*. New York: Collier, 1968.

Cook, David. *African Literature: A Critical View*. London: Longman, 1977.

Dangarembga, Tsitsi. *Nervous Conditions*. London: The Women's Press, 1988.

Davidson, Basil. *The Black Man's Burden: Africa and the Curse of the Nation-State*. New York: Random House, 1992.

Emecheta, Buchi. *The Bride Price*. New York: George Braziller, 1976.

Emerson, Rupert. *From Empire to Nation*. Cambridge, MA: Harvard University Press, 1960.

Harrow, Kenneth W. *Thresholds of Change in African Literature: The Emergence of a Tradition*. Portsmouth, NH: Heinemann, 1994.

Jahn, Janheinz. *Muntu*. New York: Grove, 1961.

Kane, Cheikh Hamidou. *Ambiguous Adventure*. London: Heinemann, 1972.

Ngugi wa Thiong'o. *Petals of Blood*. New York: E. P. Dutton, 1978.

———. *Weep Not, Child*. London: Heinemann, 1964.

Obiechina, Emmanuel. *Culture, Tradition and Society in the West African Novel*. Cambridge: Cambridge University Press, 1975.

Ogunba, Oyin. "The Traditional Content of the Plays of Wole Soyinka." In *African Literature Today*, ed. Eldred Durosimi Jones. Vols. 4–5, Part I: 4: 2–18; Part II: 5: 106–115. London: Heinemann, 1970–1971.

Okri, Ben. *Flowers and Shadows*. London: Longman, 1980.

Podis, Leonard A., and Yakubu Saaka. "*Anthills of the Savannah* and *Petals of Blood*: The Creation of a Usable Past." *Journal of Black Studies* 22 (1991): 104–122.

Porter, Bernard. *The Lion's Share: A Short History of British Imperialism, 1850–1983*. 2nd edition. London: Longman, 1984.

Rushdie, Salman. *Shame*. New York: Knopf, 1983.

Soyinka, Wole. *Death and the King's Horseman*. New York: Hill and Wang, 1975.

Tinker, Hugh. *Men Who Overturned Empires*. London: Macmillan, 1987.

Whitaker Jr., C. S. *The Politics of Tradition: Continuity and Change in Northern Nigeria, 1946–1966*. Princeton, NJ: Princeton University Press, 1970.

V

ENVISIONING SUCCESSFUL CHALLENGES:
SHAPES OF THE NEW ORDER

It is fitting, we believe, to conclude with a section that looks not to the past but to the future. The two essays that follow are both concerned with the attempts of African writers to envision alternatives to the repressive hierarchies associated with the colonial experience and its legacies.

In "*Anthills of the Savannah* and *Petals of Blood*: The Creation of a Usable Past" (a version of which appeared in *Journal of Black Studies* 22 [1991], 104–122), Leonard Podis and Yakubu Saaka discuss a confluence in the work of Achebe and Ngugi with regard to the value of traditional images in the reshaping of contemporary African culture. In *Anthills*, according to Podis and Saaka, Achebe puts forward the traditional figures of Idemili and the elder of Abazon, among other devices, as sources of inspiration for the regeneration of Kangan society. In so doing, they argue, his approach resembles that of Ngugi in *Petals of Blood*, in which Ndemi, Nyakinyua, and Theng'eta are the traditional sources upon which renewal is to be based. As we noted in the Introduction, *Anthills* and *Petals* are both intensely involved in envisioning alternatives to corrupt neo-colonial regimes, as well. Both novels are also steeped in a feminist consciousness, according to Podis and Saaka, an approach which was familiar in the works of Ngugi but new to Achebe with the publication of *Anthills*. (For differing views on the degree to which *Anthills* should be considered feminist, see Section II: A Critical Debate on Achebe's Depiction of Women.)

The final essay in our collection, Obioma Nnaemeka's "Marginality as the Third Term: A Reading of Kane's *Ambiguous Adventure*," offers a hopeful concluding note to this book. Rather than reading the condition of "other," or "third term" as that of loss, Nnaemeka sees the African's otherness as a site of gain. Particularly in light of the African (especially Igbo) worldview, she asserts, the position of "margin/periphery" is more properly seen as a "transcending [of] boundaries and not necessarily one that is circumscribed and diminished by the limits, edges, and boundaries." Rather than seeing the "third term" as inferior or "third rate," Nnaemeka elucidates a positive conceptualization of African otherness based on "thinking 'both . . . and' instead of 'either . . . or.'"

Such a radical revisioning of the meaning of this "ambiguous location," according to Nnaemeka, permits empowerment, seeing not "Shame. Danger. Loss." but rather "the possibilities and potential . . . where perpetual crossing is guaranteed and the finality of cross-over [is] denied."

Chapter 16

Anthills of the Savannah and Petals of Blood: The Creation of a Usable Past

Leonard A. Podis and Yakubu Saaka

The influence of the works of Chinua Achebe on those of Ngugi wa Thiong'o dates back to the early 1960s when Ngugi, in the wake of *Things Fall Apart*, recognized in Achebe a great novelist who had set about reclaiming the African past. Ngugi's first published novel, *Weep Not, Child*, while it focused on a much more recent past, none the less incorporated many of the features of *Things Fall Apart*: a title chosen from the work of a western canonical poet, a story line examining how things fell apart for a young Kenyan and his colonized society, and an ending in which the protagonist looks to suicide by hanging as a solution. In the years that followed, Ngugi was to exhibit some of Achebe's concerns in his own works, such as criticism of contemporary political corruption and repression and a desire to set the record straight by challenging western versions of African history. At the same time, however, Ngugi began to distance himself from the model set by Achebe, believing that Achebe, though critical both of western appropriation of African culture and of present-day corruption in government, did not provide sufficiently radical critiques of neocolonialism nor propose revolutionary solutions. By the time he published *Petals of Blood* in 1977, his own work had undergone what David Maughan-Brown (180) calls "a decisive ideological shift," creating a significant gap between his approach and that of Achebe. Ngugi's dissatisfaction with Achebe perhaps reached its height when, in *Decolonising the Mind*, he grouped Achebe with those whose use of a non-indigenous language constituted "a servile worship of what is foreign." (Ngugi 1986, 19)

With the publication of *Anthills of the Savannah*, however, we believe that the ideological gap between these two authors narrowed. Like Ngugi, Achebe turned his attention to the challenge of envisioning a radically new society out of the elements of a usable African past. Achebe's continued insistence on his belief in reform rather than revolution notwithstanding, *Anthills of the Savannah* indicates a movement in the direction of the views expressed by Ngugi in *Petals of Blood*. This essay compares Ngugi's 1977 novel with *Anthills of the Savannah* and suggests a confluence of vision on the part of two of Africa's greatest writers. As we will see, Achebe's book bears specific resemblances to Ngugi's work in the areas of plot, theme, character, narrative technique, feminist consciousness, and mythmaking vision.

Although *Petals of Blood* is not a product of Ngugi's current, most revolutionary phase, that in which he has completely abjured English for his native Gikuyu, it nonetheless offers a radical critique of Kenyan society, calling for a revolution based on the rediscovery of indigenous culture with its communal traditions. As Cook and Okenimkpe (113) observe, "Ngugi looks to the past to provide a meaningful continuum with the present and the future." In the words of another critic, *Petals of Blood* envisions a cultural "regeneration" that will "feed on the people's indigenous past." (Pagnoulle, 273) Similarly, in *Anthills of the Savannah*, Achebe appears to be identifying a usable base of tradition upon which to rebuild Kangan (presumably Nigerian) society. His previous works, some of which devoted themselves to reclaiming the past and others of which criticized the corruption of contemporary society, did not propose such a solution. As G. D. Killam noted after the appearance of *Petals of Blood* but prior to the publication of *Anthills of the Savannah*, Achebe did not view history as did Ngugi: "Achebe believes that history must be disposed of before he can look at the present." (Killam, 10) Although as early as 1969, Achebe began to see himself as a "protest writer," one who had "moved from criticizing his society to directly taking a hand in remolding it" (Ogungbesan, 40), such an activist view did not pervade his fictional works. However, with the publication of *Anthills*, Achebe appeared to take a new view of the value of history to the present and future. As we will see, both *Petals* and *Anthills* signal important attempts by their authors to reestablish the potency and relevance of African traditions as a source of value and stability for the future. Both authors see a new communality, based on traditional culture, as the most effective antidote to the decay, corruption, and alienation that afflict contemporary society.

Indeed, each work seems to represent a turning point in its author's career. For Ngugi, *Petals* is a pivotal book that stands simultaneously as the culmination of his development as a western-style esthetic novelist (Mamudu, 16) and as a new departure in his experiments with developing a more Afrocentric and a more neo-Marxist literary approach. For Achebe, *Anthills* is a work that attempts to activate the values embodied in his historical books on Igbo society in the service of solving the problems examined in his books on contemporary Nigerian society. It is also a watershed in its positive emphasis on the role of women as central to cultural regeneration, an emphasis that further brings Achebe in line with Ngugi's views.

To be sure, there are many differences between *Anthills of the Savannah* and *Petals of Blood*. In general, Ngugi's book is a vaster, more sprawling narrative, covering a much longer period of time and presenting a more comprehensive series of events. It is more a novel of character, examining the major figures in great psychological depth, whereas Achebe's book is somewhat more stylized and selective in presentation, depicting even the central characters more as symbolic types, as people whose actions are essentially representative of values embodied by the narrative as whole, not necessarily of unique personality traits. Yet despite Ngugi's greater attention to character, some of the figures in his novel, particularly the villains, are drawn more one-dimensionally. They are the sorts of characters that have prompted Gerald Moore to lament the tendency of African fiction to "erect cardboard 'baddies' who are never anything but bad." (Moore, 284) By contrast, the "villains" in *Anthills* (mainly the government officials) are generally not the absolute incarnations of evil that their counterparts tend to be in *Petals*. At the same time, Achebe remains more suspicious of human nature in general, failing to grant the idealistic goodness of the masses that characterizes Ngugi's vision. Finally, despite some similarities in narrative technique which we cite below, it is important to note that the point of view in *Petals of Blood* is situated in a lower socioeconomic class than in *Anthills of the Savannah*. Ngugi, in keeping with his Marxist orientation, situates the point of view nearer the base of the anthill, unlike Achebe, who has located it at the peak, in the ruling elite of Kangan.

Still, for all the differences one might note, it is instructive to examine Achebe's book for its strong and numerous affinities with *Petals of Blood*, reading *Anthills* as a kind of variation on a theme. At a very general level, like many contemporary African novels, both works emphasize the pervasiveness of political and social corruption in their respective countries, Kenya and Kangan. At a more specific literary and structural level, there are striking plot similarities: the existence in both books of delegations seeking drought relief, the presence of the uplifting traditional rituals of Theng'eta in *Petals* and kolanut in *Anthills*, and the conclusion of each novel with either an actual or impending childbirth. Indeed, in both books, much of the narrative centers on the relationships among a small circle of acquaintances who spend their time socializing, confessing their pasts, planning political strategy, and attempting to forge a community. There is even some resemblance between the major characters of each book, Ikem corresponding roughly to Karega, Chris to Munira, and Beatrice to Wanja. Moreover, in both works, it is women that stand at the core of the community. Additionally, in creating their network of characters, both authors have exploited the idea of the elitist old school connection, Munira, Karega, and Chui having all attended Siriana and Chris, Ikem, and Sam, His Excellency, having attended Lord Lugard College. Even in the choice of titles, there is a certain similarity, both authors having selected unsettling metaphorical images from nature to serve as a form of commentary on societal problems.

From the standpoint of technique, the works are similar in that both embody multiple points of view, projecting a series of separate voices that together constitute a communal voice. Thematically, too, both novels express, and attempt to resolve, a complex ambivalence towards sociocultural modernization, recognizing its powerful appeal, but criticizing it for its association with corruption and for its ill fit with traditional values and contemporary cultural needs. The duality of the modern and the traditional is prominent in both works, as in the case of Wanja in *Petals of Blood,* the "barmaid farmer" (Ngugi 1977, 61) who vacillates between her role of barmaid/prostitute and her role as agrarian earth-mother, and Beatrice in *Anthills of the Savannah*, who alternates between her pose as a wisecracking westernized sophisticate and her role as "village priestess." (Achebe, 96)

We will begin our more detailed comparison of the two books by returning to the three plot similarities briefly mentioned above—similarities which would appear to be more than coincidental. It is striking that in *Anthills of the Savannah* Achebe rests much of the narrative complication on a plot detail that echoes a similar plot development in *Petals of Blood*, namely the circumstances surrounding a delegation sent to the capital city from a drought-stricken, outlying region. In both instances the mission is composed of worthy citizens intent on informing officials of the dire circumstances back home. In both instances these admirable supplicants are accorded a rude reception, receiving insensitive treatment and even imprisonment for their pains. And in both instances the delegation's mission serves as a catalyst to bring about a violent climax to the action. In *Petals of Blood*, the visit from the Ilmorogians sets in motion the chain of events that "brings the beast down to Ilmorog" (Pagnoulle, 269), leading to the creation of new Ilmorog and its dispossession of the common people, the cooptation of Theng'eta, the negative transformation of Wanja, and the ultimate destruction of the oppressors, Chui, Mzigo, and Kimeria.

In *Anthills of the Savannah*, the visit by the delegation from Abazon takes on an even more central role, figuring in the action from start to finish. The visit serves as the catalyst for a series of reactions that precipitate the self-destruction of the Kangan government. As in *Petals* the authorities respond inappropriately, essentially ignoring the real purpose of the delegation, attempting to interpret the visit in terms of their own preconceptions and goals. While the reader knows the purity of the delegation's motives, the government imputes hostility and rebelliousness to the travelers, casting them as disloyal and aggressive, and arresting them. In *Anthills*, members of the delegation are reviled as part of a conspiracy, supposedly orchestrated by Ikem, to overthrow the regime. Once they are detained, Ikem delivers the speech that results in his arrest for supposedly advocating regicide; his arrest leads to his murder by security officers, which in turn motivates behavior by Chris that ultimately helps bring about the coup.

The second important plot element in *Anthills of the Savannah* which would seem to allude to *Petals of Blood* is the presentation of the ritual surrounding the naming of Elewa's and Ikem's daughter. The aura surrounding this ceremony and the function it serves in consolidating the characters into a close-knit community are reminiscent of the Theng'eta ritual in *Petals of Blood*. This mystical ceremony, presided over by Nyakinyua, fills the night "with the power of bloodnearness." (Ngugi 1977, 228) It infuses the pure of heart with positive energy and forges strong bonds of community, creating the "sense of a common destiny, a collective spirit." (240) In particular, Karega finds himself transported and transformed by the ritual. Similarly, in *Anthills*, the naming ceremony unites "all the company" present in Beatrice's "whiteman house." (Achebe, 210–211) The spiritually uplifting effect of the ceremony presided over by Beatrice and Elewa's uncle is most apparent in the reaction of Abdul, the officer of the repressive state security agency: "Abdul, a relative stranger to the kolanut ritual, was carried away beyond the accustomed limits of choral support right into exuberant hand-clapping." (212)

A third plot similarity is apparent in the endings of both books. One of the most hopeful signs for the future in *Petals of Blood* is the revelation, in the last chapter, that Wanja is pregnant, aware of "the stirrings of a new person." (Ngugi 1977, 337) As she sketches the father of her baby in order to reveal his identity to her mother, she becomes transfixed by the task: "[L]ifted out of her own self, she felt waves of emotion she had never before experienced." (338) Once she finishes the drawing of Abdulla, she feels "a tremendous calm, a kind of inner assurance of the possibilities of a new kind of power." (338) Amid the misery and disappointments that have nearly engulfed the characters by the end of the book, this occurrence brings a sense of promise for the future. Similarly, amid the sadness at the end of *Anthills of the Savannah*, with the violent deaths of Ikem, Chris, and even Sam, the birth of Elewa's daughter, fathered by Ikem, is a key event that provides a sense of redemption and strikes a positive note. Indeed, it is Elewa's pregnancy that first revives Beatrice, the "priest struck dumb for a season by the almighty" (Achebe, 204), from the "total devastation" of her grief over the loss of Chris. The beginning of her return to her rightful place at the center of the community occurs on "the morning of Elewa's threatened miscarriage" (202), as she is called on to act. Although the last chapter starts with a grim description of "a baby born into deprivation" (201), it concludes with the inspirational naming ceremony that solidifies the community and orients it towards a more positive future, centered on the child proclaimed to be "the daughter of all of us." (211)

The three plot similarities just discussed are further significant in that they are all connected, in both novels, to the central attempt of the authors to show the regeneration of community based on indigenous roots. As critics have noted, the journey from Ilmorog to Nairobi results in "a definite heightening of communal militant awareness." (Pagnoulle, 269) It begins with the recognition that "the crisis was a community crisis needing a communal response." (Ngugi 1977, 123) Moreover, the sense of common purpose, the sharing of hardships of travel, and the exposure to the indignities of their reception in Nairobi create even stronger bonds of solidarity. The specific link to the past is created by the group's connection with the tradition of Ndemi, founder of Ilmorog, a connection that is reinforced by the role of Nyakinyua. With Nyakinyua as their "guiding spirit" (Cook and Okenimkpe, 93), the delegation sets out, in the spirit of Ndemi, to fight for what is theirs. Ngugi, who has shown previous interest in founding legends (for example, the Gikuyu founding legend in the *The River Between*) has apparently incorporated the Ndemi story in *Petals of Blood* to emphasize the possibility of reinvigorating such a tradition as a response to contemporary problems.

In *Anthills of the Savannah*, the visit of the delegation serves a similar purpose. Although the book doesn't focus principally on the community of the travelers, since its main concern is with the group of characters in Bassa, it does emphasize the galvanizing effect of the delegation's presence on the formation of community among the other characters.

In *Anthills*, Achebe dwells on the legend of Idemili, daughter of the almighty, who is sent on a mission to restore order among the people (Achebe, 93), and who, significantly, relieves the drought that has plagued "parched settlements all the way to Orimili." (94) Much as Nyakinyua channels the spirit of Ndemi in *Petals*, the "bearded old man" in the delegation from Abazon perpetuates the tradition of Idemili in *Anthills*. The central link with community and tradition in this instance is the magnificent oration of this elder member of the delegation (112–118), whose stories are "reminders from which future generations can learn." (Innes, 163) Reviving the spirit of the past in his skilled use of proverbs and storytelling, the elder energizes the company, which includes Ikem, and thus helps pave the way for the climactic action of the novel. More specifically, one of the elder's main emphases is on the value of the *writer*, a non-traditional role, but one which he links to tradition by connecting Ikem's occupation with the figure of the storyteller. Appropriately, the elder himself "do [es] not know ABC" (Achebe, 112–113), yet through the elder's oration Achebe is able to establish the writer as a contemporary agent of change who is firmly rooted in an indigenous tradition. Fittingly, the elder's consummate skill in the use of proverbs, appearing as it does at the heart of Achebe's novel, reinforces the power of this vision. It is further noteworthy that the use of oral narrative serves a similar function in the journey in *Petals of Blood*. As preparations for the trek begin, Abdulla emerges from his previous lethargy and uncertainty to become once again the hero of the forest, and one of the signs of his regeneration is his ability to tell traditional stories effectively. (Ngugi 1977, 116–117)

In much the same way, the second and third plot similarities discussed earlier are relevant to the authors' views on the uses of tradition. Indeed, they need less explication than did the function of the delegations because they are more self-evidently concerned with links between past and future. The Theng'eta and naming rituals are both traditional rites that emphasize community in such a way as to prepare the members ultimately to face the future with greater resourcefulness. The fact that both ceremonies have such a strong impact on particular members of the group attests to the continuing power and usefulness of the past. As one critic has noted, the Theng'eta ceremony is an attempt both "to recapture the spirit of the past" and "to renew a sense of unity among the participants." (Johnson, 12–13) Although the community initially created is subsequently fragmented due to Theng'eta's being "abused and commercialized" by the capitalist appropriation of the drink, the ceremony nonetheless functions to convey "an indication of new resolve" (13, 15) that is built squarely on the foundations of tradition. Likewise, the birth of children to members of the community at the end of both novels works by invoking a universal symbol of hope and regeneration, childbirth, and then employing it within a context that suggests that the most promising type of future is that which is born from a present infused by tradition.

Another prominent similarity between *Anthills of the Savannah* and *Petals of Blood* lies in the casts of characters, especially in the major figures that constitute the primary communities examined in each book. As we noted earlier, three of Ngugi's main characters, Munira, Karega, and Wanja are roughly reflected by Achebe's characters, Chris, Ikem, and Beatrice. The similarities are numerous. For example, like Chris and Ikem in *Anthills*, Munira and Karega have been educated in prestigious British colonial schools. All the central figures in *Petals* are, in essence, exiles in Ilmorog, expatriates in their own country. By the same token, the main characters of Achebe's novel might be said to exist in a state of spiritual exile. Despite their membership in the governing elite, they are alienated and disenchanted. Like Ngugi's main characters, they spend time together discussing ways of changing the status quo, hoping to alter society both to improve the lot of the people and to help create a new order, one in which they can envision themselves as fully integrated participants.

We begin our more systematic comparison of the characters by examining Ikem and Karega because, despite their differences in status, they are linked by a spirit of social progressivism. Both could certainly be called ideologues, crusaders for the improvement of society and the quality of life for the populace. Although Ikem has a worldly-wise quality that urges him to reject the sort of doctrinaire prescriptions and "simplistic remedies" (Achebe, 90) that so often appeal to Karega (as when Ikem deplores a possible "democratic dictatorship of mediocrity" [148] in his speech at the university), he is, like Karega, fundamentally a man of the people. His assessments of Kangan's problems, for example, echo Karega's analyses of Kenya's woes. Reflecting on the "prime failure of this government," he muses: "It is the failure of our rulers to reestablish vital inner links with the poor and dispossessed of this country, with the bruised heart that throbs painfully at the core of the nation's being." (131) There is an affinity here to the speech of Karega, who frequently deplores the acts of the ruling elite, as in this complaint about the misguided philosophy behind the tea parties: "And what do we do with people who are hungry and jobless, who can't pay school fees, shall we make them drink a tinful of oath and cry unity? How easy . . . why, there should then be no problems in Ilmorog, and in all the other forgotten areas and places in Kenya." (Ngugi 1977, 112)

Beyond their political crusading, Ikem and Karega share a similar regard for traditional culture and see it as playing a crucial role in any positively transformed society of the future. Karega, early in *Petals of Blood,* is virtually obsessed with knowing the past, approaching such matters as tales of the Land Freedom Army's exploits with an eager reverence. Later, he is the community member most profoundly transported by the Theng'eta ceremony. It is Karega who ultimately leads the strike that will attempt to reestablish Theng'eta as a force to be controlled by the people. Ikem, too, despite his status as a modern reformer, reveres traditional ways. His presence at the elder's rousing oration, an oration that serves in large part to honor and defend Ikem's role, is one indication of this connection to tradition. There are also more overt indications. For instance, at his university address, Ikem tells the crowd: "May I remind you that our ancestors—by the way you must never underrate those guys; some of you seem too ready to do so, I'm afraid. Well, our ancestors made a fantastic proverb on remote and immediate causes." (Achebe, 146) Clearly, if one were to identify the authors' political mouthpieces in these two novels, one would have to single out Karega and Ikem. Just as Karega comes closest to expressing Ngugi's political beliefs, so Ikem seems to speak most directly for Achebe's politics. While Karega and Ikem are not the absolute *spiritual* centers of the novels, that honor being accorded to women characters in both instances, they do tend to speak for the authors politically.

If Karega and Ikem are the ideological spokesmen in the two novels, their friends Munira and Chris might be thought of as their foils in this capacity. In each case, as character foils they serve to highlight the ideological spokesperson's views and actions by deviating from or opposing the more "politically correct" course of action. In their relationships to Ikem and Karega, respectively, Chris and Munira both demonstrate resistance to the more radical courses of action that their friends wish to pursue. In *Anthills of the Savannah*, Chris constantly urges Ikem to proceed more cautiously with his crusading editorials, counseling Ikem that such militant behavior will only provoke a repressive response from His Excellency. Likewise, in *Petals of Blood,* Munira finds Karega's idealistic educational reforms too radical, and urges Karega to be more conservative. Significantly, in both books the more conservative character foil is also placed in the position of being the more radical ideologue's superior. As headmaster of the Ilmorog Primary School, Munira is Karega's boss. As commissioner of information, Chris is essentially Ikem's boss.

That Chris rises to the challenge of taking meaningful political action by the end of the novel while Munira does not (albeit Munira's crazed act of arson does have potentially desirable political outcomes) is a significant difference between the two characters, but one that shouldn't obscure other basic similarities. Essentially, besides being foils for the central ideologues, Munira and Chris both function as conflicted, ambivalent fence-sitters, the sorts of "everyman" figures with which a typical reader might identify. The sense in which these figures represent the "average" person does not rest on socioeconomic or occupational status but on the issue of political courage. Karega and Ikem have made their choices: They represent that relatively small group committed to radical involvement. But Munira and Chris, by contrast, are characterized by the kinds of doubts and indecision that more typically plague the gen-

eral population. Should they disengage themselves and ride
out the storm, as Munira is so intent on doing, or should they
become involved and make a stand, even if it is a futile stand,
in the name of justice?

In examining the third pair of characters, Wanja and
Beatrice, we wish to place our discussion in the context of another important similarity between *Anthills of the Savannah* and
Petals of Blood: namely that both works emphasize the central
role of women in the regeneration of society. Such an approach
to depicting women represents a new departure for Achebe,
further suggesting a confluence with the views of Ngugi. While
Ngugi has long been recognized as a writer who portrays
women as central figures, Achebe has generally been viewed
as one who casts women as secondary to men. Carole Boyce
Davies, editor of *Ngambika*, an influential critical anthology
on women in African literature, speaks directly to this matter.
She identifies Ngugi as "probably the most brilliant example"
of "African men who challenge the traditional social and political dominance of patriarchy and who support women's issues. . . ." (Davies 1986a, 11) By contrast with those male writers guilty of "locking women into postures of dependence and
. . . defining women only in terms of their association with
men" (14), Davies believes Ngugi has shown the way towards
"accurate portrayals and ones which suggest . . . transcen-
dence." (15) Achebe, she believes, is one of those other male
writers: "his primary concern is woman's place within man's
experience and man's lone struggle with larger social and political forces. While Achebe's works are obvious classics within
the African literary tradition, a re-examination of his work from
a feminist position reveals woman as peripheral to the larger
exploration of man's experience." (Davies 1986b, 247)

Perhaps Davies' assessment of Achebe's work was correct
prior to the appearance of *Anthills of the Savannah*. However,
the depiction of women in *Anthills* suggests an important shift
in Achebe's practices. Like Wanja, the "barmaid farmer" of
Petals of Blood, Beatrice, who is possessed of a similarly divided
consciousness, stands at the spiritual center of the novel in
which she appears. Wanja's centrality to *Petals* probably needs
little discussion. She is the source of strength that helps hold
the community together. As Cook and Okenimkpe note, it is

she "who will link together the straying, alienated characters of the story, and will animate both their energies and desires." (Cook and Okenimkpe, 95) Significantly, the first meeting of Munira, Karega, Abdulla and Wanja occurs in Wanja's hut (Ngugi 1977, 60), not, for instance, in the more likely location of Abdulla's shop. It is Wanja's energy and benign influence that suffuse old Ilmorog. She revives Abdulla's shop, becoming "the life and major attraction in the place" (74), she helps Nyakinyua with the harvest, she sets Joseph on the path to an education, and she even temporarily revitalizes Munira. Not surprisingly, when she suddenly grows restless and cynical and leaves Ilmorog (75–78), things deteriorate. The centrality of Wanja's role is further underscored by the fact that an earlier version of the novel was apparently titled *Ballad of a Barmaid*. (Bardolph, 53)

Whereas Wanja follows a line of women characters who have been influential in Ngugi's fiction, such as Mwihaki, Nyambura, Muthoni, Mumbi and Wambuku, Beatrice ("BB"), as we have suggested, represents a new direction for Achebe. Like Wanja in *Petals*, "BB" serves as the center of the community depicted in *Anthills*. She is the person in whom both Ikem and Chris confide; she is Elewa's source of comfort when Ikem is killed, and, with Abdul's aid, it is she who assists Chris in evading the security police. After Chris's death, Beatrice's apartment becomes the meeting place for the new community that is formed. It is there that the naming ceremony occurs. Complementing these facts of Beatrice's involvement in the community is Achebe's portrayal of her as the heart and soul of the novel. In connecting her directly to Idemili and in designating her a "village priestess," Achebe underscores his conception of her spiritual importance.

Of course Beatrice is not only a priestess, just as Wanja is not only a farmer. Just as Wanja has an antithetical side that opposes her more positive spiritual character, so too does Beatrice. Her alter ego is that of the skeptical, westernized sophisticate. Her fulfillment of this role is evident in her position as senior assistant secretary in the ministry of finance, and in her unique background, which His Excellency takes pains to highlight for the American journalist: BB is "the only person in the service, male or female, with a first-class honours in English. And not from a local university but from Queen Mary College, University of London." (Achebe, 68) Perhaps more important, Beatrice's own narrative voice reveals her to be a modern, westernized woman, particularly in the irreverent, almost jaded sensibility she projects. In direct contrast to her function as traditional priestess and goddess, she repeatedly denigrates the ways of her countrymen, at least in her private thoughts. At Sam's dinner party, for example, she haughtily observes that "the wines were excellent but totally wasted on the company." (70) Later she somewhat arrogantly contrasts Ikem's "string of earthy girlfriends" with the more sophisticated "yours truly." (109) While relating the story of one of her own girlfriends, she ridicules the behavior of that woman's fiancé's family, who live "in some backwater village." (81) In this instance, as elsewhere, she generally disapproves of the use of traditional proverbs, noting that the fiancé's aunt insults BB's girlfriend with an inane proverb. In this vein, she dismisses traditional "nonsense talk," sayings such as "Better to marry a rascal than grow a mustache in your father's compound" along with "a whole baggage of other foolishnesses like that." (80) She even makes light of the role of priestess in which Achebe has cast her, quipping to Chris when he asks whether she has slept, "'Priestesses don't sleep.'" (104) In BB's cynical undercutting both of traditional cultural elements and of her own more spiritual role, there appears to be an echo of Wanja's iconoclastic impulses. One day Wanja toils selflessly in the fields, the next she cynically and savagely lashes out, issuing "a stream of invectives and ceaseless complaints" (Ngugi 1977, 75), indulging in "bitter, ironic laughter" (75), and dismissing Ilmorog as a "wretched hole." (77)

Like Wanja, Beatrice is not genuinely opposed to tradition, but has been made restless and dissatisfied by the frustration and injustices that attend living in what she perceives to be a schizophrenic culture that often confronts people (especially women) with the worst of both the traditional and the modern. As we have seen, Beatrice at times ridicules proverbs, seeming to prefer metaphors in the western tradition, as when she refers to a peripheral dinner guest as someone "having no greater will for social courtesies than a standby generator has to produce electricity when the mains are performing satisfactorily." (Achebe, 71) Yet, there are times when Beatrice herself uses traditional sayings in all seriousness, as when she asks, "Haven't our people said that a totally reasonable wife is always pregnant?" (81) A good deal of her skepticism seems to stem from her feminist attitudes, which urge her to be wary of traditional ways. Like Wanja (Ngugi 1977, 38), Beatrice grew up in a household where she was beaten (Achebe, 78), and she prides herself on rejecting "male chauvinist bullshit." (80) She rejects the view that both the oppression of women and the impulse towards feminism are solely foreign importations, aspects of the colonial legacy: "You often hear our people say: But that's something you picked up in England. Absolute rubbish! There was enough male chauvinism in my father's house to last me seven reincarnations." (81)

Beatrice's mistrust of traditional patriarchy is perhaps most fittingly expressed in her response to her parents' having named her Nwanyibuife: "Nwanyibuife—A female is also something. Can you beat that? Even as a child I disliked the name most intensely without being aware of its real meaning." (Achebe, 79) In creating a central female character for the first time, especially one with the name of Nwanyibuife and one so sensitive to the injustices of traditional patriarchal society, Achebe would appear to be making a self-conscious reference to his own history of treating women characters as peripheral. As we have noted, Ikem tends to serve as Achebe's political spokesman, and his evolving views on the role of women are much discussed in the novel. During her narration, BB cites the lack of a "clear role for women in his political thinking" as "the chink in his armoury of brilliant and original ideas." (83) When Ikem tries to defend himself as an author who devoted a full-length novel and a play to "the Women's War of 1929," BB dismisses Ikem's work as an inadequate attempt to turn to women as a "last resort." (84) However, as BB notes, Ikem began to change "near the end," acknowledging that whatever the "new role for Women will be. . . . *You* [women] have to tell us." (90) In this highly self-conscious debate about the need for Ikem-as-author to change his views on women, Achebe would seem to be making a barely veiled reference to his own controversial record on women's issues and signaling a desire to move towards the type of greater feminist consciousness associated with Ngugi.

Another major literary technique that connects Achebe's *Anthills of the Savannah* to Ngugi's *Petals of Blood* is the use of narrative point of view. Both works make use of multiple points of view in order to project the sense of the many voices that, taken together, constitute the whole community. Critics have generally acknowledged that Ngugi experiments with narration in *Petals of Blood* in order to achieve such an effect. Although Lisa Curtis (199) asserts that "Ngugi is unable to sustain the collective narrative voice" successfully, most critics praise his achievement. For example, Christine Abdelkrim (43) notes that despite what initially appears to be an "anarchic" quality to the narration, Ngugi ultimately achieves "an extraordinary coherence and unity." Peter Nazareth (120) has observed that the book solidifies Ngugi's stature as a "village writer," with Nyakinyua in particular functioning "like a *griot*" narrating "the story of the village." René Cerpana (29) likewise invokes the image of the *griot*: "Ngugi appears as a modern 'griot' who is true to his self-appointed mission and faithful to his people." Aya Mamudu (19) specifically relates Ngugi's narrative technique to the idea of tradition and its role in the shaping of community: "For the larger purpose of *Petals of Blood* the interconnections of past, present and future on a communal scale are stressed. Narratively, this purpose dictates the use of multiple points of view . . . so as to emphasize the entwined complexities of the realities, facts or events which cumulatively constitute the history of a people." Mamudu also discusses the function of the "chief narrator," who is sometimes an omniscient voice, other times "an individual observer/ participant ('I')" and still other times "a member of the participant group ('we')." According to Mamudu, this overarching narrator is, among other things, "the invisible recorder of folk history, the embodied voice of the group." (Mamudu, 19) Cerpana (6) also devotes some attention to the presence of the narrative "we" that appears from time to time: "the different 'we's' represent the people living around the heroes and also the former generations. They stand for the collective presence, the communal spirit in this African novel. But they also bring in their own vision of the truth, the popular voice of numerous witnesses."

It is noteworthy that Cerpana refers to the "witnesses" that contribute to the construction of Ngugi's narrative, for in *Ant-*

hills of the Savannah Achebe heads some of his chapters by identifying the narrators as witnesses. In particular, Chapter One is titled "First Witness—Christopher Oriko" (Achebe, 1) and Chapter Four is titled "Second Witness—Ikem Osodi." (31) The narration of *Anthills* is striking not only because it is multifaceted and diffused among various characters but because none of Achebe's previous works features what might be called an experimental narrative technique. *Things Fall Apart, No Longer at Ease, Arrow of God*, and *A Man of the People* have all employed rather conventional approaches. Thus Achebe's decision to experiment with diffusing point of view in *Anthills* carries unusual significance. Once again the fact that Achebe has chosen a method that seems to echo Ngugi's approach suggests a convergence of vision between the two writers. In *Anthills* Achebe appears to be experimenting with a narrative scheme that will be commensurate with his vision of the creation of a new cultural order. Like Ngugi in *Petals of Blood*, he uses multiple points of view to reinforce his conviction that this new order will be communal, not individualistic, in nature.

In this respect, we might consider that both books function in their own right as founding legends that stand as explanations of, and exhortations toward, the promised new communal order. Both Ngugi and Achebe can, in short, be seen as engaging in a sort of mythmaking activity that draws on earlier indigenous mythmaking. Their own regard for founding legends, that of Ilmorog in the Ndemi story and that of Abazon in Ikem's "Hymn to the Sun," is reflected in their attempts to create a new type of founding legend for their troubled societies in the form of their very own fictions. In these new founding legends, there is no single specific hero like Ndemi; rather there is a whole community headed by people like Wanja and Karega, Beatrice and Ikem. Just as Ndemi and the founders of Abazon overcame the challenges they confronted, so too will the revitalized Kenyan and Kangan people prevail, and each of these books gives its particular version of how the triumph they will know originated. In these fictionalized constructs of the African past and present Ngugi and Achebe have clearly begun the creation of a usable past, a creation that may have a profound effect on the further development of African history and culture.

Works Cited

Abdelkrim, Christine. "*Petals of Blood*: Story, Narrative, Discourse." *Echos du Commonwealth* 6 (1980–1981): 37–51.

Achebe, Chinua. *Anthills of the Savannah*. New York: Doubleday, 1987.

Bardolph, J. "Fertility in *Petals of Blood*." *Echos du Commonwealth* 6 (1980–1981): 53–83.

Cerpana, René. "History and Literature: Narration and Time in *Petals of Blood* by Ngugi wa Thiong'o." *Echos du Commonwealth* 6 (1980–1981): 1–36.

Cook, David, and Michael Okenimkpe. *Ngugi wa Thiong'o: An Exploration of His Writings*. London: Heinemann, 1983.

Curtis, Lisa. "The Divergence of Art and Ideology in the Later Novels of Ngugi wa Thiong'o: A Critique." *Ufahamu* 13 (1984): 186–213.

Davies, Carole Boyce. "Introduction: Feminist Consciousness and African Literary Criticism." In *Ngambika: Studies of Women in African Literature*, edited by Carole Boyce Davies and Anne Adams Graves. Trenton, NJ: Africa World Press, 1986a: 1–23.

———. "Motherhood in the Work of Male and Female Igbo Writers: Achebe, Emecheta, Nwapa and Nzekwu." In *Ngambika: Studies of Women in African Literature*, edited by Carole Boyce Davies and Anne Adams Graves. Trenton, NJ: Africa World Press, 1986b: 241–256.

Innes, C. L. *Chinua Achebe*. Cambridge: Cambridge University Press, 1990.

Johnson, J. "A Note on 'Theng'eta' in Ngugi wa Thiong'o's *Petals of Blood*." *World Literature Written in English* 28 (1988): 12–15.

Killam, G. D. *An Introduction to the Writings of Ngugi*. London: Heinemann, 1980.

Mamudu, Aya. "Tracing a Winding Stair: Ngugi's Narrative Methods in *Petals of Blood*." *World Literature Written in English* 28 (1988): 16–25.

Maughan-Brown, David. "Four Sons of One Father: A Comparison of Ngugi's Earliest Novels with Works by Mwangi, Mangua, and Wachira." *Research in African Literatures* 16 (1985): 179–209.

Moore, Gerald. *Twelve African Writers*. Bloomington, IN: Indiana University Press, 1980.

Nazareth, Peter. "The Second Homecoming: Multiple Ngugis in *Petals of Blood*." In *Marxism and African Literature*, edited by Georg Gugelberger. London: James Currey, 1985: 118–129.

Ngugi wa Thiong'o. *Petals of Blood*. London: Heinemann, 1977.

————. *Decolonising the Mind: The Politics of Language in African Literature*. London: James Currey, 1986.

Ogungbesan, K. "Politics and the African writer." In *Critical Perspectives on Chinua Achebe*, edited by C. L. Innes and Bernth Lindfors. Washington, D.C.: Three Continents, 1978: 37–46.

Pagnoulle, Christine. "Ngugi wa Thiong'o's 'Journey of the Magi': Part 2 of *Petals of Blood*." *Research in African Literatures* 16 (1985): 264–275.

Chapter 17

Marginality as the Third Term:
A Reading of Kane's
Ambiguous Adventure

Obioma Nnaemeka

We must try to remember what the rainclouds will never forget.
—Acklyn Lynch

When something stands, something stands beside it.
—Igbo proverb

A man who wails is not a dancing bear.
—Aimé Césaire

Part I of the television series, *The Africans*, begins with two juxtaposed images—different in form but fundamentally similar in their paradox and complexity—slowly rising to our view: man/the narrator and object/a milepost. These two images are juxtaposed on a grassy knoll behind which flows the sea of time, generations of time. The man, an embodiment of multiple identities, moves forward and embraces the other symbol of multiplicity, the milepost, with its many arms pointing to different directions, from Lusaka to Cape Town, from Harare to Mecca. Unity in diversity. The man articulates the paradox of space:

To me, this place captures the essential paradox of Africa's location. You know, it's the most central of all the continents of the world. Not far from here, the equator cuts the African continent into two almost equal halves. No other region of the world is traversed by the equator in quite that manner. It is the middle continent by any standard; sitting next to what the Europeans call the Middle East. And yet the majority of our people have lived in relative historical isolation in their villages. And now, colonialism and underdevelopment have added to our problems. This most central of all continents has been pushed to the very periphery of world affairs. For the Africans, this need not be so; it hasn't always been so. (Mazrui)

The title and subtitle of the series, *The Africans: A Triple Heritage*, are flashed on the screen.

This television series examines the congruence of space and history; it is "the epic story of how geography can be the mother of history." The subtitle captures the essence of the complex drama that unfolds. As the narrator affirms, "The geography of my birth made me a walking example of three cultures: Africa's triple heritage." This triple heritage is lived simultaneously at different levels—culturally (traditional Africa/Islam/ the West) and linguistically (Kiswahili/Arabic/English). The story is an exploration of paradox, center/margin dyad, the power to name, and history. Above all, the story provides a site where the convergence of the politics of location and identity politics is rooted in the politics of history/memory loss.

To a certain extent, the complex journey of Ali Mazrui, the narrator of the documentary, is similar to the ambiguous adventure of Samba Diallo, the protagonist of Cheikh Hamidou Kane's novel, *Ambiguous Adventure*. The intensity of the dilemma of living three legacies is generated by the simultaneity of the experiencing. Yet Samba Diallo does not live three *distinct* legacies; rather, he experiences the point of convergence of a triple heritage. Like the milepost, Samba Diallo is at a crossroads. Just as Africa, by the accident of history, is "pushed to the very periphery of world affairs," Samba Diallo is pushed to the periphery; but more specifically, he is located at the juncture/congruence of peripheries. Like the patches of a quilt, the components of Samba Diallo's history are simultaneously separate and linked, exposing patches of history whose contours and boundaries are touching, but whose separate geographies are easily discernible.

To live at the periphery is to experience the vertigo and precariousness of the precipice. V. Y. Mudimbe correctly captures the liminality of this marginal site, which he designates as an ambiguous space:

Marginality designates the intermediate space between the so-called African tradition and the projected modernity of colonialism. It is apparently an urbanized space in which, as S. Amin noted, "vestiges of the past, especially the survival of structures that are still living realities . . . often continue to hide the new structures." This space reveals not so much that new imperatives could achieve a jump into modernity, as the fact that despair gives this intermediate space its precarious pertinence and, simultaneously, its dangerous importance. (Mudimbe, 5)

The pain, despair, and disease of the margin emanate, on the one hand, from the intensity of experiencing simultaneously the conflicting elements of paradox and, on the other hand, from the objectification and impotence that subtend being named. Confusion is symptomatic of the challenge of the ambiguous space or what Trinh T. Minh-ha calls "the challenge of the hyphen." (Trinh 1990) Although Samba Diallo is confused, he is clearheaded enough to articulate the discomfort and dilemma of simultaneous experiencing:

> I am not a distinct country of the Diallobé facing a distinct Occident, and appreciating with a cool head what I must take from it and what I must leave with it by way of counterbalance. I have become the two. There is not a clear mind deciding between the two factors of a choice. There is a strange nature, in distress over not being two. (Kane, 50–151)

Installed in an ambiguous space, Samba Diallo is no longer *a* or *b* but more than *a* or *b*. The margin is paradoxically a site of loss and gain; a site where one loses in order to gain. But the troubling question remains: Why is this ambiguous space always viewed as a site of loss, impotence, and disenfranchisement instead of as a location of gain, contestation, and empowerment? This is the question that this paper seeks to address.

Ambiguous Adventure narrates simultaneously the dilemma of Samba Diallo as well as that of Cheikh Hamidou Kane, a westernized African writing an African story. The African worldview celebrates the complementarity of contiguous realities in the universe. The Igbo believe that "when something stands, something stands beside it." By insisting on the word "beside" instead of "before/behind/above/under," the Igbo concept of duality differs from the conflicting and hierarchical paradigm that is grounded in the privileging of the Cartesian *cogito*. The Igbo believe that whatever stands/exists is a lack and needs the other thing beside it to achieve fullness.

Man and woman are not in conflict but rather mutually complement and empower each other. The Igbo will in all likelihood say "beside (not behind) every successful man is a woman." The same could be said for the image of the "eagle on *iroko*" that is etched on the Igbo imagination. The beauty of the eagle is admired and appreciated because it is held high and visible by the strength, height, and majesty of the *iroko* tree. Conversely, the beauty of the *iroko* derives partially from the beauty and elegance of the eagle that is perched on it. For the Igbo, and Africans in general, contiguity means mutual gain and empowerment. They embrace the theology of nearness. This way of thinking differs markedly from the Cartesian paradigm where opposites are structured vertically—the paradigm of power and oppression—or in psychoanalytical theory and practice, from Freud to Lacan, where the woman, as lack, is subaltern.

From the foregoing, one can speculate that an Igbo/African mind writing Samba Diallo's story would in all likelihood write a different story; a happier story where the different components of the triple heritage will be mutually empowering: a story of struggle but also a story of triumph. It seems to me that in telling the story of life in the margin/periphery, the Igbo would in all likelihood tell the story of a life transcending boundaries and not necessarily one that is circumscribed and diminished by limits, edges, or boundaries. This way of thinking, "both . . . and" instead of "either . . . or," is best exemplified by Thierno's conclusion at the end of his story of the gourd:

> "The gourd is of a droll nature," the teacher went on after a long pause. "When young, it has no other vocation then to achieve weight, no other desire than to attach itself lovingly to the earth. It finds the perfect realization of itself in weight. Then one day everything changes. The gourd wants to take flight. It reabsorbs itself, hollows itself out, as much as it can. Its happiness is a function of its vacuity, of the sonority of its response when a breath stirs it. *The gourd is right in both instances*." (Kane, 33–34, emphasis added)

But Samba Diallo's story as told by Cheikh Hamidou Kane is a different story; it is a story of loss and dis-connection. Why?

First, Cheikh Hamidou Kane states unequivocally that he intends to write a sad story:

> The story of Samba Diallo is a serious story. If it had been a gay recital, we should have told you of the bewilderment of the two white

children, on the first morning of their sojourn among little Negroes, in finding themselves in the presence of so many black faces. . . . But nothing more will be said of all that, because these memories would revive others, all of them also happy, and would bring gaiety to this recital of which the profound truth is wholly sad. (Kane, 50–52)

Second, the story of Samba Diallo is self-reflective; it is also the story of Cheikh Hamidou Kane's multiple orientation, particularly the fissures in that orientation. The novel's pervasive critique of the West notwithstanding, one recognizes the author's affinity with the western orientation that he critiques.

Kane's story recognizes and elaborates on the tripartite nature of Samba Diallo's orientation—traditional Africa/Islam/the West. These three legacies are embodied in the three participants who are engaged in the first *palaver* in the novel—the chief (Samba's cousin), the teacher (Thierno), and the director of the regional school. However, Kane fails to maintain this debate at the tripartite level of the conflict. He reduces the debate to a bipartite level by collapsing traditional Africa and Islam and pitching the combination against the West. The West and the rest of us.[1] The Cartesian dichotomy is consequently established. In fact, Descartes is very much alive in the novel: "'To every word one can oppose another'—is that not what one of your ancient philosophers has said? Tell me frankly if this is not still your conviction today?" (Kane, 77) It is at the bipartite level to which the debate is reduced that I will locate my arguments.

Studies of Kane's *Ambiguous Adventure* often focus on the nature of the two components in the conflict as well as the intensity of the conflict without necessarily examining the specific site in which the conflict unfolds; the no/every man's land, the ambiguous space in which one lives one's conflict. It is this location on which one stands in order to "join wood to wood," this ambiguous space, this neither here nor there space, this "other" location where one faces "the challenge of the hyphen" that I call "the third term." Samba Diallo articulates the despair of the third term:

"Perhaps I shall teach. Everything will depend on what will have happened to me by the time I reach the end of my studies. You know, the fate of us Negro students is a little like that of a courier: at the moment of leaving home we do not know whether we shall ever return. . . . It may be that we shall be captured at the end of our itinerary, vanquished by our adventure itself. It suddenly occurs to us that, all along our road, we have not ceased to metamorphose ourselves, and we see ourselves as other than what we were. Sometimes the metamorphosis is not even finished. We have turned ourselves into hybrids, and there we are left. Then we hide ourselves, filled with shame. . . . I can't help wondering if there hasn't also been a little of the morbid attraction of danger. I have chosen the itinerary which is most likely to get me lost." (Kane, 112–113)

Hybrid. Shame. Danger. Loss. Samba Diallo's story is totally sad. However, while recognizing the despair and precariousness of this ambiguous location called the third term, my paper will examine the possibilities and potential of this hybrid site where metamorphosis/change is guaranteed and synthesis/stasis denied. A study of the third term ultimately leads to an examination of the ambiguous space as a site where perpetual crossing is guaranteed and the finality of a cross-over denied. The third term, which designates the shifting positionality conditioned by the crisscrossing of ever-shifting identity vectors, is a site guaranteeing the multiplicity of energies and possibilities; it is a space of representation. The proper harnessing and balancing of these energies and possibilities of the third term is the sole weapon against the erasure/nihilism and despair that Samba Diallo finds troubling. In this regard, my paper argues for a reconceptualization and retheorizing of marginality.

The third term is not just the other of the center; it is a configuration of the center and non-center. Hegemonic discourses and power politics which thrive on difference homogenize this hybrid term in order to maintain the self/other split, from which emanate such amalgams as Third World and North/South, when such constructs defy even our basic notions of geography. The center's ability to define itself only in comparison or relation to a homogeneous other accounts for the collapsing of the hybrid third term into a coherent other with which it (the center) never coincides. The struggle of the third term should, therefore, be against what makes the split possible: the power to name. To name is an act of imposition, marginalization, and circumscription. The named is oftentimes expected to carry the burden of a history from which he/she is excluded as agent. In the act of naming, agency is denied and the limits of participation defined and imposed. Hegemonic discourses of power, which name from the center, see the ambiguous space of the third term as a marginal, "less than," negative space of loss while losing sight of the fact that this ambiguous space carries in it a configuration of the power and complexities of the center and non-center/other. The center's urge to dichotomize and exclude makes it oblivious to the possibility of self-exclusion. The center's marginalization of the third term, which carries with it parts of the center itself, is tantamount to autode(con)struction.

Any analysis conducted from the center/normative, which is obsessed with the creation of the self/other power paradigm, ignores the implicatedness of the center in the formation of the third term. In other words, Samba Diallo as the third term is an embodiment of the center (in this case, the West) and the other (in this instance, the non-West). The center's pronouncement of the third term as a marginal/less-than position could conceivably be argued for only in terms of purity and autonomy, not in terms of quantity or even quality. The third term can only be less than the center in so far as it is regarded as a point of contamination in which case it is no longer purely the center or any of the other components which form it. Quantitatively and even qualitatively (depending on who does the valorization), the third term's "more than-ness" is not as disputable as it seems. What has been disrupted is the homogeneity/purity of its individual components. But then, it is a disruption that could be empowering.

The third term symbolizes the point where separate existence is no longer guaranteed:

> Every hour that passes brings a supplement of ignition to the crucible in which the world is being fused. We have not had the same past, you and ourselves, but we shall have, strictly, the same future. The era of separate destinies has run its course. In that sense, the end of the world has indeed come for every one of us, because no one can any longer live by the simple carrying out of what he himself is. But from our long and varied ripenings a son will be born to the world: the first son of the earth; the only one, also. (Kane, 78–79)

Samba Diallo's father, the knight, sees not so much the necessity, but the inevitability of this first son of the earth—the hybrid, the third term. Although the knight is fundamentally concerned about the positionality of the architects of the new world order, he is prepared to pledge his son, Samba, not as a passive observer, but as an active partner in this hybrid space/configuration:

> My son is the pledge of that. He will contribute to its building. It is my wish that he contribute, not as a stranger come from distant regions, but as an artisan responsible for the destinies of the citadel. (80)

Survival or annihilation hinges, therefore, on the issue of agency. A study of life in the ambiguous space will not only deal with how one lives in it, but more importantly, how one can survive there. Related to the question of survival in the marginal space are issues such as perspective, balance, freedom, and agency. Perspective implies possibilities and choice, paradigm designates belonging; freedom means freedom to choose, freedom to choose to belong.

The element of ambiguity which is inscribed in the title of Kane's book remains central in the novel at different levels—intellectual, psychological, moral, and temporal. The beginning and the end of the day remain recurrent features in the novel. The spectacular dance of twilight and dawn, two sites different in their temporality, but similar in their situatedness, is repeatedly orchestrated throughout the novel (29, 58, 60, 71, 171). Samba Diallo's ambiguous positionality mimics the repeated occurrence of the twilight, whose grandeur, poetry, magic, and power lie in its situatedness in an ambiguous temporal site where light and darkness are joined in a profound drama of representation, where life and death are contiguous and simultaneous possibilities. *Ambiguous Adventure* celebrates the necessity to die in order to live. At the Glowing Hearth, Thierno hoped to make Samba Diallo "the masterpiece of his own long career" by teaching him how to die in order to live. The Most Royal Lady explains more clearly the ambiguous life/death relationship:

> [R]emember our fields when the rainy season is approaching. We love our fields very much, but what do we do then? We plough them up and burn them: we kill them. In the same way, recall this: what do we do with our reserves of seed when the rain has fallen? We would like to eat them, but we bury them in the earth. (Kane, 47)

The twilight, where daylight slides into darkness, is the ambiguous temporal site *par excellence*; it announces the setting of the sun (death) as well as the possibility of the appearance (birth) of the moon. The association of the ambiguous space to the moon raises an important issue which often surfaces in discussions of cultural alienation—lunacy:

> The potential and necessary transformation meant that the mere presence of this new culture was a reason for the rejection of unadapted persons and confused minds. (Mudimbe, 4)

These "confused minds" have been variously named schizophrenics or *les aliénés* in order to justify and legitimate their rejection and marginalization. Like Samba Diallo, the Fool had come back from the West disoriented. The Fool's positionality in the ambiguous space is demonstrated by the incongruity of his attire and the strangeness of his physiognomy:

> The age of the frock-coat, and its doubtful cleanliness over the immaculate neatness of the boubous, bestowed an unusual appearance upon this personage. His physiognomy, like his clothes, left an impression of strangeness. Its features were immobile and impassive, except for the eyes, which were never quiet for an instant. (Kane, 86)

In actuality, the Fool transcends categorization. His shifting positionality, "[t]he inconstancy of his ever-roving glance, the changing expressions of which died almost before they were born, raised a doubt, after the first impression, as to whether this man's brain could contain a single lucid thought." (86) Consequently, the society declares him "less than"/marginal and names him "the Fool." As the named, he loses power and agency: "One day he found out that he had been nicknamed 'the Fool.' Upon that, he relapsed into silence. But the nickname clung to him nevertheless." (Kane, 87) Living in the margin is not an illness, as Lucienne's allusion to a physician may want us to believe: "curing your people of that part of themselves which weighs them down. . . . [their] Negroness." (141) Samba Diallo, the Fool, and others who live in the ambiguous space of pluralism are not sick. If they are confused, their confusion stems partly from the difficulty in finding appropriate responses to the arrogance that nurtures the assumptions and conclusions of Lucienne's arguments.

The battle that rages in the ambiguous space is that between nature and the unnatural, between humanity and dehumanization. Ali Mazrui notes that the cultural arrogance of Europeans and the subsequent deprecation of Africa and African peoples generated two major types of responses from Africans—*romantic gloriana* and *romantic primitivism*. On the one hand, *romantic gloriana* claims that great civilizations, important historical moments, grandiose monuments and technological know-how are indigenous to Africa. On the other hand, *romantic primitivism* valorizes and eulogizes the natural, the simple, and nontechnological, in effect attacking Western arrogance by embracing what the West deprecates. The latter position is epitomized by the négritude literature (what I call the literature of nostalgia), from Aimé Césaire's chant of "hooray for those who have invented neither powder nor compass" to Léopold Sédar Senghor's plea to New York: "New York! I say to New York, let black blood flow in your blood." Cheikh Hamidou Kane argues against the West with a *romantic primitivism* response. In *Ambiguous Adventure*, it is shown that unlike the West that fights to subjugate Nature, Africa does not seek to conquer Nature because it coincides with Nature and, therefore, cannot set out to conquer itself:

> You have not only raised yourself above Nature. You have even turned the sword of your thought against her: you are fighting for her subjection—that is your combat, isn't it? As for me, I have not yet cut the umbilical cord which makes me one with her. The supreme dignity to which, still today, I aspire is to be the most sensitive and the most filial part of her. Being Nature herself, I do not dare to fight against her. I never open up the bosom of the earth, in search of my food, without demanding pardon, trembling, beforehand. I never strike a tree, coveting its body, without making fraternal supplication to it. I am only that end of being where thought comes to flower. (Kane, 139–140)

In contrast to Africa's oneness with Nature is the materiality, artificiality, and superficiality of the West. In contrast to the Africans for whom nothingness is fullness—"Strange, Lacroix was thinking, this fascination of nothingness for those who have nothing. Their nothingness—they call it the absolute, they turn their backs to the light, but they look at the shadow fixedly"—the West is "slowly dying under the weight of evidence" (77–78), the external, and the superficial.

On some level, Samba Diallo's journey demonstrates the futility of the search for authenticity, the failure to recover a lost origin. Trinh Minh-ha rightly notes that this search is inextricably linked to the fear of indeterminacy:

> Of all the layers that form the open (never finite) totality of "I," which is to be filtered out as superfluous, fake, corrupt, and which is to be called pure, true, real, genuine, original, authentic?. . . *Authenticity* as a need to rely on an "undisputed origin," is prey to an obsessive *fear*: that of *losing a connection*. Everything must hold together. In my craving for a logic of being, I cannot help but loathe the threats of interruptions, disseminations, and suspensions. To begin, to develop to a climax, then to end. To fill, to join, to unify. The order and the links create an illusion of continuity, which I highly prize for fear of nonsense and emptiness. (Trinh 1989, 94, emphasis in the original)

Survival in the ambiguous space is linked to memory and a deep sense of history without the enslavement to history. The major struggle in the ambiguous space is "the struggle of memory against forgetting." Thierno, the master, is fully aware of the consequences of the intersection of histories:

> "If I told them to go to the new school," he said at last, "they would go en masse. They would learn all the ways of joining wood to wood which we do not know. But, learning, they would also forget. Would what they would learn be worth as much as what they would forget? I should like to ask you: can one learn *this* without forgetting *that*, and is what one learns worth what one forgets?" (Kane, 34)

One can respond to Thierno's question in relative terms. Yes, one can "learn *this* without forgetting *that*," it all depends on how much of *that* that one chooses to forget. I argue that the knowledge of *this* and the knowledge of *that* are not mutually exclusive. To forget is to die. The pervasive juxtaposition of life and death in *Ambiguous Adventure* underscores the problematic of the ambiguous space (the third term). The third term is where one dies in order to live. Samba Diallo dies not only because he forgot, but more importantly, because he *chose* to forget. By *choosing* to forget to pray, in response to the Fool's request, Samba Diallo allows a part of him (the essence, according to Thierno) to die:

> "Promise me that you will pray tomorrow."

"No—I do not agree. . ."
Without noticing, he had spoken these words aloud.
It was then that the fool drew his weapon, and suddenly everything
went black around Samba Diallo. (Kane, 174)

Samba Diallo's death in this ambiguous location is an experience of life. Samba Diallo is like the seed that has to die in
order for the plant to grow. This location where death occurs
is an expansive, unlimited space; it is a space of possibilities.
In the dialogue with a "voice of darkness" that concludes the
book, Samba Diallo is cognizant of the limitlessness of this
space of victory, a site that is the antithesis of the debilitating
"closed circle":

> "I am two simultaneous voices. One draws back and the other increases.
> I am alone. The river is rising, I am in its overflow . . . Where are
> you? Who are you?"
>
> "You are entering the place where there is no ambiguity. Be atten-
> tive, for here, now, you are arriving. You are arriving."
>
> "Hail! I have found again the taste of my mother's milk; my brother
> who has dwelt in the land of the shadows and of peace, I recognize
> you. Announcer of the end of exile, I salute you. . . . Here is the sea!
> Hail to you, rediscovered wisdom, my victory! The limpidness of your
> wave is awaiting my gaze. I fix my eyes upon you, and you harden into
> Being. I am without limit. Sea, the limpidity of your wave is awaiting
> my gaze. I fix my eyes upon you, and you glitter, without limit. I wish
> for you, through all eternity." (177–178)

Although Kane tells a story of conflict and limits, there exists in the novel an undercurrent of expansiveness and the transcending of limits. Unfortunately, studies of *Ambiguous Adventure* often focus on the conflict between the West and Africa
without paying equal attention to the novel's insistence on the
coexistence of limits and expansion, this dance of limitations
and possibilities which creates the charm of Kane's extraordinary novel.

Notes

1 *The West and the Rest of Us* is the title of a book co-authored by Chinweizu, O. Jemie, and I. Madubuike.

Works Cited

Kane, Hamidou. *Ambiguous Adventure*. Trans. Katherine Woods. London: Heinemann, 1972.

Mazrui, Ali. *The Africans*. Boston: Little, Brown, 1986.

———. *The Africans: A Triple Heritage* [videorecording]. Santa Barbara, CA: Intellimation, 1986.

Mudimbe, V. Y. *The Invention of Africa*. Bloomington, IN: Indiana University Press, 1988.

Trinh, Minh-ha T. "The Challenge of the Hyphen." Keynote speech given at the Great Lakes Colleges Association Women's Studies Conference, Dayton, Ohio, November 1990.

———. *Woman, Native, Other: Writing Postcoloniality and Feminism*. Bloomington, IN: Indiana University Press, 1989.

Notes on Contributors

Ama Ata Aidoo is one of the foremost living writers. The former minister of education in Ghana, she has enjoyed a prolific career as a novelist, playwright, poet, and story writer. Her works include, among others, *Our Sister Killjoy, Anowa, Dilemma of a Ghost, No Sweetness Here,* and *Changes.* Her distinguished career as an educator has included positions at colleges and universities in Africa as well as the United States.

Olusegun Adekoya is a lecturer in the English Department of Obafemi Awolowo University in Nigeria.

Kofi Anyidoho, poet, critic, and literary scholar, is a professor of literature and director of the School of Performing Arts, University of Ghana, Legon. His publications include four books of poetry: *Elegy for the Revolution, A Harvest of Our Dreams, Earthchild,* and *AncestralLogic & CaribbeanBlues.*

Chris Kwame Awuyah is an associate professor of comparative literature at West Chester University.

The late **Catherine Bicknell** was head of the humanities department at Marygrove College, Detroit, Michigan.

Micere Mugo is a dramatist, critic, and distinguished educator. Formerly the head of the literature department at the University of Nairobi, she co-authored, with Ngugi wa Thiong'o, *The Trial of Dedan Kimathi.* She is currently a professor of African literature in the African American studies department at Syracuse University.

Obioma Nnaemeka is an associate professor of French and women's studies at Indiana University, Indianapolis. A prolific scholar in African feminist studies, she is the author or editor of a number of forthcoming books, including *The Politics of (M)Othering: Womanhood, Identity, and Resistance in African Literature.*

Vincent Odamtten is an English professor and chair of the African American studies department at Hamilton College. He is the author of *The Art of Ama Ata Aidoo: Polylectics and Reading Against Neocolonialism.*

Chioma Opara is on the faculty of the Rivers State University of Science and Technology, Port Harcourt, Nigeria.

Leonard A. Podis is a professor of expository writing and English and director of the expository writing program at Oberlin College. His publications include many essays on literature, language, and writing, and two books, *Writing: Invention, Form, and Style* and *Rethinking Writing.*

Yakubu Saaka, former deputy foreign minister of Ghana, is a professor and chair of the Department of African American Studies at Oberlin College. He has published extensively on African politics, including the book, *Local Government and Political Change in Northern Ghana.*

m8202-TX
77